Tuned Out
Traditional music and identity in
Northern Ireland

Tuned Out
Traditional music and identity in Northern Ireland

FINTAN VALLELY

First published in 2008 by
Cork University Press
Youngline Industrial Estate
Pouladuff Road, Togher
Cork, Ireland

© Fintan Vallely 2008

All rights reserved. No part of this book may be reprinted
or reproduced or utilised in any electronic, mechanical or other
means, now known or hereafter invented, including photocopying and
recording or otherwise, without either the prior written permission
of the Publishers or a licence permitting restricted copying in
Ireland issued by the Irish Copyright Licensing Agency Ltd,
The Irish Writers' Centre, 25 Denzille Lane, Dublin 2.

British Library Cataloguing in Publication Data
A CIP catalogue record for this book is available from the British Library

ISBN–13: 978–1–85918–443–1

The author has asserted his moral rights in this work.

Typeset by Tower Books, Ballincollig, Co. Cork
Printed by Gutenberg Press, Malta

www.corkuniversitypress.com

'If any there be which are desirous to be
strangers in their own soil and foreigners in their own cities,
they may so continue and therein flatter themselves.
For such like I have not written these lines,
nor taken these paines'

Camden (1588), quoted as preface for *The Montgomery Manuscripts – the Record of the Land Allocations of the Ulster Plantation*, compiled by Rev. George Hill in 1877

Dedicated to Evelyn Conlon

Contents

	List of illustrations	xi
	Preface	xiii
	Acknowledgements	xv
1	Sound, assumption and symbolism	1
2	'Folk' music and 'Traditional' music	7
3	Dance music and song	12
4	Loyalty, identity and religion in Northern Ireland	17
5	The myth of 'the west'	25
6	The 'sound' of music	32
7	GAA, culture and the Victorian model	39
8	Fetishising the crossroads	50
9	Religion, nationality, difference and inequality	54
10	The radical impetus of 'folk'	63
11	Traditional music in a modern world	68
12	Performance style and political identification	76
13	Dreams and realities – folk memory and Gaelic identity	83
14	The way it was?	89
15	The bridge of glass – Scotland and Ireland	93
16	'Crossing over' of tunes and songs	100
17	A music- and song-transmission cornucopia	108
18	Migration, movements and music	115
19	The fluidity of change	120
20	New nations, new times, new cultures	126

21	The creation of modern style	136
22	Tonal boundary-marking: prejudice, politics and ethnicity	140
23	Withering and blooming in the seventies	146
24	Jigging at the crossroads, 2008	152

Notes and references — 155
Bibliography — 179
Appendix: Interviewees — 189
Index — 191

Terminology

The term 'Republic of Ireland' is used throughout this text in deference to how the country is described by people today. The official title for the Irish State in EC parlance is, in fact, 'Ireland', but to avoid confusion, and to ease comprehension, it is generally not used in the pages which follow.

'Ulster-Scots' is used in single quotes only in the early chapters until the term is clarified.

'Traditional' with a capital is used selectively, generally to indicate 'Irish Traditional music' in order to avoid the possessiveness of 'Irish', the point of the book, and following musicians' conventions. However, sometimes it is used to denote simply the adjective 'traditional', hence lower case.

List of illustrations

1.1	Lambeg drums, seen here being played out of their political context at the John Hewitt bar, Belfast, for the launch of Rev. Gary Hastings' book, *With Fife and Drum*, in July 2003.	1
1.2	Strabane flute and fiddle sculpture.	5
2.1	The Loughnashade Trumpet, logo of the Irish Traditional Music Archive in Dublin.	7
2.2	An eclectic selection of instruments used in Traditional music today, as portrayed on music books published by Ossian Music in Cork.	8
3.1	Cullybackey, County Antrim musician John Kennedy OBE taking a class in County Armagh, 2001.	12
4.1	1808 Map of Ireland.	17
4.2	The island of Ireland after Partition.	20
5.1	The Blair sisters from Protestant east Belfast, playing music 1932.	25
5.2	Young step dancers in competition at the Ballymena Feis of 2003.	27
6.1	'Johnny the Jig', a bronze sculpture by Rosamund Praeger.	33
6.2	Jackie Boyce, Comber, County Down, author/compiler of *Traditional Songs of East Down*, singing at the final Ennistymon Singers' Festival, County Clare, 2002.	35
7.1	'Pan-nationalism' wall inscription on the western outskirts of Portadown, County Armagh.	41
8.1	Dancing at the crossroads – a popular fair-weather pastime in the age before dance-halls, surplus wealth, universal mobility and global culture (Charles Lamb, 1920).	50
9.1	Dancing at the crossroads in Dundee, 1940s	54
9.2	Advertisement for the Directorship of the Ulster-Scots Agency, 2002.	62
9.3	English translation of the Ulster-Scots advertisement.	62
10.1	The Weavers – post-war forerunners of modern-day 'folk' musicians.	63

xii List of figures

11.1	The Liverpool Céilí Band, formed with Irish musicians who had settled in Liverpool, England.	68
11.2	Mullaghbane, County Armagh – typical session, 2002.	70
11.3	Japanese musicians busking with Irish music in Galway, 2003.	71
11.4	The Electric Bar, Derry.	74
12.1	Roy Arbuckle with his Different Drums ensemble, which uses Lambeg and bodhrán along with uilleann pipes, flutes and various forms of percussion.	76
13.1	Jimmy Murphy playing in a casual, performer-centred session, at a bar in Charlestown, County Mayo.	83
13.2	An early banner of CCÉ's *Treoir* magazine.	86
13.3	*Treoir* editorial explaining the cancellation of the 1971 Fleadh.	87
14.1	John Rea of County Antrim playing hammer dulcimer.	89
15.1	Historical population movement between Ireland and Scotland.	93
15.2	The Irish tune, 'Rakish Paddy'.	97
15.3	Three pieces of music which are essentially the same tune.	98
16.1	An air shared by two contrasting political songs.	100
16.2	Tune with the air of the Loyal anthem 'Battle of Garvagh', a polka dance-tune commonly played in Sligo.	100
16.3	Two similar tunes: The Duke of Atholl's Rant (Scottish), and The Humours of Ballyconnell (Irish)	101
17.1	Douglas Hyde.	108
17.2	Title page of 'the Fraser collection'.	111
19.1	Early 1900s' Ediphone.	121
20.1	Byrne harp performance poster.	126
20.2	Edward Bunting.	127
20.3	Frankie Gavin playing with Malachy Bourke.	129
20.4	Melbourne flute-maker Mike Grinter.	132
20.5	Sandino's Bar session in Derry	133
20.6	Children at the village of Tocane St Aprè in Southern France playing, following a summer school in Traditional Irish music.	134
21.1	A typical session venue, the Dungloe Bar in Derry city.	136
23.1	Classlessness in Traditional music.	146
23.2	County Antrim uilleann piper Wilbert Garvin.	150
24.1	Scene from opening concert of the Glór music centre at Ennis, County Clare, in 2001.	152

Preface

This book deals with the attitudes of Protestant performers to Traditional music in Northern Ireland. It reflects on broader Protestant community views of the music through their eyes, and considers too the impact of historical literature, political statements and other interventions that have affected and shaped Traditional music today. The study deals only with what is known as 'Traditional' music – that which is played widely in Northern Ireland, in the Republic of Ireland and in Irish diaspora areas abroad. As described by the players and aficionados, 'Traditional' music is taken to mean the dance music, forms of dance and style of songs that were the one-time entertainment of rural people prior to urbanisation and the development of mass forms of entertainment.[1] More-modern musics are seen as having already influenced, and continuing to influence, Traditional music's ongoing composition and practice. Some commentators will refer to 'the tradition', an expression which indicates the historical continuity of Traditional music – its evolution, accumulation and development of repertoire, the process of its being passed on, and the styles of its implementation.

The concept of the 'Traditional' is arbitrarily bounded. For instance, the traditional political music and song of the North of Ireland are largely not dealt with in these pages, primarily because of the conventions of Traditional musicians, but practically because they merit the space of separate description and analysis. Not included in the genre definition 'Traditional', therefore, is the derivative political music which involves the traditional (Protestant) Orange and (Catholic) nationalist bands,[2] the distinct Lambeg drum music tradition[3] and the bodies of Orange and republican song,[4] except for cases where items from both are also considered as part of the general 'Traditional' repertoire.[5] While the political music is rooted in the same music traditions, and is itself a rich subject for separate study,[6] it should be said that a separation of it has never, strictly speaking, been engineered. Nor has it had to be; that has only *seemed* to occur, for it was (and still legitimately is) always there as part of each local and/or political tradition, but generally in its own territory.

The data was originally researched in 1992, in a profoundly different political climate to that which burgeons in 2008. The information is supplemented by other kinds of data, which has been gathered by others and presented in various historical, ethnomusicological, cultural and sociological texts in the intervening years. The study does not offer conclusions, but presents musicians' attitudes as a contribution to ongoing debate and assertion about culture and identity in Northern Ireland.

Acknowledgements

I must express the most sincere thanks both to those who I had the privilege of interviewing and to their families for hospitality, consideration and time. Each interviewee had their own unique take on what may typically, otherwise appear obvious. Without them this book could not have been considered. The survey could not have materialised either without the prompting and organisational energy of Constance Short, the challenge of Tommy Fegan and the support of Maurna Crozier and Tony McCusker. Use of quotes from parallel references in song analysis by Brian Mullen (BBC, Foyle) and David Cooper (University of Leeds) has been of particular value in illustrating the overall text, and for access to these researches I am deeply appreciative.

Sincere thanks to Andy Pollack, John Moulden and Barra Ó Seaghdha, who read the manuscript closely and gave valuable advice; Michael Cronin of Dublin City University for direction; Martin Stokes for thorough enablement, subtle directive and encouragement; Rebecca Pelan for information and photographs; Róise Ní Bhaoill of Ultach Trust for statistics; to Patricia and Eric, Annie Campbell and Eamonn McArdle for nudges and unrepayable patience and hospitality; above all to Evelyn Conlon for inspiration, forbearance and encouragement and to Warren and Trevor for living around the requisition of private spaces that all of this imposed.

Thanks too to the late Tony McAuley, who gave me his time and the benefit of his experience generously, to Brian Vallely, and to my parents for resistance to complacency, and to Leslie and Avril Bingham for comfort, direction, horse-sense, sandwiches and whiskey; to John Kennedy, Hamish Henderson, Gary Hastings and Geordie McAdam, Andy Crockhart, Michael Healy, Philip Robinson, Colm Sands, Robbie Hannan, Cecil Colville, Doris and Alec Crawford, Wilbert Garvin, Gusty Spence, Michael O'Doherty and George Patton. Gratitude is due to Nicholas Carolan, Brian Mullen, Tom Munnelly, Hugh Shields, Gary Hastings, David Cooper and Ciarán Carson for citations of their work here. Sincere thanks also to the several musicians who did not wish their names to appear.

Many, many others also helped the shaping of this text, mostly through conversation, anecdote and observations in the course of music-making and song gatherings; I am grateful in equal measure to all, but in particular to Heiner Riepl, Andrea Beer and Kunstlerhaus Oberfaltzen at Schwandorf, Germany, for the facility to complete the final revision.

Research for the work was made possible by funding generously provided through the Queen's University of Belfast by the Central Community Relations Unit at Stormont, Belfast; this was given with no suggestion as to desired conclusion, and with no condition beyond receipt of a final report. Research abroad was aided by the Cultural Unit of the Irish Department of Foreign Affairs, and completion of the manuscript was generously assisted by the Arts Council of Northern Ireland, and the Irish Studies' Association, Dublin. It was brought closer to completion under the auspices of the Academy for Irish Cultural Heritages at the University of Ulster in Derry, and completed and updated with facility support from the Music department of Dundalk Institute of Technology.

Fintan Vallely,
September 2008

CHAPTER ONE

Sound, assumption and symbolism

Lambeg drums, seen here being played out of their political context at the John Hewitt bar, Belfast, for the launch of Rev. Gary Hastings' book, *With Fife and Drum*, in July 2003. Hastings is a noted stylist in Traditional music on concert flute.

A Lambeg[1] drum beat out on the White House lawn in Washington DC on the last St Patrick's Day of the twentieth century. It announced a new millennium for Irish Traditional music as we know it. It marked the entry to a second millennium for *sean-nós* song, the third for the harp, and the fifth since the manufacture of the Loughnashade trumpets, which were found in a County Armagh lake in 1887. Most significantly, the Lambeg *brattle* was the symbolic inclusion of Northern-Irish Protestant identity in the imagery of Irishness, a tonal representation of key importance. Music is exercised year in, year out, to walk the ancestry of Protestantism in

Northern Ireland, but such martial music has long been abandoned as an everyday rallier among Catholics. For Catholics, traditional dance music – as an artefact of artistic culture – has come to be seen as an identifying symbol. Once part of the self-entertainment of all religions, this body of dance music was for much of the twentieth century rejected by Protestants. That such music expressions as marching music and dance music, each of them perfectly standard and with features common to all, have now come to be pragmatic signifiers of opposing identities is a matter of history. The selectivity and thoroughness of the rejection of dance music, however, has led to the 'tuning out' of Protestants from part of their own recreational music heritage and, as suggested in the quote from Hill (p. v), Protestants becoming 'strangers in their own soil'.

This study wasn't prompted by missionary zeal to heal divisions, but by a desire to set the factual record straight. It would seem that musicians should have no more nor no less responsibility to solve political problems than any other interest group in Northern Irish society, even if by their art they are statistically more likely to be present at rituals which either formalise political accommodations, or offer recreational comfort in political circumstances. One must acknowledge, however, that, because of these historically embedded associations, a polarised society does come to expect much of the musician.

As a Catholic teenager in County Armagh who began playing Traditional music during the early 1960s, I remember clearly that there were Protestants wholeheartedly involved in music at that time. My experience over the years tells me that this is still the case, but there are far fewer Protestants playing today and the music now is generally regarded by the body of Protestants as 'Fenian' (Catholic). This suggests that some vital potential in Protestants' lives may be missed out on by the exclusion of the music from their collective cultural options. This is highlighted by the enthusiasm with which the so-called 'Ulster-Scots' movement has engaged itself with Scottish music in the first decade of the twenty-first century.

Ancient sustenance

Is the absence of an ancient, historical music actively debilitating? In the sense that traditional musics throughout the world are believed to hold comforting and vital meaning,[2] might the option of the presence of such music in Protestant lives be enriching, if not advantageous? People, of course, decide what they will and will not accept as 'culture'. Perfectly good cultural artefacts are made redundant every day all over the world as populations adjust to new political, religious, social, emotional, fashion and economic environments. This happens in much the same way as a child growing to adulthood progressively abandons nursery rhymes, swings and bicycles, but the difference with music is that this is never regarded as entirely 'gone'; there have been systematic revivals of traditional and folk forms throughout the world since the late nineteenth century, so much so that some commentators consider that all music forms thrive by revival.[3] Since many people from Protestant backgrounds in Northern Ireland have already been finding total satisfaction in Irish Traditional music, it does seem that, while religious zeal and ruthless rationality – the 'old banner' and 'new broom' respectively – may be appropriate for some people, this will not be the case for all. Some hitherto sealed door may therefore be opened in the course of the pages that follow.

The interviewees

The text is based in the author's experiences and observation as a musician over some forty-five years. The arguments are gleaned from conversations and interviews with musicians and non-musicians, and from historical and ethnomusicological studies. Comment on history – both accurate and inaccurate – is included in statements from musicians on the grounds that such belief is part of their folklore and, in a phenomenological sense, a real part of the situation. The people spoken to[4] come from various class backgrounds and, for the greater part (around 80 per cent), from Protestant religions. Although the study draws largely on urban centres in counties Antrim and Down for its interviewees, it is not aimed at assessing any particular empirical data as to the actual numbers of Catholics and Protestants involved in Traditional music; rather it is the attitudes of those interviewed that are the focus. Additionally, three of the interviewees are media personnel, key observers by definition. Six of the informants were, or still are, involved in politics: two in specific Protestant-community politics; two in Ulster-Scots ideology (one of the latter is also a historian). Fourteen of those interviewed are musicians and/or singers, twelve of them involved exclusively with 'secular' Traditional music, and two engaged with both Traditional music and Protestant-community political music activities.

Scottish connections

At the time of the original compilation of this work in 1992, the Ulster-Scots identity was but linguistic idealism, and the Peace Process might only have been dreamt of. No claims were being made then by any of the players for exclusivist Ulster 'Scotsness' in music and song, although naturally (and significantly), all mentioned the popularity of actual Scottish sounds enjoyed during their lives. However, it is a well-attested fact that the popular-music Scottish influence has indeed contributed to Traditional music, not only in Ulster itself, but throughout all four provinces of British-controlled, pre-partition Ireland. While this study cannot deal in any great detail with the Ulster-Scots political movement per se (such ideology merits dedicated analysis which is done elsewhere, such as by the editor in Tonge, et al., 2008 and by Dowling, 2007), it does address vital, relevant interrelationships in music, which have existed at various times between Ireland, Scotland, England and eighteenth- and nineteenth-century France.

Tuned Out explores its territory largely through musicians. Most of these are conversant with the traditional and continued practice of Traditional music by people of Protestant-religion backgrounds and by Protestant people in predominantly Protestant areas. The observations made here do contradict some popularly held beliefs about Traditional music, proffering instead that the common ownership and identification myths are, in addition to political pragmatism, underpinned also by absence of information. The selected comments show that while the ascription 'Traditional music is Catholic music' may be popular political pragmatism, the notion is substantially superficial and uninformed: Traditional music is simply the music that was played commonly and 'popularly' on the island of Ireland by the lower classes (who had the opportunity or need, or who so desired), most strongly prior to the intervention of recording, cinema, radio and television. It is the product of much mixing and blending of the music traditions of all these islands and has survived into the digital age by economic marginalisation, revival and revitalisation, as well as by reconstruction. The very history of Traditional music among Protestants contradicts the exclusively Catholic assumption; not every Protestant sees the music as 'Catholic'. This was particularly so for older people in the 1990s, for some rural communities and generally for many who had gone through third-level education.

However, the years leading up to the new millennium do provide much evidence of hostility and confusion with regard to Protestants and Traditional music. The most dramatic demonstration of this is perhaps that which occurred on the 25 August 1993, when a bomb was placed at the back of the Jolly Judge bar in Newtownards, County Down, during a Traditional music session. The device was claimed by the loyalist paramilitary group, Red Hand Commando, who warned that venues hosting 'folk' music were viewed as part of a 'pan-nationalist front', and would be considered 'legitimate targets'. Traditional musicians in counties Down and Antrim were outraged at the Red Hand Commando's assumption that the music was only played by Catholics and that it was hostile to Protestants.

The action drew attention to the fact that Traditional music not only can be, but is viewed as an emblem of Catholicism, particularly in the

Flute and fiddle sculpture near Strabane.

working-class areas of Belfast and the major towns of Northern Ireland. A couple of years earlier, George Patton, then Director of the Orange Order, had already described the process of such belief: 'The *perception* I suppose is that Traditional music is associated with republicanism . . . And it's not! But it takes you a wee while to get that out of your mind.' In Newtownards in 1993 the gist of this was eventually acknowledged by the Red Hand Commando's withdrawal of their threat after just twenty-four hours,[5] following intervention by unionist politicians who were more familiar with their constituents' recreational pursuits. For instance, the Democratic Unionist Party's Wilbert Magill, himself a Lambeg drum player, said: 'Does this mean that if someone sings *The Green Glens of Antrim, Danny Boy* or *The Mountains of Mourne*, he is republican-oriented? The thing is ludicrous.'[6]

Other developments indicate changing awareness about musics, particularly about ambiguity in a mixed-religion society. A dramatic visualisation of this is Maurice Harron's sculpture (above), which is located at the

Strabane, County Tyrone, Derry/Lifford route roundabout, close to the Donegal border. Part of a circle of five five-metre figures – a snare drummer flanked by a fluter and fiddler who stand facing two dancers – it is entitled 'Let the Dance Begin'. The composite of stainless steel and copper strips was commissioned by the Strabane–Lifford Development commission, Sustrans, the Northern Ireland Arts Council and the Ulster Wildlife Trust. Unveiled in 2001 to the music of players from local schools, the image strives to balance music identification between the polar certainties of fiddle and snare drum, with the ambiguity of flute or fife standing in the middle, which can be interpreted either as the recreational, Traditional music of concert flute or the marching repertoire of band flute and fife. Charlie McHugh, chair of Strabane District Council, who cut the ribbon on this presentation, cited inspiration from his father and grandfather, both musicians in the area. Local Arts Officer, Karen McFarland, oversaw the placing of the project, which was conceived of as a vision of cross-border partnership and reconciliation.

Therein, of course, still lies the assumption that political music indicates Protestants and dance music indicates Catholics. This book will adopt a contrary attitude, that regardless of religion it is a core current of artistic engagement that sustains interest in Traditional music.

CHAPTER TWO

'Folk' music and 'Traditional' music

The terms 'folk' and 'Traditional' have very definite usage and meanings in music, but are often misapplied by writers and commentators whose primary expertise is outside that field. Within music, use of the terms may also be revised according to the purpose of the commentator, as analytical thinking gels or clarifies.[2] They will be explored here in order to ease comprehension of subsequent chapters.

The Loughnashade Trumpet, logo of the Irish Traditional Music Archive in Dublin.[1]

'Folk' has been used to indicate the culture of earlier eras since the eighteenth century and has been used to denote the idea of 'indigenous music of place' since the mid-nineteenth century.[3] 'Traditional' has been in currency in Britain since at least 1876[4] and in Ireland since 1913. The Irish Traditional Music Archive (ITMA),[5] the major information centre for Traditional music, notes in its documentation that: '"Traditional music", which lays emphasis on transmission, is nowadays preferred to the term "Folk music", which emphasises origin and circulation.'[6]

'Traditional' music

The most useful definition for the purpose of this study is that adhered to in Ireland by Traditional musicians themselves. In this (as outlined in the Preface and in Chapter 11) 'Traditional music' is considered to be a body of song (in the Irish and English languages, the material in English often being older than that in Irish), music (slow airs, dance-tunes – jigs, reels, hornpipes, polkas and marches) and dances (artistic performance and social forms).[7] Most succinctly put by the Irish Traditional Music Archive,[8] the music includes 'many different types of singing and instrumental music, music of many periods . . . an essentially "oral" character . . . a tradition of popular music in which song and instrumental music is created and transmitted in performance and carried and preserved in

An eclectic selection of instruments used in Traditional music today, as portrayed on music books published by Ossian Music in Cork (*Picture courtesy Derek Spiers*).

the memory ... essentially independent of writing and print'.[9] The ITMA further refers to 'Songs performed in Irish and English ... quick or slow, strict or relaxed in rhythm ... The bulk of the instrumental music played is fast isometric dance music – jigs, reels and hornpipes for the most part; slower listening pieces composed for an instrument or adapted from song airs form only a small proportion.'[10]

Traditional-music instruments

The instruments used define Traditional music more precisely: 'fiddle, whistle, flute, uilleann pipes, concertina and accordion ... '. They produce a particular sound in a particular manner: 'Certain timbres are considered traditional, and certain stylistic techniques are used which arise from the nature of the instruments.'[11] The body of instruments is not static, but changes gradually to incorporate new and migrated sympathetic devices.[12] It responds to invention, to changes in technology and international exchange, thus guitar and bouzouki have been introduced and accepted as the dominant accompaniment instruments, and electronic keyboards have almost totally replaced the upright piano in dance bands.

Traditional-music process

It is *process* that is seen as marking Traditional music most succinctly: 'Three crucial factors in folk music [place] it apart from other forms of musical expression: continuity, variation and selection. Continuity . . . a song has been known for many generations . . . Variation . . . as each singer learns the song, he or she adds personal changes . . . Selection . . . a community of people will select the songs that they choose to pass on . . .'[13] The ITMA does note, however, the issue of nationality and boundaries, or indeed, the lack of them: 'Irish Traditional music is best understood as a very broad term that includes many different types of singing and instrumental music, music of many periods, as performed by Irish [including Northern Irish] people in Ireland or outside it, and occasionally nowadays by people of other nationalities.'[14] Composition is a core element, with a particular meaning and significance in folk music. Always a personal, creative act, it involves both originality and amendment; individuals may make new material, bend a tune to suit their own style or instrument, or may add to a piece if deemed suitable or if a part has been forgotten: 'folk music is composed by individuals, but . . . subsequent to the original act of composition, many persons make changes "communal re-creation"'.[15]

Traditional-music transmission

Oral/aural transmission is a major undisputed ingredient of 'folk', even if it is not an exclusively or conceptually definitive feature. Most popular and rock musics and many of the non-Western classical musics are learnt by ear, and many Traditional musicians also sight-read when learning tunes (but 'reading' is not done in the course of performance). All musicians have to learn the notation of tunes by some method, but whether by ear or by note is (arguably) not important. Direct learning from other players may be either a passive process (osmosis), or an active one (person-to-person teaching), without the use of text or notation. In this the emphasis is on listening and thus on stylistic reproduction of what has been heard. Whatever way music is learnt today, once a piece has been memorised, then learning how to perform it begins. Thus the aural (heard) element is of greatest importance in the oral (passing on from person-to-person without the intervention of visual aids). The essential 'aural' involves picking up the subtle rhythmic nuances of Traditional music which, in common with all other music forms, can only be achieved by listening to established and/or respected stylists. The aural/oral also applies to learning the music from such stylists via recorded sources.

Another core element of a traditional music is its value in a community which is at ease with it. Such a music genre is always assumed to have some form of local origin, but it is, and always has been, subject to change. This is expressed as a process by ethnomusicologists: 'folk and traditional music . . . is music that is accepted by all or most of the people in a cultural group as their own'.[16] Folk music and its transmission processes so defined, one would imagine that Traditional music in Northern Ireland should reflect not only the inherited cultures of both the native Irish and the Plantation settlers, but the intermixing of both of these, as well as the ongoing influence of outside and more 'popular' sources. Leaping back over the years which followed the partition of the island of Ireland – as the present Traditional music repertoire does – this can be seen to be the case. The late nineteenth- and early twentieth-century Irish dance-music collections show an overlap with Scottish music.[17] The song repertoire in Ireland owes much to the Lowland Scots and English ballad traditions. Of particular relevance to this study, in Ulster folksong John Moulden identifies three strains: 'Irish, originating in the form of Irish language poetry – English and Scottish – from planters and other long- and short-term migrants'.[18] These proportions are estimated at 70 per cent Irish, 20 per cent English and 10 per cent Scottish.[19]

Whether 'folk' or 'Traditional' is used to describe indigenous music on the island of Ireland is not of any great consequence to appreciating the music. Terms such as these, however, may be of great relevance in popular media commentary, where the trivialisation implied in the use of 'folk' can sometimes have artistic or economic consequences for performers. For instance, one journalistic view is that both the Twelfth of July Orange parades and the All-Ireland *fleadh cheoil* are equivalents: 'major Folk Festivals'.[20] Some of those involved in Traditional music today contest the use of the term 'folk' at all, contending that the dogged continuation of the music affords it genre status: 'Whatever need existed at the beginning of this century for proof of the meaningless distinctions between "folk" and "art" music, there is hardly need for it in the final decade – even if no proof has been offered in the interim . . .'[21]. Yet artistically, the coining of the term 'folk', the refining of it to 'Traditional', and the use of both terms in musicological research, definition and debate have been key issues in the course of Traditional music's argument for the cultural recognition upon which developmental and educational finance were dependent. This book is part of that process, and requires understanding of not only the distinctions between the major music genres on the island, but appreciation of the finer distinctions between 'popular', 'folk' and 'Traditional'. Attention will now be turned to applying some of this thinking to indigenous music in Northern Ireland.

CHAPTER THREE

Dance music and song

Cullybackey, County Antrim musician John Kennedy OBE taking a class in County Armagh, 2001.

Traditional music in Northern Ireland is, by religion of birth, mixed. In general it is mainly Catholic with a small number of Protestants, in many areas it is exclusively Catholic, and in some is exclusively Protestant or may be Protestant with a small number of Catholics. Musicians can be classified loosely as pre- and post-revival. Pre-revival musicians might be regarded as those who had learnt through their families, or where music had been a constant presence in their locality; most of these were born before 1945. 'Revivalists' are those who began to experience music or to play after their teens, or through influences from outside their immediate environment (such as radio, TV, bar sessions, festivals or the *fleadh cheoil*); generally they were born after 1945. Since revivalist players have now reared families, those of their children who play – from thirty-five downwards – are usually regarded as 'part of the Tradition'. Most musicians – Protestant and Catholic – from all of Northern Ireland (and indeed the whole island), are revivalist, but in more remote pockets of all counties there are also those who have been playing or participating in the music in an unbroken continuity through the generations. Fermanagh is notable in this regard in Northern Ireland.

The gender balance within the public and performance scene of Traditional music over the whole island of Ireland is generally mostly male, reflecting the situation in other musics. In Protestant music circles, however, there appear to be even fewer women involved. This is likely to be a consequence of the more recent, relative absence of a cultural value being put on the music in the educative stage of life in the home, if not at school. As with other forms of music everywhere, in Traditional music in Catholic areas girls generally outnumber boys at the learning stage (eight to sixteen years) by ratios of between 2:1 to 8:1. After that age they seem to lose interest. Boys on the other hand go for physically expressive pursuits which, when they do play music later in their teens, makes the camaraderie of the music-pub scene more attractive to them than to girls. Older women have tended not to be involved as much in, or not to have continued with, playing instruments, but have always sung and danced. All this, of course, is related to having and rearing children, attitudes within that being trend-responsive and constantly in flux. In this sense the gender expression of Traditional music is similar to that of rock music – it is male oriented and it is a *do*-ing music: 'Trad music's not a listening game – it's a bit like rugby, you don't watch it you play it.'[1]

Over all of Ireland, more males will play, more females will listen or be there for the crack,[2] the real human purpose of the pursuit. It would also appear that an increasingly educated, liberal, middle-class cohort are playing and following the music (similar to the folk music scene in England, Scotland, Wales, Europe and the USA). The music is no longer the only, or most easily available music option open to rural communities. Indeed it takes great effort and patience to help children to learn, and money is needed for classes, recordings and instruments. Free time, disposable income and transport are required for obligatory performance and/or competition travel. In order for the music to be handed on, or made available to children, the altruistic parents need to be spurred by some ideological or educative motivation (just as in choral, baroque, classical, jazz or any other genre). Catholics in Northern Ireland have been overwhelmingly more applied to Traditional music in this regard than Protestants, even to excess in some circumstances: 'The Catholics would push their young ones more to learn I think than Protestants would ... and some of them unfortunately makes their children miserable.'[3]

Migration to the cities has decreased the significance of rural areas in the roll of 'big names' in Traditional musics everywhere. However, the pastoral aura remains treasured for its vital, comfortable and approving environment of support and validation. For many, the epitome of performance and listening pleasure is still the country or small-town venue. Whether urban or rural, however, the players from Protestant backgrounds come from all of the professions, including the prison service and police force (hardly remarkable, considering these have been largely Protestant). As applies in Catholic areas, the underlying ethos of accessible self-entertainment which is the fabric of session and festival performance means that Traditional music is likely to be better appreciated by those in rural, rather than urban areas.

Politically partial lyrics

There are many songs wherein explicit political loyalties can be displayed, but these appear to be of no more consequence than political opinions, as care is taken in when and where they are performed. Older song includes both loyalist and nationalist genres, each with applicability in their own areas. Robin Morton vividly recalls loyal song in Traditional idiom being sung in private Protestant company in mid-twentieth century Portadown,[4] and most Catholics too have had similar experience of nationalist lyrics. However, the body of lyrics relating to the Napoleonic era and the 1798 rebellion of the United Irishmen are considered a key part of the Traditional repertoire. Stylistically these are often artistically substantial, lyric-melodic works, and since this period involved both Protestant and Catholic the material is considered to be non-sectarian. Of course, to a modern-day loyalist the sentiment is not favourable to the Crown and may therefore be considered politically repugnant. However, singing is not a major part of the general session scene, and anyway, at both that level and the professional, performers are location-sensitive about repertoire. Therefore, the issue of Traditional music being particularly disfavoured on account of party politics expressed in song-lyrics seems unlikely to be a major factor in the music's retention or uptake. Generally, inclusion or exclusion of political song is by choice; indeed for many Traditional singers of either political persuasion, a good song is a good song and a certain pleasure may be taken in performance of the political songs of the 'other'. Most Protestant singers recall that this was the case also in their parents' generation: 'Me mother sung. She liked the traditional singin. Her own mother was very good, and she had some good rebel songs too . . .'.[5] The same applies to playing anthems as it does to melody: 'Canon Cahill . . . asked if it'd be possible to have a concert and a wee bit of a dance . . . he says: "Yous fellas'll play The Sash?" It was definitely a Catholic area. I says "We will, but you'll come up and announce that you asked us tae play it and you'll stand beside us while we're playin it!" He says "I will!" An' he did!'[6]

The more 'party' political songs are often considered lyrically, if not melodically, trite by Traditional musicians and singers, but there are many good songs in the 'loyal' and 'rebel' repertoires. When Traditional singers find a song they like they do not discriminate, even when they don't concur with its political sentiment: 'I heard a fellow on Downtown Radio the other night saying that only Catholics can play "Catholic" music and Protestants "Protestant" music. That's a lot o' nonsense! I've heard Paddy Tunney [a Catholic singer] singing "The Bould Orange Heroes of Comber" – an' there was naebody to beat him!'[7] No trivialisation is intended here of the actual contextual meaning of political musics. Clearly musics have many faces. In all of them they fulfil important functions and inspire receptive souls.[8] The spirit of the literally political song, regardless of lyrics or tune, is associated with solidarity and political cohesion of its milieu. Being a Traditional sound in its local and/or ideological community it has a unique galvanising effect on and suggestive power for the approving listener. Put in the words of a loyalist Protestant: 'What really stirs my blood is our own music – Ulster Orange music.'[9] This of course encourages the view that music forms indulged in by other cultures are similarly politically experienced.

By contrast, Traditional music per se is experienced by musicians – Protestant and otherwise – more cerebrally:

> How I learnt [the fiddle] was I used to think about this wonderful sound . . . it was the funny head on them – these boys playin' these things and these wee funny curly heads on them [the fiddles] . . . I loved Traditional music . . . I play Irish music because I like it. I wouldnae care if Pope John wrote me a hornpipe, I wouldnae care if Ian Paisley was to write me a jig . . . I only play the stuff I love.[10]

> One thing I feel very strong about – music is a godly gift. I would relate it to something with a higher power than politics. I get a good feelin when I think about it that way. Every wee boy or girl has that in them – if we could get the right approach to them. Every'nt has a different style . . .[11]

Traditional music also has a separate socio-artistic value, and for many, particularly in Europe, is indulged in as a reaction against the pressures of the greater political life: 'I'd got really sickened of all the subcultures in London, wanted to divorce myself from all of that. Irish music was like cleansing, purging the soul. I took it up with a great deal of abandon and fanaticism.'[12]

Songs and music with a direct political or ideological agenda have always existed in Ireland as the recreational side of political culture,[13] as a necessary boundary-marking device, comforter, morale-booster, cenotaph and everlasting flame. This might be particularly so in the north of Ireland where everyone has lived for almost four centuries in some degree of fear or discomforting alertness. The actual music – in particular the song-airs, upon which as non-political tailors' dummies any shape, size, colour, style or gender of aural or emotional clothing could be hung – was simply a resource;[14] it was absolutely taken for granted. Outside of politics, and unless religious or moral strictures discouraged it, it was available for the entertainment and diversion of the plain people, regardless of religious or political affiliation. However, modern entertainment practices, prompted by the invention of moving pictures, film documentary and recorded sound, undermined these older music and song practices. By the 1950s, what we know today as 'Traditional' music was at a low popular ebb. This situation was reversed by a revival or repopularisation process, a dramatic resurgence throughout the latter half of the twentieth century. The 'revival' effectively means the totality of attitudes and activities in music since the setting up of Comhaltas Ceoltóirí Éireann[15] in 1951. Its ideological seeds had already been sown by the previous century's Irish Romantics and music collectors (many of them Protestant), and had been productively fertilised by the politicising influence of the Gaelic League from 1893 onwards.

CHAPTER FOUR

Loyalty, identity and religion in Northern Ireland

Map of Ireland in 1808, with the four historic provinces (Ulster, Connacht, Leinster, Munster) and the close proximity of Scotland indicated.

People in Northern Ireland generally have no problem knowing the religion of strangers. Because of religious and consequent political polarisation, surnames maintain distinctive roll-calls that still echo the seventeenth-century Plantation of Ulster. An act of conquest, expansion and control by the English monarchy of the day, this brought in Scottish and English Protestant settlers. Popular analysis based in historical writing, seventeenth-century statistics[1] and present-day rural demography, show that surviving Catholics in general moved from being in charge of their territories, into exile, or to the status of tenant,[2] the latter most likely on the poorest land:[3] 'up in the sticks, up the hills and the mountains and the Glens, in the Sperrins . . . those are Catholic areas. Where there's bad land it's where you get Fenians playin Fenian music still with a continuity . . .'.[4] Such a view of the past persists up to modern time where there are opposing 'blanket' ideologies – unionism and nationalism.

'Unionism' denotes the favouring – economically and/or ideologically – of the Union of Great Britain and Northern Ireland. The term is sometimes loosely – but often inaccurately – used by political commentators to denote 'Protestant'. 'Nationalism' denotes the favouring of unity of both parts of Ireland independent from Britain – ideologically, and usually economically. It is a broad term, often used as synonymous with 'Catholic', which is reasonably accurate in that nationalists are mostly (but not exclusively) Catholic.

The Orange Order

The major Protestant/unionist organisation is the Orange Order. It is well covered by analysis and descriptive material elsewhere, and will not be dealt with in detail here because it plays no direct part in, or has little interest in, Traditional dance-music promotion. The Order is heavily involved with the promotion of agitational and band music, both of which are, ultimately, connected to dance music, but considered distinct subjects of investigation.[5] The Orange Order is a politico-religious, Masonic-type, male organisation begun as a declaration of loyalty in 1795 and institutionalised in 1815; it spread throughout the world wherever its members emigrated. Its aim was to protect the British monarchy and the Protestant faith,[6] implying strong opposition to the perceived threat of Catholicism, which was personified in the eighteenth and nineteenth centuries as the native Catholic Irish and their co-religionist international allies, and today by Catholic nationalists. The Order's objectives remain largely the same in Northern Ireland today, but abroad it may be quite different. For instance, in the Atlantic provinces of Canada it is substantially a welfare organisation which does such charitable works as providing meals to senior citizens of all religions.[7]

Loyalism in its present active form could be said to have been formalised as a reaction to 'Home Rule' for Ireland in the period from the 1890s up to 1912, in tandem with republican developments. Northern loyalists were unionists from the old province of Ulster, substantially representing the political interests of the descendants of those who arrived as a consequence of the Plantation. Southern loyalists, from the rest of Ireland, were predominantly the descendants of earlier colonisation and plantation in other provinces. The Home Rule crisis arose when parliamentary independence from Britain was proposed for Ireland; northern unionists threatened insurrection, the Great War intervened and the British government relented. The agitation revived and solidified the Orange Order and defined loyalism as we know it today. These events in particular, being alive in the memory and experience of today's oldest Protestant generation, and having been described orally to the next, fuel political, social, cultural and religious beliefs and fears, and colour attitudes to things 'Irish' – including Traditional music. In the later twentieth century Loyalism incorporates a more aggressive ideological support for Union with Britain, suggesting an absolute antipathy to all things material and ideological which could be perceived as undermining it – such as the Republic of Ireland, Catholicism, republicanism, nationalism, socialism and any political accommodations with them. Since 'loyalist' came to imply potentially militant organisations, it should not necessarily be assumed to mean 'Unionist', still less 'Protestant', although its concurrence with both is common.

'Republicanism' is the militant expression of nationalism, an applied ideology which originated in the late seventeenth- and early eighteenth-century Enlightenment and was motivated by events in eighteenth-century France. The Society of the United Irishmen, formed in Belfast in 1791, led by Protestants Thomas Russell, Wolfe Tone and Samuel Neilson, promoted the principles enshrined in Thomas Paine's *The Rights of Man*. It inspired the 1798 (in the north largely Presbyterian) rebellion,[8] and developed in the late nineteenth century as Irish republicanism, adhered to by the (mostly Catholic) political independence movements. During the Irish 'Romantic'[9] or 'Celtic revival' period in the latter part of the nineteenth century (which began before, but overlapped with, the Home Rule crisis), republicans supported the movement for the revival of and interest in identified Irish 'cultural heritage' – notably language, antiquities, song, dance and games. Their espousal of the Celtic revival contributed to the political interpretation of Irish music and dance events. The fact that some of these – such as *aeridheachta* (outdoor concerts) and *feiseanna* (Irish step-dance and music competitions) – were banned by the British authorities[10] contributed to institutionalising music, song and dance as decidedly political. Republicans have maintained this support for Irish 'culture' (nominally, but not usually literally), down through the years. By the late twentieth century republicanism and its organisations (largely Catholic, and again with military activity) were espousing socialist philosophies, and still persisting in demands for political and economic

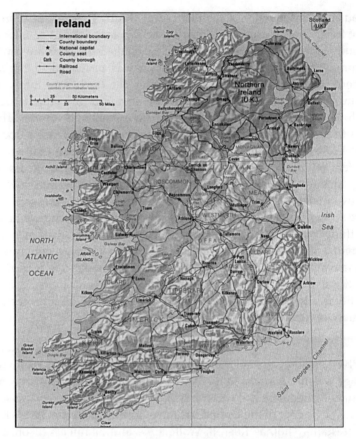

The island of Ireland after Partition.

unification of Ireland. 'Republican' should not be confused with – although it is likely to overlap with – the catch-all loose term 'nationalist', and still less so with 'Catholic'.

Fuelling all nationalist demands is Partition,[11] the division of Ireland into two separate political units. The largest of these is the twenty-six-county state of the Republic of Ireland, which is independent from Britain, and known now within the European Union as 'Ireland'. The other portion has six counties, and is entitled 'Northern Ireland' (a region of Britain, a component of the United Kingdom of Great Britain and Northern Ireland, UK or United Kingdom for short). The old term 'Ulster' – historically, until 1921, the northern provincial unit of the island – geographically includes three of the present-day counties of the Republic of Ireland. 'Ulster' is often used as a metonym for the cumbersome 'Northern Ireland', but usually only by unionists; nationalists tend to regard Ulster as comprising the nine historic, geographic counties.[12] Unionist usage of 'Ulster' dates in particular to 1912 – the peak of the Home Rule crisis – when the loyalist slogan was 'Ulster will fight ... and Ulster will be right'. The expression 'the troubles' or 'the trouble' originated with political unrest in Ireland in the early part of the twentieth century, but came to be used by Northern people of both communities (often tongue-in-cheek, usually politely so) to denote the upheaval after 1969.

The term 'ethnic' is used in its loosest sense in some of the chapters that follow, and takes cognisance of the process of its incorporation into the vocabulary of first, anthropologists,[13] and second, journalists and historians. It is not considered applicable to Traditional music in the sense used by MP John Taylor,[14] and implied by MEP Dr Ian Paisley.[15] If such views held any water at all, all Catholics would appreciate Traditional music (most, in fact, do not, and popular or rock music are indeed often the entertainment at republican functions) and no Protestant would play Traditional music or should even like it (many do both, the Arts Council of Northern Ireland on one occasion hosting it in a loyalist club).[16] In any case, the views of the (Protestant) musicians interviewed in these pages strongly refute such an exclusivist view.

Symbols for identities are used frequently in music. The shamrock, the emblem of Ireland, represents Irish cultural identity occasionally, as the thistle, the emblem of Scotland, represents Scottish influence. The tricolour – a vertically barred green, white and orange flag – is the official Irish (and republican) flag; the union jack – interlocked diagonal, horizontal and vertical red, white and blue crosses – is the British (and loyalist and unionist) emblem; the blue 'X' form of St Andrew's cross (Scottish emblem) is utilised occasionally by the Ulster-Scots, the red '+' form of the St George's cross is used to indicate or support Englishness (in football in particular). The only emblem enjoying use by both Protestants and Catholics is the 'red hand'. This is used with equal conviction by Loyalists to represent a separatist Ulster (Protestant, British identity), and by nationalists to indicate the pre-1921, old Irish province of Ulster (all-island Irishness). There are many other organisations involved in Northern Ireland cultural and political life, most beyond the limited focus of this music study.

Definition and assertion

The definitions given here set the scene in which Traditional music is observed in relation to people of Protestant background and/or religious practice – not necessarily (but possibly) of unionist or loyalist political beliefs. The terms 'Orange', 'Protestant', 'loyal' and 'unionist' may on occasions be interpreted interchangeably in Northern Ireland life, but there, and in the pages that follow, they are often so used (where not otherwise confusing or inaccurate) for the sake of avoiding repetition of words. Mention is sometimes made (mostly by news media) of a distinct

'Protestant traditional music'. This usually indicates the dominant public music associated with unionist ideology – the Orange songs and the Lambeg and band music traditions, music participated in or appreciated publicly by Protestants in political contexts. For example: 'Ulster Orange music ... is the music of the people ... this is what binds people together and is the heart of traditional music ... it relates one person of the same group to another'.[17] But there are also Irish Traditional musicians who are politically unionist, some of them loyalist. This book views all political-agitational music as a separate territory of investigation and takes the view that the nationalist equivalent to the politically definitive Orange music is the republican song and band heritage, equally unrepresentative of what is known as 'Traditional' Irish music.

Thistles among the shamrocks

The close proximity of Scotland cannot be ignored in matters of music, and much will be said on this later. The linguistic profile of an isolated landmass is what most clearly defines it, but if it utilises a shared language, then the only ultimate stamp of distinctiveness can be its local range of accents. So too with Traditional musics: while tune types and melodies may be shared with neighbouring regions, it is how they are performed, accepted and utilised that makes them of the place, and part of, or the basis of, its 'Traditional' music. The music of Ireland overall includes a body of Scottish Gaelic and Lowland tunes (the eighteenth-century composers of which are established in print), all of which are played with distinctive Irish accents in different localities. Most relevant to this study is the fact that a grave distinction is necessarily made between 'Scots' and 'Scottish'. The former indicates 'Scots', the language/dialect spoken in Lowland or North East Scotland. The latter indicates 'of Scotland', and includes Gaelic-derived song and music, some of which predates the Ulster Plantation. Related to these is the newest component of twenty-first-century cultural considerations for Northern Ireland, the Ulster-Scots phenomenon.

'Ulster-Scots' and genetic reappraisal

One major consequence of the 1996 Belfast Agreement has been the searching for, formalising of and consolidation of cultural identities among Northern Ireland Protestants. Driven by the perceived tenacity of Irish identity, but likely also inspired by post-1989, national fragmentation in Eastern Europe, the strongest strand of this has been the 'Ulster-Scots' movement, which harks back to roots in Scotland. This is a political movement that works towards Ulster Protestant cohesion through 'Ulster-Scots' identity. First it should be said that it only applies peripherally to the subject of this book; in relation to seventeenth- and eighteenth-century origins, it potentially represents only perhaps half of Ulster Protestants, and of these it does not interest or involve many, or most. The term is initially used here in quotation marks, not least because of its newness, but on account of its politically considered departure from meaningful English-language descriptions of broad identities. This feature will be looked at briefly in relation to territory and language.

Firstly, since 'Scotch-Irish'[18] is the long-established term (meaning 'the Irish who originated in the land of Scotland'), it should be expected that 'Scotch-Ulster' be used for the same origin group today as 'Ulster' is desired as the primary descriptor of the place in which they now live. But this cannot be done because the object of the 'Ulster-Scots' movement is to distance itself from all connections to Irishness. It would follow logically that an actual Ulster Scot can only be a person from the province of Ulster (including counties Monaghan, Cavan and Donegal), who has subsequently become a resident of Scotland, just as a 'French-Canadian' is a French-speaking citizen of Canada; so too with 'Irish-Americans', 'Swedish-Americans', 'Russian-Finns' and indeed the Anglo-Irish. Secondly, coming at identity from a linguistic angle, an 'Ulster-Scot' may see themselves as speaking an Ulster version or dialect of the actual Scots tongue. Since, manifestly, few do this, least of all the hierarchy of the movement, the term 'Ulster-Scots' remains inappropriate. In all of this chapter 'Ulster-Scots' is used therefore to indicate only what it actually is – the (perfectly legitimate) *political movement* which is driving (in this case) a music acquisition exercise, one which to an artistic mind, however, is a profoundly ahistoric, unartistic stab at irredentism.

Music has been a secondary consideration of the Ulster-Scots movement; its original focus was linguistic.[19] The linguistic aspect did not show any signs of success and so music was addressed; the idea was pursued that a unique Ulster-Scots music tradition might support the thesis that a Scots-origin section of Northern Irish Protestants are 'different'. The movement does not draw for resources on the surviving extant Traditional music, but disregards Protestant participation in this, and instead looks for role models in Scotland. Practically, as an adoption or borrowing of Scottish music, this is no less valid than learning a foreign language, or playing jazz. And since all styles have had to be invented by real people somewhere, and even if such music aspiration might take many decades, the notion of a modern construction – 'Ulster-Scots music' – which might have features exclusively appealing to the politics of Scots-Irish Protestants who are scattered among those of English and native Irish descent over all Ulster counties, is hugely interesting and challenging. However, so far it has proven difficult to identify such a Scots-Irish tune. But the matter is possibly easier with song (where words carry unambiguous meaning), where Scottish songs sung in Ulster, and Ulster-made songs in Scots style, have been well collected, and many are still sung within the corpus of the 'Traditional' in Ireland. But outside of Ulster-Scots linguists' desires to establish a validating culture, the idea of musicians splitting hairs over such minutiae as semantic origin seems as pointless as, for instance, the idea of Ireland, England, Scotland, Canada, the USA, Scandinavia and France trying to ascertain which of their landmasses produced which of the intermixed tens of thousands of instrumental pieces which they have all inherited from the nineteenth century.

What is being presented publicly today as 'Ulster-Scots' music[20] largely falls outside the remit of Traditional music as practised in Ulster; going by its demonstrated and desired stylistics it is more appropriately classified as 'Scottish'. Its main music ingredient has indeed a modern – 1950s, popular – Scottish feel, and its dance forms are dominated by Scottish country-dancing, which is largely brought in and newly taught in modern time. Since the Scottish tradition is dealt with comprehensively in many extant Scottish publications,[21] consideration of the Ulster-Scots music in Ulster can be given here only in so far as it has been part of established Ulster music traditions. Since none of the interviewees for this publication gave any indication of identity beyond Ulster-Irish or Ulster-British, the intriguing Ulster-Scots phenomenon must be left for a different form of social or political study and considered formatively irrelevant to analysis of Traditional music practices.

CHAPTER FIVE

The myth of 'the west'

The Blair sisters from Protestant east Belfast, playing music in 1932.

Prior to the 1970s, the most prevalent popular assumptions about any Traditional musics were that they are 'hick', 'redneck', 'peasant' and, in Ireland, 'culchie'.[1] The film *Deliverance*[2] did much to verify – if not signify – this; therein the 'noble peasant', implicitly inbred hillbilly was cast as possessing great virtuosity on banjo. The film *Zorba the Greek*[3] did the same for the music of the bouzouki and of Greece.

On the Atlantic islands of Europe 'Traditional' and 'folk' musics are associated with the western, poorer land, peripheral marginalities and with interior mountainous regions, and with people who are certainly more economically/geographically challenged. In Ireland such communities were even more backward, their music servicing the needs of those left behind after the less loyal or home-oriented, more ambitious or rational people had gone to more fruitful financial lives in the USA, England or at least Dublin. In Northern Ireland too, regardless of religion, Traditional music is first coloured by a regional bias. This was the case even as far back as 1970: 'When people think of Irish folk music and song they seem unconsciously to direct their minds towards the West . . . Certainly they never think of this province [Northern Ireland]. Yet you have only to list some of the names of our singers and musicians to realise that the tradition is very much alive "up North".'[4] Twenty-two years later, after forty years of revival and repopularisation, the same idea was still current: 'I would assume that if I wanted to hear Traditional music I would have to head into the West somewhere.'[5] But the most important view of Traditional music is that it has the ability to represent national, religious and political identity – a view shared by Protestant and Catholic non-musicians alike – and that it suggests 'Irishness': 'I identify "traditional" music with Irish traditional music. When I hear it I first think "That's Irish music", and that's it. I think I might be inclined more to say "That's *Southern* Irish music", rather than *Northern* Irish music too.'[6] Some Protestants have given consideration to where this attitude came from: "Whenever the Revival happened in the sixties – Protestants didn't buy it any more . . . Catholics can, because it was still their culture, for various reasons. But the Protestants can't because it's called "Irish" now.'[7] Most can recall sufficient first-hand memories to establish that Protestant antipathy to the music was not always there: 'But the Clancy Brothers[8] . . . it wasn't even ten years before the Troubles started because I mind[9] them. I was only a cub like. But they were goin in sixty-three [1963], four, five, six, and they were goin' a bomb. And me ma and me da used to go to their concerts in the Ulster Hall and the rest of it, and that was "Irish" music. But after 1970 it was definitely Irish with a big "I".'[10]

The Belfast city experience of Irish music in the 1940s and 1950s for non-musicians was of ballads and dances, pub life and ballrooms, rather than the kitchen. Perhaps remembering with a rosy haze and possibly analysing retrospectively with later-century terminology, one person recalled: 'The Traditional music was always a part of the life [on the Shankhill Road in Belfast]. I remember my elder brothers and sisters whenever they would have went up to the "Jig" as it was called in those days, to some of the local dance halls, the Rialto or the Court Ballroom or whatever. They would've asked what band is on: "Is it a traditional band or a modern band?" cos they wanted slow fox-trots and stuff like that, whereas Traditional bands would have played the more traditional type of music . . . Coaches Street was a little dance hall which was on the border [between the Shankhill and the Falls roads]. Both Protestants and Catholics went to Coaches Street. They would'a played Traditional music, all types ... You had the Irish Traditional music, which we all hum and sing, there was no problem.'[11] These remarks may use terminology which was not common in the 1960s, but they do also indicate that all balladry and popular Irish song was seen as at least Irish (and relatively uncomplicatedly so), if not actually 'Traditional', and associated largely with past life rather than Irish political identity. One interesting facet of Shankhill Road Protestant life concerns solo/artistic 'display' or group step dancing, so-called 'Irish' dancing (which has been a major symbol of Irish culture and Irishness, particularly in the USA), where centred around competition – like the relationship between elocution and speaking – the dance there might be as much concerned with deportment as with 'culture'. But it has also had – and retains – Protestant participation in County Antrim. The dance has always had a close association with Traditional music and, following Partition, it acquired a formidable organisational structure, courtesy of the new Irish state, for which it was emblematic.

Such step dancing, with elaborate choreography and dress code, has had a life separate from the music revival after 1951, but it often overlapped for occasions such as a *Feis*[12] or concert. Step dancing in Northern Ireland, particularly in North Antrim, was also kept alive in Protestant communities. Its social life involved, and continues to involve, the annual Feis at Ballymena. Irish dancing was taught in

Young step dancers in competition at the Ballymena Feis of 2003.

Belfast too, in both Catholic and Protestant areas, although much more determinedly in the former. On the Protestant Shankhill Road, the street is remembered as a rehearsal space: 'We were dancin' in groups, you know, round in a circle thing. I don't remember any names cos I took the rheumatic fever and I had to give up the dancin' after that, but I really loved it . . . You got wee capes and all, just like the Catholics. We wore all those . . . we had competitions with other schools . . . in them days religion didn't come into it when you were competin'. They usen't ask you were you Catholic or Protestant, just the same as sport today. Like boxin' . . . We always done it out on the open ground. There was a swings – and we called it the Hammer – and our school, the Getty Primary, was just on the corner and we used to do all our displays and all, fiddles and all were playin' for us. I'd still like to be livin' in those times again . . . It was always Irish music we sang. Even when I'd put on the television I'd sit and sing away til it – ballads. I got the Furey Brothers tapes, cos they sing a lot of the Irish . . . at my age I'm into Country and Western now . . . '.[13] Up until the 1950s in Protestant– Catholic interface areas, in local communities grounded by common poverty, there appears to have been some degree of socialising by young people 'across the boundaries', and the portable music of the day on at least some of these occasions of display was of the 'Traditional' kind: 'Fifteenth of August was Our Lady's Day, and you went down to Townsend Street and there was always a bonfire there and you danced. There was always an accordion and an oul fiddle there . . . and then you went down to get the hussies too . . .'[14] Country and city were two different places and the influx of migrants to Belfast provided evidence of a different culture: 'Orange Hall dances in the country would have had Irish music. You had all types, you would'a had the odd jig or reel, but there wasn't too many knew how to do the jigs and the reels. You were taught in school, but those people who came in from the country took to it like a duck to water. They could'a got up and done the jigs and the reels . . . but these would'a been more a Scottish tradition of jigs and reels than maybe an Irish tradition – *The Australian Ladies, Duncan MacInnes, Leavin Port Askaig . . . Blue Bonnets over the Border* stuff like that, strathspeys – *The Marquis of Huntly* and the *Muckin o' Geordie's Byre*. The Irish tunes – *The Dawnin of the Day*. The ballads – Percy French was very popular, *The Rose of Tralee, Mooncoin* . . .'[15] As in Catholic areas, the common ballads on accessible themes were what people sang on the (Protestant) Shankhill Road in the 1940s and '50s: 'They were singin' in the public houses and all the old songs were sung, and in some of the public houses some of the old songs are still sung. Irish songs . . . I remember when *Galway Bay* came out at first, I was a wee bit hypersensitive about "The strangers came and tried to teach us their ways" – y'know? But you got over it – "The women in the uplands pickin praties, speak a language that the strangers do not know"?[16] You would'a got people's heckles riz a bit. Whenever I would have had "one or two"[17] maybe – which is not too often – I would give a renderin' myself. I'm very fond of *The Rose of Tralee* . . .'[18]

In the post-war period, such commercial ballad singers as Bridie Gallagher[19] performed these kind of innocuous, place-praise, emigrant-nostalgia songs to popular acclaim. Céilí bands[20] played too, mostly in Catholic venues, for dancing which had to be done to Traditional music, but other dance forms were popular, the military two-step for instance, as well as barn dances, highland flings and ballroom-style formats. John Kennedy of Cullybackey, County Antrim, a flute player and teacher and also a marching band tutor, played all such tunes in a semi-professional repertoire that contained local and Scottish marching tunes as well as Traditional dance pieces. Outside of the city too, through the Counties Derry and Antrim Country Fiddlers Association, Protestant and Catholic musicians played together with equal confidence, if not unself-consciously, continuing a contact that pre-dated organisational formality. This loose organisation was founded in 1953, 'To preserve the art of country fiddling in as pure a form as possible, free from commercialism, and to encourage juveniles to take up and carry on this art, as did their fathers before them . . . To become a strong and real brotherhood . . . in keeping alive one of the very few remaining arts by which the executants make their own entertainment and at the same time give great pleasure to their countless admirers.'[21] Its founder members included Alex Kerr of Newtown Crommelin, an Orange Lodge grand master, and Mickey McIlhatton of Glenravel, a noted Republican. Its membership was from both religious traditions and it gave performances in aid of charity in Catholic and Protestant church halls and in Hibernian and Orange halls. Many of its gatherings involved singers.[22] All of this developed as part of the revival, and it would have been impossible for younger Catholic musicians in Ulster counties not to be aware that Protestants also played the music, not least because the usual religious or political assumptions could be made on the basis of knowing any player's surname or locality, as in any other walk of Ulster life. Among Catholic players the dominant feeling about their Protestant counterparts was positive, even if implicitly or explicitly coloured by a nationalist perspective. For instance, in relation to membership of a CCÉ branch in Newry, County Armagh, in the 1960s, uilleann piper Wilbert Garvin could remark: 'I think there was a certain pride in that branch of Comhaltas[23] that they had a Protestant in it.'[24] The assumption of religion based on the evaluation of surnames indicates how little players really intruded on each others' private lives. Indeed, the wrong conclusion could be reached by this at-a-distance association: 'We all knew a flute player, Chris "Charlie" Ferguson, who went to live in London. Charlie would'a been a Catholic, although he was from Bangor. He thought Séamus Tansey[25] was the bee's knees, but Tansey had never met him. And when Charlie died [tragically young] he left his flute to Séamus. Next thing Séamus Tansey comes on the Tommy Sands programme on Downtown [local NI independent radio] and said that he'd been left a flute by this man Chris Ferguson who was from "the other side of the house".'[26]

It is not difficult for a largely Protestant rural area to remain unthreatened by the kind of hostile perceptions of Traditional music that might prevail in the more politically savvy city. Some such Protestant musicians from mixed rural areas declare that national identity and religion associations do not enter the picture for them at all: 'In Ballymena there is no perception of Traditional music being one tradition or another that I'm aware of. But maybe that's very unusual. For instance when I was in Newry, I would have perceived it as "Catholic". . . I suppose I would have been the only Protestant in that local branch of Comhaltas . . . there is such a thing as the collective consciousness, and certainly I would be very concerned if Trad music and the Gaelic language and the dance were perceived as being synonymous with Catholicism . . . if you go through history that wasn't always the case . . . '.[27]

The balance among players verifies in fact that there are mainly community-based preferences for Traditional music. Two contrasting statistics emerge, in this case relating to playing from the 1950s to the 1990s: 'Ninety per cent of the musicians I mixed with were Catholic here [in the North] and down south. But there were no Catholics playin' the music where I live.'[28] The older Protestant musicians in County Antrim in 1991 appeared unconcerned about whether or not the music was labelled 'Traditional' and 'Irish'. They believed that it had a superior, artistic validity that cut across community divisions: 'I do think it should be taught in schools. You see it's part of our culture, there's no gettin away from it. It's the country's music and should be treated that way . . . now you would get an element about Belfast who would turn up their noses at it – just refuse maybe to learn it . . . but I don't think for one minute the country children would be so dogmatic . . . '.[29] This reasoning is conditioned by classic rural–urban differences; the player quoted here had learnt his music in a rural environment, and only later did he and his wife (also a musician) move to the city, where the music was not smiled upon by new urban-sprawl, working-class Protestant neighbours: '. . . we lived out near Whiteabbey Hospital, then they built up that Rathcoole area . . . and after the troubles started we had to stop playin'. You know there was resentment. Well, there would have been . . . You couldn't have brought a crowd you know to the house for an out-an'-out session, you couldn't have had that . . . Of course the music had to stop. And the year before that I can remember us havin' people in the house and . . . they would have played' til maybe one or two on the mornin' in our house and nobody would have said boo.'[30]

CHAPTER SIX

The 'sound' of music

> One night some of the studio crew decided they would play a little joke – and it was meant only to be a joke. They put up a list of performers on the caption stand and a leading caption. It read 'Taig-Time with Tony', after an old Ulster Television programme called 'Teatime with Tommy'. I was being told: 'This is your music, and this is Fenian music or Taig music or Catholic music'.[1]

Just because the music might often be played exclusively by Protestants in certain Protestant areas is no vaccination against derision or suspicion. There are many cases where Protestant musicians come up against criticism for playing 'Fenian' music, and where they are not known locally they can suffer embarrassment or danger when hasty judgments are made: 'We had an hour to wait for the train to Ballymena, so myself and John Kennedy went over to a bar that was seen as a loyalist establishment for a drink. He was still flyin' after a long weekend of singing and music. "Irish Traditional music's the best music there is!" he declared, smackin' his lips after the first mouthful. "I hope," says a menacing, sunglassed voice from the bar, "that y'mean Traditional *Orange* music?".'[2] Tensions and tolerance levels about music rise and fall with the political barometer outside and at one point a notable session, which was always generally exclusively Protestant (but never obligatorily so), in the course of the UWC[3] lockout in the 1970s, popular anecdote reputes that its landlord pinned a notice on the door of the music room: 'Irish Traditional music – played by Protestants'.[4] The minority – and dwindling – Protestant practice of Traditional music was reflected in Northern Irish television, where performance standards were critically important. In the early days of the 1960s, producers could not find enough Protestant musicians of a high enough standard to 'keep up the percentages' of religious representation in their programming. UTV dealt with this ussue: 'We had no policy on religion of musicians, but Brian [O'Donnell, from a Catholic background] would have made sure that we wouldn't have avoided looking for Prods if they were good enough. Where these

'Johnny the Jig', a bronze sculpture by Rosamund Praeger (1867–1954), located outdoors at Hollywood, north County Down. The plaque indicates simply that the artist 'loved children', it did not specify religion and suggests that the concertina was an instrument popular enough in Northern Ireland to depict in public sculpture. Otherwise, the concertina is promoted as emblematic of the Traditional music of west Clare.

conversations [about religion] came out was at fleadhs when somebody with a few too many jars and the wrong flag [the Irish tricolour] wrapped round them would say: "Aw Brian, we'll get there in the end!" O'Donnell would go mad, thump the table and say that music is for all of Ireland, and music is nothin' political, was an expression of people and he would put the best of musicians on – whatever they were . . .'.[5] BBC had a similar problem: 'On TV, I didn't want it to look like a series of programmes that only featured Catholics . . . to avoid the accusation "This is a Fenian series", biased . . . I came across Len Graham and Joe Holmes. I searched long and hard for people who could do it to a degree that was radio broadcastable . . . but it was always a problem . . .'.[6]

Given this situation, in their eagerness to represent everyone, it is hard for media personnel to avoid seeming patronising to Protestant musicians: 'But you do get a sickener – I get approached by RTÉ every so often and what they want is "Irish-speakin, house-trained, flute-playin Protestant". A lot of them boys down there [in Dublin] haven't a clue and when they find an Irish-speakin, house-trained, flute-playin' Prod, they're highly intrigued: "Isn't it wonderful!".'[7]

Stylistic supremacism expressed by the southern-centred Comhaltas Ceoltóirí Éireann, in the form of rejection of Northern singing, can be assured to alienate the Northern Protestant musician too: 'I felt totally betrayed by Comhaltas when a certain famous Free-State adjudicator[8] criticised the Ulster style of Jackie Boyce, a Protestant singer from Comber.'[9] Working-class Protestant musicians are not shy about admitting to negative attitudes towards Traditional music within their own communities; they have to live with the consequences: 'The music has always been called Fenian music, but only since the Troubles has there been aggression about it – never before . . . I must be the only person ever to have been called a Fenian bastard and a Protestant bastard in the one night – in the same pub, all for playin' Traditional music . . . I've been called a Fenian bastard by people walkin' past me own house who heard the fiddle playin' through the window . . .'[10] Because of such assumptions, discomfort is caused for Protestant musicians, even if they understand and/or support the ideology which generates the attitudes, and patience can sometimes be rewarded: 'On the first evening playin' Traditional music at the gig in this pub in Newtownards, we heard a crowd of young lads doin' a flute band practice in a room out the back. They came in afterwards and one of them says to us "I hope yous aren't goin' to play Fenian music?" I says "What's Fenian music?" "You know," he says, "diddley dee stuff." Now I knew the lad from his da who played in a pipe band, so I says to him, "Well, your da plays diddley dee?" "No he doesn't." So I plays "The Athol Highlanders" [a Scottish Traditional tune] on the fiddle: "That's diddley dee, right?" "That's not a diddley dee tune," he says. "I'm afraid it is, son." The same night me mate took out his big black [concert] flute and left it on the table. Well it wasn't too long before a wee B-flat one was produced and left beside it. "Yis can't play that one," says the lad. So I asked him, "Do you know 'Jock of Hazeldene'?" "I do," says the lad. Then I says to him "D'ye play two parts or three?" "There's only two parts in it," says the lad. "Wrong," says I and played him the three parts on the wee flute. After that they had to learn[11] the third part and thought it was great. From then on they came into the session every week after their practice, offered me fifteen pound a week to coach them, and joined into the session with songs and stuff ...'[12] Still prevalent in the 1990s, these attitudes only confirm what had been current as far back as the late 1960s: 'X played traditional music. When people were being evacuated out of his [Protestant] street in sixty-nine,[13] his next-door neighbour was a wee woman who was very nervous and distressed. So her sister arrives in a taxi to move her stuff. There was

Jackie Boyce, Comber, County Down, author/compiler of *Traditional Songs of East Down*, singing at the final Ennistymon Singers' Festival, County Clare, 2002.

talking on the street and X's wife comes in ragin' and says, "D'you know what she's after sayin?" – "I suppose yous'll be alright because he [her fiddler husband] plays Fenian music."'[14]

Instrument style

The very style of instruments used in Traditional music has itself become emblematic of identity, but what is familiar in the city may not be so in the country. Political assumptions aside, the rural folk in many areas by the 1960s had very limited experience of any sort of music variety, or different or modern instrumentation. A degree of bafflement about instruments was common, and perfectly understandable: 'We went back to somebody's house with the guitars after the concert and they had a great spread ready for us. And then after a while the woman said "Boys, will yis not take out yer banjos?" So the man went over to the corner to pass me the guitar. He looked at it for a while, made a few moves – couldn't figure out how to pick it up – and then kind of awkwardly put his fingers through the sound hole under the strings. His wife got very embarrassed: "Here!" she says, "Don't hould it be the wyers!" They were so unused to music and instruments he was totally confused.'[15] Political critics in the city, however, shoot from the hip and the first line of identification there is quite simply the visual: 'Fiddles and banjos are automatically associated with "Fenian" music, no matter what sort of music is being played – Traditional, country and western or bluegrass'.[16] Again: 'I had got a spot on a TV show with our bluegrass group. One night I was sittin' at home with my wife, and a couple of friends are in. Then our band came on the TV, and I hadn't said anythin' about it comin' on. He [one of the friends] doesn't recognise me on TV: "Turn that oul Fenian music off!" he says. A week or so later the same friend was enjoyin' our music at a function and I put it to him what he had said about the TV show. The lad says: "Did I say that? Well, yiz looked like Fenians."'[17] Given a more philosophical view it is *difference* that is the main thing: 'Certainly the pipes [uilleann pipes] would not be perceived as a Catholic[18] instrument, if I can be as blunt as that. It's the *oddness* of the instrument, not its connection with any preconceived idea about the musician . . .'.[19]

Translated into the city environment with a younger audience, mystification and wonder can transform to physical reaction when tempered by a pragmatic political awareness. Reflecting this, the city view of song style can be the same as that applied to banjos and fiddles: 'The thing that led me into the whole performin' arts [multidenominational music] thing, was me standin' in a pub singin' one or two folksongs and bein' called a Catholic bastard. That sorta thing shocked me, especially since I was singin' "The Green Fields of France",[20] and this guy was actually shoutin' with such hatred – callin' me a "Catholic bastard". I said to myself, "Hold on, what is goin on here?" The fact that that song could be considered Catholic . . . Well, the person *was* drunk, but that is not acceptable that a person should get angry over such a strong anti-war song.'[21] Non-Catholics born outside the Irish cultural climate can be more blunt. Untroubled by cumbersome history and unburdened by reconciliation obligation, they can perhaps more objectively acknowledge the religion-conditioned 'outsider' perceptions that have been learnt in constant session-playing: 'Protestantism is really divorced from the music. It is *in spite of* their Protestant background that Protestants play Traditional music. It's frowned upon in their community very often if they're from a working-class background: you're not supposed to play what largely seems "Taig" music . . . Traditional musicians who come from Protestant working-class communities . . . live in places where they really are afraid to be known to play "Irish" music. One man would say he played music of his own particular area. He played square dancing for barn dancing. It's Irish, but it's very much *Ulster* music . . . People livin' in . . . nice little twee places, have been told "If you want to be one of us, don't you be playin' that Fenian music". Another player was told to come back into line with his religion and church and stop playin' Fenian Music . . .'.[22]

Rejection

All of this points to an active suspicion or a process of rejection of Traditional music by Protestants in urban areas, creating distance from it by conferring on it a Catholic or nationalist (political) identity and therefore hostility to loyalism: 'Especially in the last twenty years . . . a lot of Protestants have rejected everything Irish. So if it's "Irish Folk", it's not theirs; "Irish Traditional", it's not theirs.'[23] There is, of course, an awareness in the Protestant community of Traditional music as simply music, but this is found more in rural areas, among educated or middle-class Protestants, and where there is a broader world-view: 'As we get older we progress, we realise that it is not "Republican" music. So if the kids can realise that at an earlier stage [through the EMU[24] in schools] so much the better, because despite all that's said about us [Protestants] and despite what some of our people do, we would like our people to respect others' traditions. We aren't going to give our traditions up, but we would like to be able to respect people with an opposing tradition. Sometimes the track record of some of our guys is not good. We hold our hands up to that – we're human, but that is what we preach . . .'.[25]

The reasons for rejecting the Traditional as 'other', or 'Fenian', are of course political, but also quite simple: 'At one time I would have assumed that people playing Traditional music were politically involved nationalists. Not any more. It's maybe unique – but because once *we* join a band, a marching band, that is an extension of *our* political culture – we are joining a band that will be out on parade on the Twelfth. It's a strong political statement. So we would tend to see it the other way as well: if you're playing your Traditional music then you must correspond to me playin' "The Sash" on the flute. That's the perception that we grew up with.'[26]

CHAPTER SEVEN

GAA, culture and the Victorian model

This study has so far observed attitudes to Irishness and to Traditional music from within Protestant communities in Northern Ireland. Reference has been made to issues located outside those social groupings, but which can also exert influence on them. The most important of these is the single biggest Irish cultural organisation, the Gaelic Athletic Association (GAA). This will be considered in a historical context, which locates its ideals within a framework of cultural/artistic values reflective of its period of origin in the late nineteenth century.

At a 'Cultures of Ireland' conference held in Ballyconnell, County Cavan, in 1994, the British Ambassador to Ireland, Mr David Blatherwick, perplexedly asked the question: 'What exactly *is* this Irish "culture"?' One might have expected a man in his position to have had some previous intelligence brief, but his bewilderment is perhaps understandable in the light of the utter confidence with which Irish people in the street just *know* what it is. 'The culture' is, of course, wee girls in embroidered dance dresses, Gaelic games, the Irish language and some version of Irish music. Few people are bothered about the broader view that academic disciplines take of various strands identified as comprising 'culture'. Longman's dictionary offers three different windows: 1. '... enlightenment and excellence of taste acquired by intellectual and aesthetic training ... the arts, humanities, and broad aspects of science as distinguished from vocational and technical skills ...'; 2. ' ... the pattern of human behaviour and its products that includes thought, speech, action, institutions, and artefacts and that is taught to or is adopted by successive generations ...'; 3. ' ... the typical behaviour, customary beliefs, social forms, and material traits of a racial, religious, or social group ...'. This condenses to enlightenment expressed through the arts, human behaviour and institutions, social, racial and religious beliefs. Sociologists and anthropologists consider the uniqueness of the human species to be that it has 'culture' – 'webs of significance man himself has spun'.[1] All societies have constructed cultures, and these survive substantially from generation to generation. Religions are run by them, and wars are fought where they conflict; the world is a mosaic of unique music forms on account of them. Alterations in cultural traditions can pass unnoticed, or be accompanied by upheaval; they can be simultaneously hailed as 'innovation'[2] and damned as 'betrayal'.

'Culture' is a cocktail of talent and imagination ruled by political preferences, state subsidy and commerce. All musics have their internal politicking: their conservatives and liberals, dictators and democrats, rich and poor, fashionable and rejected, the promoted and the suppressed, serious and popular. But Traditional and folk musics have other particular problems, for they have already long ago been 'used up', by the relentless process of evolution and inter cultural borrowing and exchange that has already produced classical, jazz and popular musics, and, latterly, 'fusions' and 'crossovers'. Yet folk and Traditional musics have *also* managed to survive with social function into the twenty-first century, with an actual use or application value for celebration, recreation and ritual. Since they thereby still retain an active function in their host societies' remote and marginal political, social and economic extremities, they are an enigma, if not an embarrassment, an affront to progress and development. In travel, medicine, industry, literature, political thought, entertainment and media we are content to move with the times. But not in religions, languages, foods and musics. These contain the scents and the sounds of national and ethnic distinctiveness, the deepest reserves of self-identity (imagined, perceived and real), preserved in an aspic of ritual by the nurturing care and power of relays of earlier generations, which have made sure that they still retain graphic oral memory.

Cultures were once only the templates necessary for living. Nowadays they are, additionally, raw-material and economic resources. The human race is constantly trawling the waters of its accessible pasts in search of meaning for the lives it lives and the opinions it holds. The gauge of the nets used is the measure of societies' needs and their perceptions of worth – governed by learned or politically conditioned predispositions. Approval is sought from dead ancestors whose lives are ransacked for energy that will shine a spotlight of validation – or narcissism and profit – on today's inheritors.

Political debate in Northern Ireland is tied up in such affairs. For 'cultural' in this context we could read 'political', for 'political' we could read 'religious'. Additionally, 'Irishness' is what Catholics are perceived to be about, 'Britishness' is what Protestants are perceived to be about – or, as presently split off, 'Ulster-Scotsness' too. Each of these terms denotes territory in the political, and hence the cultural, mind. Since culture is part of the political process, a partitioning of the main symbolic Irish cultural artefacts – sport, language and music – has been steadily following the geographical partition of Ireland that was instituted in 1921. This process is effected by selective rejections and affirmations. Most

Protestants have a rule-of-thumb method of labelling certain cultural artefacts as 'Catholic', usually defined by who is seen to be involved in them. Traditional music is one of these practices – heard from afar over the fields, or on radio and TV, or at mixed social functions. Gaelic games and the Irish language are others, the former blatant by its outdoors, Sunday practice.

Most Catholics and nationalists can at least recognise things that are seen to be 'Irish'. Many will identify with them, some will promote them, and a minority reject them. But steadily too, the term 'Irish' is being abandoned as a label of self-identity by Protestants; it is used instead to delineate the opposition – both 'Catholic' and 'nationalist'. Why music, language and Gaelic games should be considered to be Catholic and nationalist, as opposed to just 'Irish', is well documented in writings relating to the pre-Partition period.[3] The rise of their significance dates from the Act of Union in 1801, and gathers momentum from 1829 with Catholic Emancipation, which gave political and, in the process, cultural recognition and thus identity to Catholics. Such cultural items are perceived by many Protestants to be common across all nationalists' interests and political experiences, even marginally participated in by many liberal or left bodies: a 'pan-nationalist' cultural agenda.

'Pan'-nationalism

In 1992 Sinn Féin President, Gerry Adams, talked of a different form of 'pan-nationalist alliance' – as a coalition of nationalist politicians united on a minimum political agenda (not, as the wags asserted, the coming

'Pan-nationalism' wall inscription on the western outskirts of Portadown, County Armagh.

together of a poorer class of person fed largely via that most popular Ulster culinary implement, the frying pan). After that date the term was taken up by loyalist paramilitaries (UDA/UFF) as a contemptuous criticism, and later by unionist politicians. One of these was Rev. Ian Paisley of the Democratic Unionist Party, who saw 'pan-nationalism' in the nationalist, nineteenth-century sense, as a creeping tide of Fenianism imposing its culture and swamping Protestant identity, something that would ultimately drown the Union. He is reported using it so on 15 February 1993, saying that 'the Catholic primate, Cardinal Cathal Daly, was part of a "pan-nationalist conspiracy" to get the Queen out of Northern Ireland'.[4] By their activities and comments, unionists (collectively and objectively) demonstrated, however, that they had identified two particular cultural areas in this 'front': one was sport (represented by the GAA), the other was the Irish language and Traditional music.

Games, music and identity

Sports practised in Northern Ireland are similar to those practised on the rest of the island. However, soccer on the island is divided organisationally, with loyalty to two associations: in the North, the Irish Football Association (IFA), and in the Republic, the Football Association of Ireland (FAI). It is the same game of course, and both feed into the British and world systems. The other big game is Gaelic football. Some Protestants may be seriously interested in Gaelic games, but with a small exception they are not involved. This is because the GAA represents much more than the game; it has an ethos of distinctive 'Irishness', and has been associated with militant nationalism.[5] This body must be considered here not only because it is seen as symbolic of nationalist identity, but also because it has associations with the promotion of Traditional dance music.

The Gaelic Athletic Association (GAA)

The GAA was formed in November 1884, an initiative led by Michael Cusack who interpreted in British sport a degradation of Irishmen by varieties of competition in which they might readily be defeated. He also wanted the artisan and the labourer to participate, hence the introduction of sport on the work-free Sunday afternoon (which seemed calculatedly offensive to Protestant Sabbatarianism).[6] Ironically, such a tone for cultural affairs was originally set by Victorian Britain. In any case, Irish sport's emphasis was on morality, health, organisation, codification and competition, the same as the ideals in operation throughout all the

British colonies, and universally in the industrialising world of the time: '... the philosophic heightening of their meaning, the moralising, the nationalism, were everywhere of the same order ... iron laws of paradox dictated that [Ireland's] sports revolution, when it finally came late in the nineteenth century, would follow the pattern, set and continuing, of the dominant culture. Even the use of sport to proclaim national distinctiveness was a British invention ....'.[7]

The GAA dedicates itself to 'Gaelic games', identified as hurling, football and handball. Hurling was played in different forms in different parts of the country prior to the nineteenth century; sets of rules for it were drawn up in (Protestant) Trinity College in the 1870s,[8] and an effort in the early 1800s to revive the game had a significant Protestant membership.[9] Gaelic football seems to have no clear history. Rather it is like a combination of soccer and rugby – not quite a ball-propelling exercise, not quite a ball-carrying one.[10] Handball, however, was played much more widely, and in the older RUC barracks in Northern Ireland there were still ball alleys in the 1990s; the Protestant Royal School in Armagh has one, now converted to a squash court.[11] The GAA was set up in 1884 with a decidedly anti-Union ethos to preserve and cultivate 'national pastimes', to provide 'rational amusement for the Irish people during their leisure hours'.[12] It developed a republican leadership in its early days, but since Partition its ethos has tended towards nationalism rather than republicanism. In music, literature, art and language, a similar process and linked to the GAA's ideals was taking place in the same late nineteenth-century period: 'Leaders of thought studied ancient manuscripts for information about Irish history and civilisation. They realised that vestiges of this ancient culture remained in the music, storytelling and customs of the Irish-speaking population ... They began among scholars – historians and antiquarians – who were essentially middle class, but then gradually filtered through to the whole country, so that a people who had been told for years that they were savages, with a barbarous language and no evidence of civilisation, were persuaded that this was not so.'[13]

Emblems, archaeology and museums

The use of visual artefacts denoting Irishness – national emblems – both commercial (souvenirs) and political, also dates from the same century, Queen Victoria capping it by decreeing in 1900 that soldiers in her Irish regiments should wear shamrock on St Patrick's day.[14] Within this period, Darwin's theory of evolution[15] was in fashion too. The Irish 'peasant' was being caricatured in *Punch* magazine cartoons as 'a retarded creature with a low forehead, bulging eyes and a heavy jaw, generally slobbering at the mouth, who comes low on the evolutionary ladder between apes and Englishmen',[16] and the stage-Irishman[17] was performing in the music-hall. Carl Stumpf, founder of the Berlin Phonogramm-Archiv, a key institution in the development of analysis of Traditional musics, writing in 1908 illuminates such depiction by observing its opposite: 'When one leafs through old, illustrated travel writings, one is amazed at the Europeanized facial features of the "savages" as they used to be called . . . It was simply not possible for the draughtsmen to see objectively . . . The pencil is not guided by the eye, but by the brain . . .'.[18] Stumpf's conclusion is a sharp correction to those who would maintain prejudice after its sell-by date: 'This unfortunate state of affairs has been abolished by the introduction of photography . . .'. Views on racial inferiority ultimately developed in twentieth-century Europe as fascism (of which Stumpf's major colleagues were victims), today surviving as racism, but en route some of it found its way into partitionist loyalist ideology. The clichéd legacy of this mis-Darwinism continued to contribute to the descriptive imagery of modern loyalism up to the 1970s, if not more recently. Characteristic of this writing is Moore-Pim: ' . . . these people [loyal Protestants] are as different in appearance from the average nationalist as a Canadian is from a Red Indian. The loyalist type in Ireland is a well set-up individual, with clear, straight, honest eyes, a clear skin, and well formed features such as are found in the case of human beings of the highest type. His hair is usually fair, or if dark it has a fine texture . . . Every loyalist knows the nationalist type – a person with thick, black hair, or hair of a pale mouse colour, with shifty or dreamy eyes, a complexion – among the men – which is curiously dull or very red; and features which proclaim it as belonging to a low order among civilised peoples . . . There are many exceptions, owing to intermarriage and to the influx of pure Ulster and pure Southern loyalist stock into the nationalist ranks . . . these people are the ancient servile caste of Ireland and Ulster . . . the people with the "putty" nose, and the huge upper lip, the typical "Paddy" . . . The race distinction has persisted . . . in the country districts everyone knows how marriage is based on equality, and alliance with an inferior is almost unknown . . . and so we have the ruling caste and the original servile caste under our very eyes at this moment.'[19]

Elizabeth Crooke observes that archaeology in the nineteenth century complemented this, 'moved from the learned academy to the Popular society',[20] and in this context notes that Rev. Patrick McSweeney of the Catholic seminary at Maynooth, eulogised archaeologists as 'national heroes'.[21] She identifies an 1840 appeal by the Royal Irish Academy and its local committees, which was addressed to 'every friend of Ireland', as evidence of an enthusiastic atmosphere of identity accession in which people were exhorted to recognise the 'importance' of a national museum of antiquities. The minds of the sympathetic were 'worked' with pride and guilt inferences in terms such as 'ancient Irish art', 'disgraceful apathy', *'national* antiquities', 'antiquities of Ireland', 'zealously contribute', 'perpetual preservation', and 'national design'.[22] Thus, in her interpretation, objects and their classificatory or museological context become political fibres in the weft and warp of the greater political narrative.[23] A further observation made by her is that the new Northern Ireland state may indeed have seen value in this partitioning of the spoils of history: '. . . it is also possible that many of the items of treasure trove, being symbols of Irish nationalism, were considered by the unionist authorities as not being of significant worth because they were not part of the identity that they hoped to nurture for the six counties'.[24] Crooke thus highlights an issue – the dumping of artefacts – which, as with Traditional music, is of considerable importance in the search for Ulster identities today: 'If this was the case, this exclusivist policy denied Northern Ireland some of its material heritage.'[25]

Cultural numerology

At present the GAA has some 200,000 players over all of the island of Ireland; these are organised into 2,500 clubs, attached to which are a large number of other people such as officials and social-club members (who include former players and helpers). Northern Ireland contains 411 of the clubs, with 583 in geographical Ulster.[26] This indicates a figure of some 30,000 players in Northern Ireland, with perhaps twice as many more other members, in addition to a vast number of observers/supporters. In rural areas the GAA clubs and the Orange Order and other Protestant halls provide some kind of focus for the community; in urban areas these are supplemented by other institutions and premises. The GAA has promoted set dancing (quadrilles) for many years, these organised around competition involving older members and non-footballers. It has also significantly facilitated music tuition and competition, making music, song and dance of iconic significance in some clubs.[27]

The Orange Order is claimed as 'the largest Protestant organisation in Northern Ireland, where it has a membership of at least 60,000'. It is organised in Ireland into some 900 numbered 'lodges', which typically meet in meeting halls known as Orange halls.[28] The Orange hall, like the GAA club premises, as a venue for socials and refreshments has traditionally provided recreation facilities as well as party ritual, but does not organise sports as an energy outlet for, and cohesive bond among, local Protestant youth. For Protestant society in the twentieth century such social/aesthetic function has been fulfilled partly by band culture, which has a political focus and an active interest in the political status quo. Associated with this are some 3,000 religious, political and musical parades annually. The GAA, of course, is ideologically political too: nationalistic energy is funnelled into the body and expresses itself through the foot; the spirit of the local community is invested in the players as warriors who do battle with neighbouring parishes, regions and counties. But it is an internal affair among 'Irishness'; it does not engage with political opponents of Irish nationalism, even though the cohesive force is found along the spectrum of opposition to Partition, or simply exists through being born a Catholic. The same thing happens with band organisation, rehearsal and competitions within the Protestant structures where the cohesive force is shared religious culture and/or the ideology of 'the Union'. There are more than a thousand bands in Northern Ireland. The exact number is difficult to establish on account of widely different affiliations, band types and purposes, seasonal versus year-round performance, instrumental combinations, political loyalties and umbrella organisations. By far the greater number of bands are Protestant, but not all of these have political affiliations, and many have decidedly no such connections.[29]

Both GAA games and Protestant band structures depend also on a large uninvolved participation (often retirees from such activities) – or consensus – which takes part, listens, discusses and views the particular proceedings approvingly as 'convention' or 'tradition'. Protestants have no particular interest in taking part in the GAA: they see its thirty-two-county structure as symbolising the claim of the Irish Republic to all of Ireland. This is no more remarkable than Catholics not having an interest in taking part in the Orange Order, since for them it ratifies colonisation and Plantation, and symbolises British territorial claim over Northern Ireland, if not Protestant supremacy. Each organisation is a social and political reflection of the other. Each has its mythology, history and roll of honour, its own legacy of dedication and selflessness, general political direction, its contradictions, black sheep and shady associations. Each is participated in by all opinions, from the benign to the militaristic. Therefore the issues of Protestants and the GAA, sectarianism and the ban on security forces,[30] are pedantic: the GAA is properly recognised by Protestants as a Catholic community organisation largely symbolic of Catholic opposition to Partition.

The Irish (Gaelic) language

The Irish language is not so clearly partitionable, however. It was the language of the native Irish at the time of the Ulster Plantation, and at that time was (and still is) substantially the same as Scottish Gaelic, the language spoken by a section of the Scottish Presbyterian settlers in the seventeenth century.[31] Presently it is taught in all areas of NI, but mostly only in Catholic schools; it is not spoken widely in secular circumstances, but is used as an everyday tongue among certain groups of people. As a first language, however, it can be heard presently in its vernacular state only outside Northern Ireland in one or other of the *Gaeltachtaí*[32] of the Republic, or – in the case of Scottish Gaelic – on one of the Scottish west-coast islands.[33] In Ireland the religion of Gaelic speakers in Gaeltacht areas will almost always be Catholic; in Gaelic-speaking Scotland the southern part of the Northern Hebrides is Catholic, while the Northern part is Presbyterian. In Cape Breton island, Nova Scotia, Canada, the Scottish Gaelic speakers are Catholic, sourced from Catholic regions of western Scotland. While the Irish language is not per se a badge of any specific political identity (even if republicans do pay lip service to it), it is a significant commitment to 'Irishness'; this is underlined by its status as the official language of the Republic. Its campaigning organisation – Conradh na Gaeilge (the Gaelic League) – was the language's original promoter and, similarly to the GAA, was a strong body within the ideological structures which energised the nineteenth-century Home Rule movement. The Gaelic League's power and heyday are now of course long gone, but its embracing of non-sport 'Irish' artefacts was indicated in 1902: 'The Gaelic League . . . aims at the creation of an Irish Ireland. It hopes to accomplish this by the spread of true national ideas. Once those ideas are grasped, a development of Ireland from within, embracing language, literature, art, industries and music will necessarily follow.'[34] Today the Gaelic League has no agenda of religious discrimination or politics in any of its structures.

Being surplus to economic life, however, the practice of the Irish language is more a pastime and dedicated interest than a challenge to the spoken 'Queen's' English, even if many of its practitioners hold deeply entrenched views of its importance to their sense of Irishness. Outside of the Gaeltacht, these people are, by income and lifestyle, more likely to be middle class. 'The language' impinges little on popular cultural life in Northern Ireland, and since it is taught in Catholic secondary schools as an official subject, most Catholics get an opportunity to learn it, and will retain at least a few words, while many achieve a basic familiarity with it, some pursuing it to full fluency. According to the Ultach Trust, in the 2002 census 10.4 per cent of people in Northern Ireland (168,000 approximately) claimed some level of knowledge of Irish, from reading skills to full fluency. Of these, 23,000 were non-Catholic, including 7,400 Protestants.[35] The previous (1991) census indicated around 13,500 non-Catholic Irish speakers. The Protestant engagement with the Irish language involves Ian Adamson, a former unionist Lord Mayor of Belfast and instigator of Ultach, the Irish-language trust; of its eleven trustees in 1999, five were Presbyterian.[36]

Since speaking language is a private affair, occupying little space, and not too noisy, it has not been particularly challenged as undermining the

Union with Britain. A related interest is the study of place-names, which are mostly Gaelic in origin. Following the abandonment of the uniquely Irish-island 'townland' system of place-naming by the British Post Office in 1972, the Federation for Ulster Local Studies, an umbrella organisation for various community groups, campaigned to have the decision rescinded;[37] County Fermanagh opted not to implement it at all, and there has been a resurgence of interest in townland names in, for instance, County Antrim. One champion of the issue was DUP MP and Armagh Rural District Councillor, Douglas Hutchinson.

Partition and the view of Ireland from the North

All Irish cultural activity through the latter part of the nineteenth century paralleled and interwove with the major movements around Irish independence, and personnel were often shared between the straightforward political and the 'cultural' organisations, the GAA and the Gaelic League. The ideology was the same, the activity it was expressed through was different. Partition, which followed this period, took place before the revolution in technology before land and air transport were subject to mass development, and when telecommunications were in infancy. There was no public radio, the gramophone and cinema were still a wonder, and what we regard today as 'live' entertainment was a simple, unpromoted (in the modern sense of the word) social life: sports, bands, drama, music hall, dancing and house céilí-ing. All of this was the backdrop to Partition, which if it cut off southerners from interchange with Protestant culture, certainly had a much greater effect in ensuring that a large proportion of Northern Ireland Protestants would circulate ideologically within an 80-mile-square area, the only exit (nowadays) being an air or expensive ferry journey to Britain. By the 1990s most Protestants had not travelled, or else had a reluctance to travel, across the border within the island of Ireland. The popular newspapers read by Protestants in Northern Ireland were essentially local, the *Belfast Newsletter* and *Belfast Telegraph* and the regional county presses. These gave the provincial and parochial dimensions; those seeking further knowledge generally read some of the myriad English press. A small number of mostly middle-class Protestants read the Dublin-published *Irish Times*. A small percentage of Northern Irish Protestants would view the Irish television stations RTÉ 1 and RTÉ 2,[38] but the vast majority would not; broader knowledge was sought from the British television media networks' news bulletins – BBC 1 and 2, ITV and Channel 4. Since the period of this study, satellite broadcasting has made Sky, CBC and other international channels available, but their coverage is still more international than provincial. This means that for the majority of Northern

Protestants, their knowledge of and perceptions of the Republic by 1992 came filtered through the British national media, or from the odd political item on BBC Northern Ireland or Ulster Television. Small wonder that the popular Protestant picture of 'the South' could at times appear rooted in imagery – some accurate and some malicious – retained from the all-Ireland press of the pre-Partition period: a picture of ignorance, backwardness, poverty, ass carts, drunkenness, priests and nuns, submissive and uneducated peasants, hellfire music and dancing in the open air at crossroads, without even a dance-hall. For those who didn't travel south or read *The Irish Times*, perpetuation of such jaded rumours and clichés about the nature of 'Irishness' had at least the (challengeable) excuse of ignorance.

CHAPTER EIGHT

Fetishising the crossroads

Dancing at a Northern Crossroads, 1920 (Charles Lamb, 1883–1964, private collection)

> 'Much as I enjoy the Irish and admire many of their cultural pursuits, I have to remind them that we in Northern Ireland are not Irish – we do not jig at crossroads . . .'
> (John Taylor, Ulster Unionist MP, 6 December 1993)

'Irishness', and all to do with it, is a vital topic in Northern Ireland's politics. Protestant opinion on self-identity runs the gamut from 'British', 'Ulster and British', 'British and Ulster', 'Ulster Irish', 'British and Ulster Irish', 'British and Irish', 'Northern Irish, 'British and Northern Irish' to just plain 'Irish'. In everyday life people are who they are, and nobody ever has to spell this out unless interviewed, so it is not as contentious a point as, say, the decision whether or not to utter the words

'Londonderry' or 'Derry', 'Northern Ireland' or 'Ireland', or whether or not to get a British or Irish passport – or both.¹ But outside of the island of Ireland it is extremely difficult for Northern Ireland people – Catholic or Protestant – to be seen and heard as anything other than Irish, as indeed every long-haul lorrydriver knows, as many Northern and Southern Irish soldiers and marines in the British services are aware. Indeed, the Northern Ireland Tourist Board has addressed this sameness materially in its literature.² No one makes a mistake about the Irishness of the accents, just as no one fails to recognise one of the (hugely varied) Scottish or Welsh accents on the neighbouring islands. Further afield in Europe few people are as overtly concerned about intra-Christian religious differences, consequently there is difficulty (and much confusion) about being recognised abroad as a 'British Ulster-person'. The simplest way 'British' turf can be distinguished within Northern Ireland is by colour-marking the kerbs and lamp-posts in red, white and blue, or by painting King Billy and paramilitary murals on gable ends, as is done in many Protestant working-class areas. While this means that for some, political identity can be bought in a paint shop, it is more difficult in middle-class areas, where that kind of thing is felt to be tacky. Hence the pressure to define difference is expressed more strongly in the area of popular 'culture', leading to decisions about what is acceptable and what is not. If one doesn't want one's gate painted in the Union Jack's colours, how does one define one's self as unionist? If one is a Protestant living in a respectable middle-class suburb how can one be different to one's middle-class Catholic neighbours?

Making myth of the crossroads

One attempt at describing distinctiveness was made by Official Unionist Party MP, John Taylor, on 6 December 1993, in an address to a Unionist Association meeting at Newtownards, County Down. His perception of the cultural differences between Catholics and Protestants illustrates the critical divisions that are preserved (at least in the imagination) among what is otherwise sameness, yet which are great enough to make the idea of 'the two communities' coming together unworkable: 'Much as I enjoy the Irish and admire many of their cultural pursuits, I have to remind them that we in Northern Ireland are not Irish – we do not jig at crossroads, speak Gaelic, play GAA, etc., though we respect these activities, just as we wish you [those who see themselves as Irish] would begin to respect us . . . '.³ Pursued the following day in the uproar of outrage which followed publication and broadcast of these words, he elaborated his shaky logic further: 'we're two distinct races – there's the British people and then there's the Irish people . . . My constituency is ninety-five per cent British, I do have a five per cent Irish minority in my constituency . . . that's our problem of course . . . you can be in Ireland without being Irish. The Irish have a certain cultural background, and a Traditional background, an interest in sport, many things which are totally different from the interests that British people have. The Irish wish to develop the Gaelic language, they want to play Gaelic football, they like Irish jigs at crossroads . . . but we British people don't want to pursue these things . . . we are not Irish in Comber or Newtownards, we are Ulster people, not Irish, we have no interest in the Irish cultural activities, and although Sam [McAughtry, a Protestant journalist from Belfast, who was also participating in the show, but identified himself as 'Irish'] says he's Irish, I doubt if he has much interest in Gaelic or in GAA, or in jigging round a crossroads, I think he's bluffing . . . '[4] He illustrated this by describing his own, Protestant, origin as: ' . . . Lowlands of Scotland. We moved over to Northern Ireland[5] about thirty years before the battle of the Boyne and we took part in that victorious event, and I have the sword that my family used . . . it's been handed down generation to generation'.[6] Harried again by presenter David Hanley on RTÉ's morning news show the next day, he remained consistent: 'We're British here. You are Irish in the southern part of our island . . . we're Ulstermen, and British. We're certainly not Irish. I look upon you as a different race, with a different culture, different interests. I enjoy being with you, but I do not feel part of you . . .'.[7]

These statements describe Irish racial identity as depending on the practice of a certain set of cultural pursuits. They define non-Irishness as the absence of the practice of these. But in contrast to the Scots and Welsh, who have strident senses of national identity maintained in music and language despite being within the UK (and now rationalised in devolved assemblies), Taylor's statements define 'Britishness' as involving, predominantly, subscription to the central Westminster parliament. His sentiments are not irrational, and highlight a significant and down-played ingredient of the cultural process in Northern Ireland since Partition: progressive, selective rejection of once-common cultural artefacts, and the construction thereby of a new politically pragmatic, oral history deficient in certain ingredients which in all other cultures are necessarily present and recognised as aesthetically valuable, if not essential. In light of the previous chapter's observations on pre-Partition Protestant mythology about Ireland, Taylor's remarks are illuminating. Crossroads dances were a feature in many rural areas in the early twentieth century, and indeed in Protestant lowland Scotland too. Except for revival purposes, however, they disappeared with the introduction of the 'hall' or ballroom, and aside from occasional display, there has been little such recreational activity on the island since the 1950s. John Taylor was, at the time of his remarks, a frequent visitor to the Republic and, one assumes, was aware of social patterns there, so one must presume that by the 'jig at crossroads' he was referring not to dancing in the open air, but, metaphorically, to the present-day popular practice of Traditional Irish music and dance. His repeated reference to the notion seems so slight as to suggest that he is at a loss to define any critical differences between Protestant and Catholic other than religious and political affiliation.

His statements therefore suggest that he was appealing directly to what he knew to be a (common?) stereotyped image among Northern Ireland Protestants of a particular, assumed backwardness in Southern Catholic social life (an absence of indoor recreation spaces). It conflated (deliberately?) Charles Kingsley's prejudice[8] and the oft-misquoted Éamon De Valera's utopian dream.[9] It also drew upon a well-established routine of visual and aural cliché that has been used since the earliest days of music-hall, through film and into television, for the portrayal of Irishness.[10] Mainly though, it reflected the popular Protestant perception of Traditional music as Fenian music. While such stereotypical characterisation may be conditionally acceptable where dramatic licence in artistic and visual expression is concerned, it does seem odd (even foolish) when utilised by political commentators and politicians. Firstly, the jig is well documented by music historians as being more typically an English dance form,[11] and was, in the sixteenth and seventeenth centuries the most popular ballad and dance form among the London masses. Secondly, John Taylor's 'jig' remark – like Democratic Unionist Party MP Peter Robinson's painting of a slogan on Clontibret Church of Ireland school – is an invalid assumption. This is because a significant number of people in Taylor's constituency played and enjoyed Traditional music and were, in fact, Protestant; they had been behaving like this in continuity for as long as Catholics and people across the border had been. As a senior politician it is surprising that he was not aware of this at the time of his remarks, particularly since the Jolly Judge pub, scene of the music-session bomb just four months earlier, was in the constituency adjoining his own. But, apropos the thrust of this study, it is highly unlikely that this politician could have been aware of the fact that the same 'dancing at the crossroads' practice was merely a universal of poor-society life in the past, and was being done as recently as the 1950s in lowland Scotland, the asserted homeland of his own familial ancestors.

CHAPTER NINE
Religion, nationality, difference and ineqality

Dancing at the crossroads in Dundee, 1940s
(Source: from an old postcard displayed on the Jimmy Shand website)

Northern Ireland's internal conflicts at a class level have generally taken second place to the overriding religious dualism of Protestant/Catholic. The members of each 'community' perceive a common (political/religious) identity that distinguishes them from the other. Maintained within each such community are separate and distinct economics-based hierarchies. Overall the situation approximates most closely to an ethnic caste system[1] wherein the perceived socially superior caste is Protestant and British-identifying (from liberal unionist to extreme loyalist, but still implicitly loyal), and the inferior caste is Catholic and Irish-identifying (from mild nationalist to militant republican, implicitly disloyal). Along with these is the new financial middle class – increasingly nominally Catholic – which, while it may exhibit its traditional birth-community's loyalties, nevertheless chooses to live outside the ghetto in neutral urban or rural 'quality' areas. Internally, both Protestant and Catholic components of Northern Ireland's society generally respect age as implying experience and prestige, and both have their systems rooted in merit.

Protestant society enjoyed 'preferred' status in the past mainly through what had become by 1966 'traditional'[2] economic privileges, but the efficacy of this is under systematic, continuous erosion from industrial recession, education opportunities, Civil Rights and European legislation, and in particular by the legislative and psychological destabilisation which followed 'peace' after 1998. By now, for most, this status appears to border on the illusory, even if the exception has always been, until recent times, the predominantly Protestant security industry,[3] which in all its forms and interdependent branches is a huge employer. This radically changing situation leaves the most vulnerable of Protestants out of work and disillusioned, feeling under siege, disapproved of and abandoned.[4] The situation is not new: 'Durin' Civil Rights we all should've been out fightin' for our rights. I came out of the British Army – I was in Cyprus – after fightin' a war [1955–69][5] and I came home to my wife and two children and no house, no job and no vote. I lived with my father and I had no vote, I was not a householder, and I was one of the Protestant ascendancy and you can't get any luckier than that.'[6] The Catholic in a similar poor economic situation feels strengthened by this dismantling of what is perceived of as Protestant supremacy, even if their own economic life is depressed, and remains unchanged; they believe this to be the inevitability of 'justice prevails'. Generally linked into this comfort is nationalist ideology, which in its early nineteenth-century manifestations was profoundly millenarianist.[7] However, due more to changed legislation than to ideology, most Catholics perceive a steady improvement of the general Catholic 'lot': property acquisition and wealth accumulation is interpreted as encroachment on Protestant power (buying 'back' the land); wearing wealth 'on the sleeve'[8] is an unmistakable manifestation of the underdog making good.

Crossing the boundaries

Both Protestant and Catholic societies tend (ideally) to be endogamous. This has as much to do with political solidarity, control and ghettoisation as with religious strictures. But in practice there is much peripheral mixed marriage, especially among those who have been through the melting pot of third-level education. This, however, in Catholic–Protestant interface areas in the past, has invited the distinct possibility of intimidation, serious injury or death. Mixed marriage has become increasingly difficult for working-class and unemployed people who live largely in the ghettos; by 1993, at the time of this study, half of the population lived in areas that were either 90 per cent Catholic or Protestant.[9] Those most likely to marry 'out of the faith' are former college students, or those involved in, or whose families are involved in, cross-religion pursuits, like musics. Protestant band music is an exception to this, since their public performances are typically connected with religious or political occasions: 'I was going out with a Catholic girl myself for about three weeks, and I had to give it up. I'd have to leave the band if I continued with her, and the music meant more to me than the girl.'[10]

Education is strictly segregated by religion: Catholics are generally educated in voluntarily built (but state-maintained) Catholic schools; Protestants in the National (state-controlled) schools (nominally non-denominational). Again, among the middle classes and where distance and perhaps educational standards[11] are concerned, there is some crossover, and there are also the beginnings of an integrated school system. This has the same difficulties as mixed marriage, and in the opinion of the ACT (All Children Together), an integrated education group, mixed religion education is 'a very radical form of reconciliation'.[12] Myth, ancient and modern, occupies a high place in cultural life in Northern Ireland, is a potent political motivating and mobilising force,[13] and was accentuated by deprivation and vulnerability in the twentieth-century economic climate. The society as a whole has had a high proportion of non-kin associations and groups, most of the more political being male-dominated, and typically 'uniformed'.[14] Overall, they run from the open to the secret, are concerned with politics, labour relations, extra-state military, gender equality, religion, prisoner welfare, poor relief, helping the aged, disability, addiction, literature, drama, music, painting, sports and intellectual pursuits. They are generally voluntary. The political and military have operated mostly outside the state structures and typically their object is to frustrate these, although in the case of loyalist militarism its purpose is objectively to augment and/or precipitate sympathetic state action. Music and sport are different to other organised activities, and in both parts of Ireland, in their perceived, ascribed and claimed Irish-national forms (Traditional music and Gaelic games), they reflect and generate opinions on the greater political situation. Of these two, Traditional music exhibits the most contradictions, because of music's time-honoured role in accompanying all the rituals of life, and because it is played by both Catholics and Protestants (while Gaelic games are played almost only by Catholics).

Religion and identity

The terms 'Protestant' and 'Catholic' do not necessarily signify that people attend church, and do not guarantee that those so labelled even believe in a god. They denote the culture into which one has been born, to which one feels one belongs, within which one feels secure in relation to the other major culture. Consequently there is the Belfast questioning of alleged religious impartiality: 'Aye, but are you a Catholic Atheist or a Protestant Atheist?' Muslims in Northern Ireland also face a similar qualification for their religion, depending on where they decide to live in the various towns.[15] The Opsahl Report in 1993 had to admit: 'Although we are still forced to use the language of stereotypes for analysis, the stereotypes no longer apply.'[16] To make any sense of the attitudes towards music which have been expressed in the previous pages of this chapter it is worth looking at the two communities' make-ups.

Catholics

An anecdote relates what is primarily expected of religions in their political manifestations: 'A parish priest is remonstrating with a drunk parishioner about his low moral state and non-practice of the articles of his religion: "I'm worried bout you, Charlie." "Ah, Father," says Charlie, "I don't have much time for mass and confession – but I'm wild *bitter*."'[17] In 1993 Catholics were estimated to be 42 per cent of the population of Northern Ireland.[18] They are presumed to be the descendants of the native (Catholic) Irish who were displaced and dispropertied by the seventeenth-century Plantation and its consequences, and by subsequent economic migrations. Although some are unionist, Catholics in general ideologically secede from British identity, instead looking to the Republic of Ireland (95 per cent Catholic), the governments of which they are often cynical about because of the sense of abandonment that the 1921 Partition represents. Catholic 'disloyalty' to Britain is a byproduct of both the Reformation and its European political alliances. Because of it, from the beginning, a series of measures aimed at guaranteeing Protestant (loyal) domination – maintenance of the Union – were built into the Northern Ireland state. Sectarian riots and pogroms, sporadic republican military activity and parallel nationalist parliamentary politics expressed the tension associated with this. In 1966 Catholics set about a different form of protest – the Civil Rights movement[19] – to overcome their political disabilities; this escalated into the 'Troubles' years, followed by the peace process that characterised entry into the twenty-first century.

The attitudes of Catholics to their sense of origin and identification are collated in the following table.[20]

TABLE 1:
Catholic attitudes to national identity over a spread of years

Year	Irish %	British %	Ulster %	N. Irish %	Island Irish %
Late 1960s	76	15	5	?	81
Late 1970s	69	20	6	?	75
1989	60	8	2	25	87
1993	61	12	1	24	86

These figures show a rethinking, but formalising, of attitudes during the period of Traditional music revival, which overlapped with both the Civil Rights movement and the 'Troubles'; therein, close to 90% of Catholics identify with the island of birth for their nationality during the latter decades of the twentieth century. This facilitates a strong disposition towards favouring in Traditional music the idea of an 'indigenous' music of the island.

Protestants

The Protestant population, in all its denominations, was 58 per cent of the population of Northern Ireland at the time of the 1993 census. It comprises the descendants of Scottish and Northern English settlers from the seventeenth-century 'Plantation' and later migration, and some old Protestant Irish. It sees itself as sometimes 'Irish', sometimes 'Ulster' or 'Northern Irish' (more recently 'Ulster-Scots' has become an option), but almost always as 'British'. It is sceptical of British commitment to preserve the Union of Northern Ireland with Britain; consequently its state of siege against the Republic and nationalists is aggravated by the omnipresent, potentially dishonourable behaviour of British governments. Paradoxically, many of the ancestors of Northern Ireland Protestants who colonised the eastern states of America translated this type of suspicion and survival mentality into the War of Independence (1775–83) against the mother country, and participated with confidence and conviction in the development of, ultimately, a multi-ethnic state in that continent,[21] marked most notably by the 1861–5 Civil War. Anthony Buckley describes the Protestant use of history in Ireland under three headings: as a political rhetoric of superiority, a charter which provides a set of guidelines from the past for action in the present, and a focus for allegiance as defining their ethnic separateness.[22] He concludes that these uses come together in the daily definition and implementation of ethnic boundaries.[23] He also asserts that the distinct Catholic and Protestant ethnicities are mutually interdependent, but implies that, while Protestants have difficulty with identity, Catholics do not.[24] From this analysis it could be concluded that cultural artefacts – like language, sport, music, entertainment, 'colours' and passport – which are needed to express Irishness would be claimed by Catholics and rejected by Protestants, who must build instead on 'Ulsterness' or 'Britishness'. The degree to which individuals in either group possess these depends on such things as their social status, wealth, family pressure, confidence or occupation. As the range of available cultural options constricts, the national identity of individual Protestants – especially those involved in Traditional music – can consequently appear a conundrum:

> Look – I'm Irish. There's a political division here in Ireland, but that doesn't alter the fact that I'm Irish . . . in private other people would say that too. You see I'm Irish, but I'm peculiarly British. And I'm British, but I'm peculiarly Irish too. I'm born and reared in Ireland . . . in an Irish atmosphere . . . we have traditions here too which are purely Irish and you're proud of them – the way you talk, some of your colloquialisms, some of your cynical views perhaps . . .[25]

> My grandfather would have considered himself Irish. From the creation of Northern Ireland and more specifically in the last six or seven years most lads my age and younger no longer consider themselves Irish within my tradition. If you ask me what I am, I'm an Ulsterman. We live in the island of Ireland, there's an Irish input, but I'm Ulster and British; my Grandfather would have considered himself Irish and British.[26]

> I would simply say I was Irish for I was never out of Ireland. I was only in Scotland one half day in my life. British? Before 1921 we were all the same. I never had a passport! . . . I would rather go to RTÉ [Irish National TV, Dublin] than to Havelock House [Independent Television (ITV) Northern Ireland]. I was always made feel very cosy there.[27]

> I would call myself Irish because no-one in Ireland thinks that I'm English, and my vocabulary and turn of phrase is Ulster. Other people can be sometimes quite disturbed when they learn that this singer whom they had assumed to be a Catholic, and certainly a native Ulsterman, has a strongly English background . . . there might also be Protestants who think I ought to be representing my 'side' better . . .[28]

> I would consider myself as an Irish citizen . . . me bein' brought up in Ireland. I wouldn't really connect myself with Britain very much. Culturally – Ireland.[29]

> I'm a British subject. But if I'm abroad I'm Irish. If there was such an animal I'd be Iro-British, but I have no concept of labels or boxes. I'm a bit of a maverick, I don't want to be labeled or boxed.[30]

The acid test is hotel registration, in any part of Ireland. It can be like a juggling exercise with four balls (flying a flag, causing a row, feeling insulted, and unwittingly being insulting): 'We were over fishin' in Mayo, and I was checkin' into the hotel. The woman asked me "Nationality?" . . . I says, "Would Ulster do?". . . it wasn't suitin' her register so she said, "Maybe 'Irish' – aren't we all Irish?"'[31] Such confusion imposed by the greater political situation is more easily worked out at present than it often was in 1992. Firstly the emergence of Ulster-Scots identity side-steps the question of Irishness by offering a new view of the past and thus a fresh option.[32] In the peak period of Traditional music revival therefore, paralleling the Troubles, a majority of Protestants had opted for allegiance to British identity, but with a significant (for Traditional music) 28 per cent identifying with the island of birth.

TABLE 2:
Protestant attitudes to national identity over a spread of years

Year	Irish %	British %	Ulster %	N. Irish %	Island Irish %
Late 1960s	20	39	32	?	52
Late 1970s	8	67	20	?	28
1989		68	10	16	29
1993	2	69	15	11	28

It can be seen from this table that, by the latter years of the twentieth century, less than a third of Northern Irish Protestants wished to be associated with a primary identity from the island. The process of how this identity labelling developed is statistically described with great colour in Brian Walker's *Dancing to History's Tune*.[33]

Shared identity?

It seems reasonable to state that all nationality-expressive cultural trappings are perfectly simple, arbitrary and universal items and concepts until claimed, and that the same item can serve many different bosses. For instance, Gaelic language in Scotland can suggest Scottishness with either Presbyterianism or Catholicism; Gaelic in Cape Breton, Canada, indicates Scottish ancestry and Catholicism; Gaelic (the same language) in Ireland almost always means Irishness and Catholicism. This being the case then, one might expect common areas of cultural identity in Northern Ireland. If these are not acknowledged as such, it is likely that this is for political reasons. In practice neither of the two main religious communities has any problem in identifying with low-profile cultural paraphernalia, like soda farls,[34] potato bread and local accents. But, as already mentioned, the very dramatic, and public, recreational activities, like sport and music, are polarised, highly media conscious and political. Such are pragmatic and political decisions: 'The English tradition in Ulster is clear. You've got a mother tradition that you couldn't call Irish and you couldn't call Scots because there's no difference between them. And those traditions were the common cultural clothing of the Scots settlers and the native Irish at the Plantation. You would have to prove that somehow or other music was an exception to all of these other rules.'[35] Confirming a common style of music in the past is the case of older people in the rural, mixed communities where Protestants have grown up with Traditional music as a part of their environment. They consider that the music is a shared heritage:

John Junior and Bill Hardie [Scottish fiddlers] and them was comin' over here and the hall was too wee, so I asked . . . the master of the Orange Hall. I says 'By the way, there'll be all shades of opinion – anybody [meaning 'Catholics too'] will be comin' for the music.' 'Well,' he says, 'The hall's there, we keep our banners hangin up on the wall, do you want us to take them down?' I says, 'I'm sure nobody'll mind', so the banner was kept up on the wall, King Willie and all, [Laughs] and we had an outstandin' concert, they even made the tea. We supplied the sandwiches and all. Me mother baked about six dozen buns for them kind of carry-ons, it was a great success. And who do you think's plonked right below the big banner – Mickey McIlhatton – the King of the Glens.[36] Mickey's sittin' to the banner playin' away. [Hoots with laughter] I says to Mickey 'Not a very good surroundin' to have to play in?' He says, 'Sure dam the hair I care – it's nice music . . .' The master of the lodge, he was the boy who made the tea, he thanked everybody for comin' and hoped they'd a very enjoyable night. And there you had at the back of the hall four big [Lambeg] drums sittin' up in a rack and you'd a banner [of the local Orange lodge] sittin' at the far end, so you couldn't've been any more offensive![37]

This information emphasises all the more how it is in urban areas that Protestant culture finds difficulty in coping with sharing cultural features with Catholics, how Protestants in urban areas *choose* what is *not* to be regarded as included in their culture in order to preserve distinctiveness. In 1996 this was challenged somewhat with the Harryville, County Antrim, blockade and marching disputes, which marked an extension of urban ideological practice to rural areas.

'Ulster-Scots'

Since the 1990s the issue of 'Ulster-Scots' has arisen as a new politically defining force, exercising influence in such fashions or tokenism as the advertising of public-service occupations.[38] The strength of this has yet to be accurately assessed outside of massive internet-site self-publicity, but it is certainly utilised to indicate loyalty to the locality of birth, and consequently to cultures of the place. Therefore it is likely to increase interest in Traditional musics, albeit, on the evidence so far, not in Ulster or Irish music, but in *Scottish* music and dance as Chapter 3 describes, and as the opening photograph in this chapter illustrates.

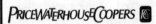

Advertisement for the Directorship of the Ulster-Scots Agency, 2002.

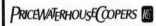

English translation of the Ulster-Scots advertisement.

CHAPTER TEN

The radical impetus of 'folk'

The Weavers – post-war forerunners of modern-day 'folk' musicians. These were a professional group, with a huge following, but they cemented a fixed, political validity for 'folk' culture, which was perceived as vanishing in the western world and beyond.

The modern apprehension of 'folk' and 'Traditional' musics owes much to the after-effects of the 1930s economic depression in the USA. For the younger college-going generation there, the liberal philosophy of leftism laid to rest the myth of 'the American dream'. Meaning for life came to be sought in the 'real people', particularly rural people. The 'folk' were idealised, then 'their' music was interpreted, not only as a signifier of honest incorruptibility, but also as a potential mobiliser of awareness and action that would assist the reinstating of 'real', egalitarian values in society. Proletarian singers like Aunt Molly Jackson were 'discovered' and fanned to new and different lives, sometimes by people whose interest was less the songs' lyric subtleties, or the singer's unique intonation,[1] but more *who* was singing. A lost world had to be recovered, and the folk-songs and the Traditional musics were identified as vital keys to gates of the pure past.

In the ideal of the 'old time', songs were presumed to have been learnt 'on the fly', as one learns a language and begins to speak in an accent, by interaction with parents and neighbours. In the 1920s, however, radio frustrated this process somewhat, introducing popular song like that of Bing Crosby, but the airwaves' specialised programmes also encouraged the re-learning of older songs. From 1923 onwards, records had already been foddering a whole generation of taste (continuing that which had been done earlier by sheet music, and further back by printed 'broadside' ballads). Singers were therefore popularised now via 78 RPM discs, among them country/blues singer Jimmie Rodgers.[2] This was the beginning of 'popular' song, a form that crossed boundaries which had thereto been culturally closed.

Folk music in the USA was interpreted somewhat differently, however; it was seen as involving past to present continuity, variation and selection. The southern states from Virginia down to Alabama and Tennessee became the blueprint for US folk-song culture. The ethos was a reality, but in this new take-up a myth also, fulfilling as it did a need for emotional orientation via the past. The creation of this home territory for down-home worthiness had been prompted by awareness of the disappearance of the American small farmer, and the loss of contact between the majority of people and food production.[3] As a populist movement the National Farmers' Alliance and Industrial Union had begun to address the arresting of these trends as far back as 1890. This was the period of the birth of 'movement culture' – organised challenge to the status quo hierarchies within societies: 'to dare to be autonomous in the presence of powerful new institutions of economic concentration and cultural regimentation'.[4] Understanding this, it was argued, was the key to appreciation of the popularity and development of Traditional musics,[5] the way in which collective efforts could gain 'psychological space'. Record companies were talent-scouting the southern US states during the 1920s in search of commercially viable singers.

In contrast to this, musicologists John and Alan Lomax began recording and collecting in 1928. Their activity overlapped with major strikes in the region, which between 1929 and 1933 attracted journalists, labour organisers and revolutionary tourists,[6] the struggle and poverty fusing to create radical ideology, class conflict and rural ballad-making traditions, all of which produced 'topical songs using old melodies to set off intensely stark and militant texts in ideologies as diverse as Karl Marx, Abraham Lincoln and Mikhail Bakunin'.[7] Radio and recordings in this era maximised audiences and accelerated the rate of diffusion of songs. So, a fascination for the pre-industrial was stirred up by challenges to capital and mass-consumption technology, with shadows perhaps of William Morris's notion of utopia[8] a century earlier. Such a combination made an attractive, durable, cultural commodity of the authentic music of the underdog, producing 'an acceleration in the process of creation, diffusion and transformation of the "topical ballad"'.[9] Interest was created 'first for intellectuals, especially those around the Communist Party, seeking the "real" and "proletarian" America in music, but later for virtually anyone writing advertising copy"'.[10] Such visual and tonal, rural and old-time snapshot imagery are familiar in Ireland today in television advertising, where the idealised past is still a much more attractive place than the present, its seasonally regulated authenticity more desirable than something from a clock-metered production-line, and where the idea of 'community' might evoke 'more than a place or local activity ... an expectation of a special quality of human relationship'.[11] But idealising the past and 'the folk' has never been just fanciful. It also has acute reality in that it represents 'an ideal and a hope for alternative modes of existence to the alienation and atomisation experienced in a society subject to increasingly rapid transformation',[12] much too important to be dismissed by excessively literal interpretations of historical revisionists' 'invention' and 'reinvention' catch-all theory, or hasty knocking of the tenability of 'myth' itself.

Thus US 'Folk' dates to the search for authentic folk songs and singers in the 1930s by people like the Lomaxes. Their 'discoveries' – Leadbelly, Sonny Terry and Brownie McGee (who played in Ireland in the 1970s), and Woody Guthrie among them – entered the Valhalla of folk studies, their style and ambience having been recovered courtesy of the new media. Woody Guthrie made a thousand and more songs, some – like 'This Land Is Your Land' – continue to be sung agitationally and symbolically today, often with inspirational effect. The political intervention of the folk-song promoters was not lost on the post-war USA government, which proceeded to ban key figures as part of its paranoid culling of communist ideas during what became known as 'the McCarthy era'.[13] Singer Pete Seeger, reared in an atmosphere of folk music ethnography and collection as the son of ethnomusicologist Charles Seeger, was one of those who fell foul of this policy. Pioneer of the folk banjo and a guitar stylist, he was the key player in the seminal and popular Almanac singers group during the 1940s, and the Weavers, both of which were chart toppers. Blacklisted for the political conviction he expressed in songs and censored from television, Seeger was persecuted by Congressional committees, and was still being refused performance space right into the 1960s. His key song 'If I Had a Hammer' (a subtle allegory on toppling power structures) became inspirational world-wide, and hugely popular. 'We Shall Overcome' was another song identified with him, one which he considerably reworked from its Gospel origins to its present-day familiar lyrics and tune – 'one of the most influential political anthems in history'.[14] This he developed at the Highlander Folk Center in Tennessee, a facility founded to train trades union organisers, and which was to become closely associated with the (USA) Civil Rights movement in the southern states.[15] Seeger himself was prominent in that campaign, and also in that against the Vietnam war throughout the 1960s. His sister Peggy, also a singer-songwriter, in partnership with unequivocal Marxist singer and songwriter Ewan MacColl, bridged this USA experience to the Campaign for Nuclear Disarmament (CND) in Britain, and to the work there of politically motivated singer and collector A.L. (Bert) Lloyd. Peggy Seeger, Lloyd and MacColl visited Ireland, where they undertook key recordings of Irish Traditional singers in the field, and also gave space to the major Irish voices at 'The Singers' Club' in London during the 1960s and 1970s. In addition, MacColl performed in folk-style clubs in Ireland, and was well-known among Irish singers and ballad audiences for his hugely well-known 'Shoals of Herring' and 'Freeborn Man', songs which are still popular today. The communism bogey in the US also had repercussions in Ireland, where in June 1953, popular singer Danny Kaye's projected appearance at the Dublin Theatre Royal that August was blocked on account of his having been cited in the 1948 California Senate Fact Finding Committee on Un-American Activities; harmonica virtuoso Larry Adler was also banned in Ireland.[16]

The years following World War II in America produced a large proportion of college students who were alienated from a society which was top-heavy with control and mass-media manipulation. 'Folk-song' became a popular, accessible, do-able form of protest and implement of change. Various American groups and individuals evolved to front this attractive, fluid movement in various forms from the 1950s onwards: the Kingston Trio (with the song 'Tom Dooley' in 1958); the Weavers ('Goodnight Irene', 1950s); New Christy Minstrels, Peter Paul and Mary and Joan Baez ('We Shall Overcome'); and, of course, Bob Dylan ('The Times They Are a-Changin'). Between 1963 and 1968 'folk-rock' arose seamlessly out of this style as almost experimental, a meeting ground of the iconic Guthrie, Jimmie Rodgers, Carter Family, Hank Williams, Doc Watson and Bill Monroe and the older black blues artistes like Mississippi John Hurt as well as younger singers like Muddy Waters. Thence the direction was rock.[17] Traditional Irish performers such as sean-nós singer Joe Heaney had participated in this too.

'Folk' and 'Traditional' music and song in Ireland had quite a different base. In the West, sean-nós song still survived as local entertainment, and in the whole island's much tighter society the instrumental music in particular retained an active role in rural popular dance through to the 1950s, and lingered strongly into the 1960s. The 'revival' for Ireland was more a 'revitalisation', a dig in the ribs, a wake-up call about putting more value on what was already being practised. As a movement it applied itself visibly not to overtly agitational republican music (which had its own momentum, related to the diaspora Irish in the US and Britain), but to the recreational and artistic. The old practitioners of Irish Traditional music, whether Protestant or Catholic, may have been variously romantic, sentimental, conservative, republican, loyal to the British crown – or just plain indifferent. But the new, young blood, which was the adrenaline of a relentless 'folk/Traditional revival', was fired up by the enabling momentum of the highly political US movement. This has been noted by writer Ciarán Carson, former Traditional music officer with the Northern Ireland Arts Council: '. . . the so-called traditional music "revival" of the sixties . . . has been attributed to many factors . . . the influence of the early fleadhanna ceoil, instigated by Comhaltas Ceoltóirí Éireann in the fifties, is undeniable, as is that of "ballad" groups like the Clancy Brothers and the Dubliners. But it also seems to have been part of a wider cultural phenomenon which, for the urban young, would have included such diverse characters as Bob Dylan, Joan Baez, Woody Guthrie, Ewan MacColl, Bert Lloyd, the Watersons, Bert Jansch, the Incredible String Band . . .'.[18]

The US experience led our modern apprehension of popular Folksong. Its figureheads became known in Ireland and Britain, where indeed many of the songs unearthed by this movement had originated and still survived. It also paralleled both the British folk-song movement (familiar to many Irish singers) and the widespread and growing awareness of, and concern for, the preservation of the indigenous Traditional music and song within Ireland. In the US and Britain, Labour, left-wing and Marxist ideologues were important among those who successfully collected, revived, promoted and fronted folk-song. The songs that were so assembled and popularised set a style and a standard that came to be expected of 'folk' music (and which still persists in Britain and Ireland today), with associations that in fact were energising and empowering, especially to the confident and growing labour-left in Ireland. In other regions – notably Latin America, and in particular Chile – struggles for democracy were linked inevitably to folk-song. This was not only by virtue of the lyrics' function as, traditionally, 'the peoples' voice' against imposed landowner culture, but also because such singers and songs were (for those reasons) outlawed by the state as subversive. Some such Chilean performers spent time as refugees in Ireland during the 1980s, where they sang at political rallies to gain international support for the campaign for a democratic Chile. With such a pedigree and roll of honour, the concept of 'folk music revival' could be accurately interpreted by radicals and conservatives alike as desiring – if not heralding – the dismantling of the conservative structures of power that had produced two world wars and the nuclear bomb (and had all the appearance of generating the ultimate blitz). Quite regardless of the intrinsic worth of songs and music and of the individual performer's interpretations of them, this was a considerable propellant for folk-song. Such a distinctive anti-imperial, anti-state political character was welcomed by labour-left thinkers and activists within Northern Ireland's Protestant community, but was not favoured by conservative Ulster loyalists.

CHAPTER ELEVEN

Traditional music in a modern world

The Liverpool Céilí Band, formed with Irish musicians who had settled in Liverpool, England. This is a typical format for such a band, which was a major part of the 'popular' music of the 1920s–1950s. In Northern Ireland a number of such bands were composed of Protestant players, or involved Protestant players.

The promotion of interest in Traditional music in Ireland generated a considerable wake in the 1960s, ripples from which continue to effect change. Because it involved such an apparent reversal of modernity and music development, the process has engendered heated debate. In fact the music incurred substantial rejection in Catholic areas, in the very community of which many Protestants popularly see it as emblematic. A (Catholic-area-born) panel-speaker at the 1990 'Whose Music?' conference in Enniskillen raised the point that few Catholics know very much about Traditional music at all. He spoke of 'a danger, in talking about this music, of an assumption that it is the most popular form of music? It is a minority taste, even among the nationalists . . .'.[1] The revival of Traditional music, as a profound restoration and revitalisation,[2] is taken very much for granted by both Protestants (where they are aware of it) and by Catholics; it is simply part of 'the tradition'. The broader implications of such revival within twentieth-century politics and social upheaval have been outlined in the previous chapter, yet, despite the active process of revival and the impact of its organisational forms in Ireland after 1951, even in the 1960s it was unusual to hear what is now known as 'Traditional' music in either part of Ireland. This contrasts with the fact that today it is a thriving entertainment and industry in many city-centre pub and concert venues in the major Northern and Southern Irish cities of Belfast, Dublin, Galway and Cork. It currently has a talent centre in the town of Ennis, County Clare,[3] and by 2000 could be heard also in practically every town on the island, with 1,500 and more 'session' nights weekly.[4] This new status, which in Dublin obscures the memory of 'No singing allowed!' notices (common in pubs during the late 1960s),[5] has developed its own value system, rituals, hierarchy, professionalism, academia, media and, above all, community. Prominent in its presentation is the standard music format, the 'session', a term probably borrowed from American blues and jazz music by Irish-exile, social recreation in pre-World-War-II USA and developed within Irish music from the 1950s onward.

The session

The session is typically a group of people who play dance tunes – reels, jigs, hornpipes, polkas, slides, slip-jigs, waltzes and marches – often interspersed with songs and melodic slow airs. Sometimes the music is played for 'set' dancers. It takes place in a seemingly unorganised way. The instruments used will generally be some combination of fiddles, concertinas, flutes, uilleann pipes, tin whistles, banjos, guitars, bouzoukis, accordions and bodhráns.[6] The music is performed differently to other musics – it is quite casual, apparently independent of, if not oblivious to, any audience, often tolerating a formidable volume of conversation. Since the 1960s it has been tolerated by publicans and drinkers who might even have been slightly in awe of it where they were not so with popular music. The musicians may sometimes appear stoic and emotionless in their application, and while some listeners observe intently, others seem to pay attention only during lulls in talking. But most of those present are there *because* of the music. Often functioning like conversation, this is music that is played 'out'. Since the 1950s it has been heard in venues otherwise reserved for conversation, whereas other forms of music could be heard only on the stage or in the concert hall.[7] Live music in Irish bars began formally between the 1950s and 1960s, with a fashion of singing lounges where people congregated

Mullaghbane – typical session, 2002.

enthusiastically to sing all sorts of songs.[8] Traditional music became somewhat dominant in the 1960s, peaking during the 1980s. Session playing pre-dates the modern trend of musak entertainment – live or piped – which is a feature in almost all drinking establishments today.

In the past, the music played at sessions was mostly Irish, but nowadays may also include some Breton, American country, bluegrass or cajun. Cape Breton music from Nova Scotia is particularly popular too, on account of the area's 30 per cent Irish, 60 per cent Scottish make-up. Scottish music itself is a strong ingredient in the older Irish tunes repertoire, but is long naturalised in Ireland where it is played with a different accent to its present practice in its home country; more modern Scottish pieces are played by fiddlers in particular. Traditional music in 'sessions' is popular not only in Ireland, but in the Irish population centres in London and other English cities, in Europe and in the USA. It has a broader interest-community too, one which has no other connection with Ireland. For instance, in Japan, a group of native Japanese players of Traditional Irish music have performed for the Emperor there on each St Patrick's Day since 1992;[9] in 2000 Bewley's restaurant (an Irish enterprise), in Tokyo, also held regular sessions. In Brittany, Irish Traditional music has a popular currency both in local marching bands and among Breton dance-music performers, while France itself has scores of Irish Traditional concert bands. Irish music is played by a substantial number of Jewish American musicians, by touring concert bands in northern Italy both on its own and in conjunction with Friulian and other Italian Traditional

Japanese musicians busking with Irish music in Galway, 2003.

musics. Throughout the European-influenced world and beyond too, this music genre can be heard as the aural décor of Irish-themed bars.[10] Arguably Irish Traditional music has in fact become the lingua franca of Traditional music enthusiasts of many different ethnic and religious backgrounds:[11] 'I went to Gormanstown [the All-Ireland Fleadh Cheoil Scoil-Éigse], a music summer school one year . . . and I was amazed one day to see a little Japanese fella with a miniature set of uilleann pipes and he was playin' Irish music as well as any of the other pipers that I had heard. And his father standin' beside him. I couldn't get over it.'[12]

Organised music

Traditional music also has a highly organised formal life which underlies the seeming casualness of the sessions. This is expressed in competitions, organisations, casual performance sessions, professional performance, media shows, music-, song- and dance-teachers, second-level teaching, third-level teaching, postgraduate study, web coverage and magazines. Looking at these individually helps one develop a sense of the field of practice.

Competitions

These are based on a classical music type framework and are organised in a regional, county and provincial structure covering both parts of Ireland and all areas of Irish population abroad. These are complemented by classes, summer schools and concerts. The focus for the competition structure is the *fleadh cheoil*[13] at which the casual sessions as described above also take place. This network was initiated by and is administered by CCÉ.[14] Since 1997 a classical music style 'grades' system has also been administered by the London College of Music, and in 1998 another was introduced by CCÉ and the Royal Irish Academy of Music.[15]

Organisations[16]

Local and national bodies organise teaching, festivals, summer schools, workshops and specialist events, often focusing on individual instruments.

The 'session' scene

This is an independent, fringe, cultural phenomenon in pubs, where typically a couple of musicians are paid a small fee to be in attendance on certain nights. They may act as a catalyst to encourage others to come in and play, but certainly they guarantee the publican and the casual visitor some sort of live music. The session is the most accessible of the music's performance spaces for player and listener alike.

Commercial professional and semi-professional practice

This includes most of the best-known names and groups in Traditional music, who play both in Ireland and to Irish and general folk-music audiences all over the world. It is well established and involves big-stage shows, club gigs, formal concerts, radio and television performance, recording, film scoring, advertising jingles and tourism promotions.

Media shows

These incorporate specialised radio and television performance,[17] magazine and documentary presentations, some tight-format shows, all usually occurring weekly though others can be more sporadic. Ulster Television (UTV) has had several series over the years, as has BBC Northern Ireland.

Local music-, song- and dance-teachers

Teachers operate both independently and in organisational structures, teaching either in one-to-one or in group situations. Students are usually young people between the ages of eight and seventeen years.

Second-level education

Since 1977, Traditional music has been present as a performance option in Irish Junior and Leaving Certificate music education curricula in the Republic. In 1988 it was introduced as a performance option in the Northern Ireland O- and A-level secondary school music curricula.[18]

Third-level education

An optional module is offered by many of the university and Institutes of Technology music departments on the island. An undergraduate degree in Traditional music was initiated in the Dublin Institute of Technology (DIT) in 2000, one in the Irish World Music Centre (IWMC) at University of Limerick in 2002; London College of Music (LCM) offers degree status in the music also. Waterford Institute of Technology and Dundalk Institute of Technology offer Traditional music specialisation in music degrees; University of Ulster offers Traditional music as a study module, and Queen's University Belfast appointed a lecturer in the music in 2006.

Postgraduate study

Postgraduate study in Traditional music is facilitated by most university music departments, notably University College Cork. University of Limerick's IWMC is the specialist in this, with several taught MA courses rooted in ethnomusicology. Dundalk and Waterford Institutes of Technology host valuable postgraduate research projects in the music. University College Dublin's Dept. of Irish Folklore has been heavily involved in song collection and associated education work.

The internet

A huge number of 'official', semi-official, private, personal and commercial websites and chat fora are the major communicational media of the music today. By 2005, entering the term 'Irish traditional music' in a search engine would generate close on four million items.

Magazines

Four of these give the music substantial promotion: *Irish Music* (fanzine style), *Journal of Music in Ireland* (*JMI*, academic), *Treoir* (the internal organ of CCÉ) and *The Living Tradition* (also covers Scotland). Most newspapers run occasional features and reviews, with the *Examiner, Belfast Newsletter* and *Sunday Tribune* having had specialist columns for many years. Among the daily press, *The Irish Times* (Dublin) consistently covers the music as an art form, while *The Irish News* (Belfast) presents performance features on it.

The commercial life of the music is a consequence of many taste, economic and political factors. The educational side is beginning to inform a younger generation at a core development stage and is likely to lead to an eventual greater level of sophistication in interpretation and appreciation, but the most widespread practice of the music remains in 'the session'.

City sessions

'The session' was once an event organised to provide a regular weekly or monthly opportunity for people to come together to play. Particularly in the 1960s, a session might have had a strong sense of mission or purpose, subversive to a world which was hostile to the music. This ethos gave it strong 'underground' appeal for musicians and aficionados. With the increasing popularity of the music, the beleaguered attitude has disappeared and enthusiastic confidence has taken over. 'Voluntary' or 'casual' sessions were, and often still are, spontaneous and unadvertised and may be private or semi-private affairs which use public space in the same way as groups of conversationalists or sports fans utilise bars. Sessions are also organised as a regular weekly or monthly event for CCÉ branches, usually involving young and old members of the branch if they play music, and/or players from other branches, and/or unaffiliated people who simply drop in. More common today is the 'paid session' (with a couple of anchor musicians, by now the coalface of public music playing), where most music is to be heard in an informal environment. While in general all age groups and classes may attend or take part in sessions in Northern Irish towns, the greater political situation imposes controls. The clientele of listeners in Belfast tends to be mixed, but this in the sense that the Protestants present (like the Catholics) will generally be non-politically intolerant, or not overtly interested in politics. The

The Electric Bar, Derry. The 'hole in the wall' effect on this Derry session pub suggests the music session as a separate world within outside reality.

loyalist and working-class Protestant will not normally drink in such places anyway, since the music is generally not a feature of their cultural upbringing (and hence has no attraction). Catholic working-class drinkers may often be present. Protestant office workers, teachers, academics, students, business people, etc., are in a different category: they *may*, and *do*, in their everyday economic life cross the barriers freely, when they don't have any personal impediment such as – prior to the early 2000s – membership of the RIR,[19] RUC Reserve, etc. Fear of abuse or attack is not the major disincentive to Protestant musicians in these mixed establishments, but for some there is undoubtedly a certain discomfort caused by the political label and the apparently largely Catholic support which the music developed.

Rural areas

In rural areas the situation is different in that the tensions there may only be a shadow of what they are in Belfast; people of different religions live together but not in tightly packed ghettos, and normally they have to get along with each other at some level. Allowing for modern bungalow isolation and TV/video-bound recreation, they are very often as close – or as separated – as any neighbours anywhere in the western world. Rural audiences and participants may be mixed and in certain places will enjoy the music in equal measure, each viewing the music aesthetically ('Traditionally') rather than politically. Generally the 'house' (venue) where the music is played will be a Catholic-owned pub, or will be 'neutral' – a hotel. In areas where the music has survived with continuity – such as in County Fermanagh, North Antrim or East Down – an establishment may be Protestant-owned and identified, and the players there may be mixed, be predominantly Protestant or totally Protestant. All permutations happen. Throughout counties Down and Antrim – the rough focus of this book – in the early 1990s there might have been a dozen venues where music was heard weekly, and others where Traditional singing and dancing were indulged in during the winter months. Each session is different, each area has its peculiarities. Each pub owner has particular attitudes and perceptions, as has each musician or group of musicians.

CHAPTER TWELVE

Performance style and political identification

Roy Arbuckle (facing camera) with his Different Drums ensemble, which uses Lambeg and bodhrán along with uilleann pipes, flutes and various percussion forms.

Traditional music's most common and accessible venue is the pub session. As a process this caters to several needs, including the artistic: the fulfilment of the players' compulsion to play and explore the music aesthetic with others as well as facilitating the music lovers' own aesthetic engagement. It also allows utopian escapism, in the desire to keep in touch with the 'folk' values of an idealised or ruralist past. Finally, there is identity, – empathy with various aspects of personal, local or indigenous Irish identity – artistic, 'cultural', political and national.

Each of these needs applies to all musicians and followers. The first (artistic) is a given for most, and the second (escapism) applies across many other interests, from budgie-breeding to vintage cars. In musicians' minds there are different attitudes to what is going on, but first it has to be assumed that they enjoy the process: 'Irish music's a way of life, you've been workin' all week, you like to get out and have a few pints and have a couple of tunes and enjoy it. That's the way that I always knew it . . .'[1] However, it is the issue of identity which is closest to the subject of this book, for it relates exclusively to those who are so disposed – perhaps mostly to Catholics who are nationalist-minded (but not all Catholics are so), yet also to some Protestants also for whom either the notion has meaning, or who appreciate the shared legacy of the music on the island. Since each of the three points reflects what occurs in equivalent Traditional music subcultures in other countries, they will now be considered individually.

Artistic considerations

Of all the arts, music involves most mystery because of its capacity to simultaneously engage the intellect, craft/skill, creative impulse, ideology, emotions and the subconscious. It transports the performer and the listener to 'another place', a liberated state of mind which may be quite indescribable. For this reason, and in its finest aesthetic sense, music is popularly regarded as a 'gift', 'a domain of a special, almost extra-social, autonomous experience'.[2] Music can be written about fancifully, fetishised by superficial consumers (people whose understanding of it may be cliché-ridden and quite different from that of the performers), while in specialised media it is usually described somewhat profoundly by professional critics and aficionados. But all non-performer interpretations can conflict with what the actual performers feel, for their consciousness (while undoubtedly aesthetically driven) may also be conditioned by local community, greater society, folkloric, political or media-promotion attitudes. By its nature, music performance rises completely beyond such easy pigeon-holing, and from the player's perspective music remains largely a personal thing, even in a session environment. Expressivity for the Traditional musician *may* involve performance in a public dimension, but it also has a fundamental privacy and artistic self-indulgence, something which is common to all cultures: '"If I feel like it, I will play one [Zimbabwe, mbira[3] music] piece all night long," one performer, Ephat Mujuru, explains. "Listen to what I am playing and then come back in a half hour and I'll be playing altogether differently."'[4] In the Irish context: 'There's lots of fellas and when they're seventeen or eighteen, this kind of red mist comes down over them. And all there is in the world for them is music. And them's the best musicians! Them ones go "boom!" That red mist came over me, completely, I had lost all control, everything went out the window except music . . .'[5] A powerfully expressive metaphor, the idea of the 'red mist' is not unique to Irish music, and probably has been picked up from jazz or blues; Tony MacMahon, for instance, speaks of experiencing 'a shaft of blue light', and others reference 'blue light' or 'blue mist'. Such self-description indicates strongly the quoted musicians' self-perception as *musicians* and provides a strong validation of the artistic integrity of the genre.

Utopian escapism

A sense of escapism is of underlying importance to the political acquisition of musics. In all twentieth-century struggles for emancipation from imperial control and suppressive annexations, the notion of past and rural pureness has played a vital role, but such ideals have been extra-nationally independent too, part of the ethos of 'the Beat generation' and often related to craft skill, as evidenced by hippy movements, crofting in Scotland and equivalent tendencies in England, Wales and Ireland. Since the movement prompted by Bishop Percy,[6] 'folk' or, today, 'Traditional' musics are felt to embody pre-industrial values, attitudes and cultures, which are more pleasant than the pragmatic rationalisation of the urban blue- and white-collar working classes and their perceived absence of 'culture': '. . . popular or "people's" music [is] part of a continuing effort to create forms of community in response to social transformations – the trauma of modernisation – that empty out all the 'little worlds' . . . on which people live . . . Human existence is conceived as a quest for community, or more specifically, for "free spaces" and "utopias" to which popular culture is a manufactured response.'[7] Some performers have to hand an abundant rhetoric with which to voice the inexpressible in this regard. In *Irish Minstrels and Musicians*[9] American collector Francis O'Neill provided a valuable inspirational, intellectual rationale and language of aesthetic interpretation, which arguably seeded twentieth-century Traditional music revival. Richard Henebry's ethno-musicological analysis in the same period[10] illuminated yet other facets of consciousness and confidence. Elements of both of these views are still heard from today's more opinionated musicians: 'The singing of the birds, the ancient chants of our forefathers the calls of the wild animals in the lonely countryside, the drone of the bees, the galloping hooves of the wild horses . . . The wind, the rain, the flowing rivers that shaped the mind and passion of our ancient forefathers, inspiring them to harness together all those sounds of animal, mineral, bird and insect so as it moulded itself into a melody . . .'.[11] Such reverence for the superiority of the past is important in the expression of identity of the Protestant participant in Traditional music in Ireland. It is of course the motivation also of Catholic musicians, but for them the option of self-expansion through the music within a greater and clear *political* identity of 'National culture' is not only real and pervasive, but easy and acceptable in their own community. It is also greatly advantageous to enthusiastic engagement with the music.

Identity

As one performer puts it:

> When I perform our traditional [Zimbabwe, mbira songs], I feel like a man who wants to show the greatness of our forefathers . . .[8]

Perceived 'native' musics are very often seen as galvanising forces in bringing together the people of one territory or land-mass. This has been witnessed in television coverage of the secessions of various nationalities from the former Warsaw Pact states. The potential for successful application of music, however, depends on the relative strengths of political forces and is predicated on the essential that all sections of a population share perceptions both of identity and of who their enemies are. Such a common view can only ever be a summary of attitudes and therefore may be at great variance with reality. Music can be shaped to suit a dominant, prevailing ideology or may be moulded to serve a radically different or even personal one. The case of African-American Chicago bluesman, Carey Bell, illustrates this; in 1966 his initial reaction to having being wrongfully arrested was to take revenge on the police after he got out of jail: '. . . I went to buy me a gun to kill that cop . . . then it came to me to go to a music store and buy some harps [harmonicas] . . . so I bought the harps instead of the gun . . .'[12] Again, suppression of identity in Nigeria found reprise through the popular ju-ju music: 'The political mobilisations of the fifties were a noted showcase for ju-ju bands and those from other genres – Yoruba [ethnic] identity had to be seen to be expressed in a traditional symbol of authority – music . . . Much of the material was recorded on disc and is still banned from public broadcast.'[13] During his country's 1830s uprising against Imperial Russia, Polish composer Chopin's 'late romantic style itself denoted revolution, and the struggle of the individual against the world; a highly-appropriate image for the ideologues of a new nation-state . . . This formulation was however entirely reversed in [twentieth-century] socialist Poland. Chopin [therein] was celebrated for his adherence to his roots and his refusal to conform to the bourgeois aesthetics of romanticism.'[14] A 'national' sound in music is desirable for the modern nation-state, especially where there are different ethnic identities: 'It has been the policy of the government [in Afghanistan, before the Russian occupation which pre-dated the Taliban regime] to break down local allegiances and divisions, and to instil in the people a spirit of nationalism . . . Music may serve as an area of shared experience which helps to delineate the boundaries of a nation; perhaps at a deep level the sentiment of Afghan popular music is a sentiment of national identity.'[15]

National representativeness

Many people, particularly in the south of Ireland, have expressed hope that Traditional music revival might serve a reconciliatory role in Ulster in the climate of sectarianism. This suggests that a common sense of identity might be arrived at through 'the music'. Earliest among these idealists were many of those involved in CCÉ, especially when it expanded its remit to include Northern Ireland in 1956. Amongst the organisations supporting this view has been the cross-spectrum peace body Co-operation North,[16] whose 1990 'Whose Music?' conference[17] was dedicated to this topic. Applying the idea of a rescue remedy, a panacea in the form of music, to Northern Ireland, may seem at face value to be so simply perfect – it involves an appeal to demonstrably very real, shared, past cultural characteristics – but it has difficulty in incorporating the political loading which all things 'Irish' have accreted and have had thrust upon them since 1921, music forms in particular.

The incorporation of musics as 'national' is well established as a feature of identity marking and cultural consolidation in recently ex-colonial states. Indeed, without such tonal distinctiveness, in the age of multinational industry and global entertainment values, international usage of mediational languages such as Spanish and English, and with the gaseous mobility of capital, a nationality based on national territory alone might seem to make no sense. If 'persistent "production" of culture and attribution of value becomes an essential bulwark against the cultural imperialism of the political and economic centres',[18] it becomes clearer that a major contradiction between Catholic and Protestant Traditional musicians lies in the political potential involved in being Catholic within that music. Since Traditional music is the music which is popularly viewed as the 'national' music of (the South of) Ireland, Catholics – those in the South, and those in the North who are nationalist – have that as their opening option on how to regard it. Even if they have no other aesthetic considerations they have the immense comfort and confidence of this popularly ascribed belief. In contrast, there is *compromise* involved for most Protestants, who for political reasons are potentially unionist, potentially antagonistic to the most basic level of acceptance of the Catholic musician. Contradiction or no, this has not prevented the Northern Ireland Tourist Board utilising cross-religion cultural aspects productively. For instance, part of its 1993 advertising campaign (a pull-out in the Northern Ireland *Yellow Pages* commercial telephone directory) displayed photographs of Traditional musicians. Some of them were indeed from Northern Ireland, but only accidentally so, as the location of photography was actually a well-known music venue at Lisdoonvarna, County Clare – in the South. In this regard the performance style of Traditional music takes on a new significance. Its 'casual' nature may on the one hand certainly be part of an aesthetic, but on the other, it also marks 'time out' from the political situation, a permanent Christmas Day in no-man's land.

'Celtic', 'Gaelic' identity

Beyond these three major features of engagement with Traditional music, the music also mediates other deeply felt ideas of earthy spirituality in a direct line from ancient times. Thus, it can share with revived folk music everywhere a role as a cause in itself – for many Protestants as well as Catholics – generally, but somewhat vaguely perceived and felt as an active link with the remote, or Celtic past, especially in the heritage-conditioned imagination of the culture-tourist in whom the Irelands, Northern and Southern, have significant vested interest. Whether or not this is a learned experience courtesy of eighteenth- and nineteenth-century romanticism is another matter, but maybe, like the other attitudes that govern satisfaction within our cultural lives, it is hardly remarkable. 'Irish Irishness' in Traditional music within Ireland may not visibly seem to be of much concern, but looking at a parallel example, that of Scottish Traditional music in Scotland in the 1900s, in a development/revival stage, 'Scottishness' certainly was critically important, and it remains a strong factor in the identification process of many Scottish musicians: 'Scottish Music can really only be played by Scottish people – it's genetic I suppose . . .'[19] Some Protestant Traditional players in Ireland do feel the Celtic or Gaelic identity just as strongly as their Catholic counterparts: 'Most of the Protestant Traditional musicians I know are not anti-Catholic, but very anti-Irish. I can't understand this. They're all against Irish nationalism – I find it's hard to understand. They play as dedicatedly, but it seems to have somethin lackin'– they take it very, very serious. They want to sit in a room and they want everybody to be very quiet . . . I don't know what way they see it. I find it hard to think – if you don't consider yourself Irish – that you have a love for the music and I don't think you can play it right if you don't love the music. And then nationalism has to come into it . . . some people say that I live in the Celtic Twilight . . .'[20]

The late twentieth century made a great play of rationally distancing itself from cultural manifestations from bygone eras (other than those in politics of course). This, understandably, was considered as 'progress'. The same period is also marked by active demands for de-partition in Ireland, and (by now partially fulfilled) for autonomy for the other great 'Celtic' monolith, Scotland. In this atmosphere Traditional music is often experienced as a validation of Celtic identity in the face of what is perceived as English blandness and soullessness. The fact that the condition which these perceptions seek to affirm or articulate is also a reaction against the relentless march of technological progress (which objectively places little value on the past other than as a series of stepping stones to arrive at the future) is unimportant; Traditional music is felt as having the political mission of, at least, the retrieval of past aesthetic values. In the renewed life of its revival period since the 1950s, the casual 'session' format is therefore soundly established as representative – an unassuming, classless, unpretentious and *proper* way to conduct an affair which is felt to carry within it the coded folk memory.

This chapter has developed major interwining and often interdependent dimensions of expressivity in Traditional music: the artistic, the utopian and identity. These variously condition the inclination or compulsion to play the music, and have underlain the enthusiastic reinvigoration of Traditional music on the island of Ireland throughout the later twentieth century. The following pages will continue on the theme of psychological engagement with the music, and will explore the elasticity of the term 'folk', its ability to encompass and become the political, with consequences in political interpretations of Traditional music.

CHAPTER THIRTEEN

Dreams and realities – folk memory and Gaelic identity

Jimmy Murphy playing in a casual, performer-centred session, at a bar in Charlestown, County Mayo.

Depending on an individual's age, religion, political circumstances, class, cultural upbringing, region, personality and education, the notion of 'folk memory', with fabulous elasticity, can accommodate many different things. These include the political (dispossession, plantations, partition and political oppression), the human condition (the heartbreak and hardship of poverty, emigration and exile), the suffusive, wholesome visions of the 'quality' of life long ago (wake, wedding and fair, passing the winter nights, hay-making, hunting and harvest, blissful uncomplicated love and cosy céilí-ing). The lives of past political heroes accrue escalating glamour as time goes by and/or as political needs call incrementally. So too musicians from the past are looked back on with nostalgia, as in an account of two fiddlers who 'lived in a wee cottage . . . great wee men, just perfect gentlemen . . . There were big slabs of stone for the floor and one of the men slept in a wee bunk beside the fire – a big open grate. There was a big sky-blue, painted cast-iron wheel and he'd sit in the chair and wind the wheel; the bellows were all under the floor . . .'[1] Romanticising the local player is wonderful, and understandable, as the music is rightly seen as having been preserved by the tenacity of such players. There have always been, in all classes, such 'fireside' musicians as those described here, as such a site for performance was the only available venue in poor society. These players both made new tunes and/or explored music intensely with what, judging by repertoire, can only be described as artistic consciousness. So-called 'amateurs' (in the original French sense of passionate lovers of, dedicatees to, stylistically and aesthetically discerning about, and technically expert in, music) are the music thinkers and aesthetes of their time, and still persist today in spite of the numbers who are drawn to seek empathy from audiences via stage and studio, and via popular and other musics. Before the major, transforming technologies and social behaviours of the twentieth century, the rate of change in music style was so slight[2] and politically uncomplicated that it was never really an issue. Whether or not musicians in the past invested either nostalgia or national aspirations in Traditional music now seems quite unimportant, however. The music – since its revival out of a progressively atrophying and potential slide to redundancy in the 1950s – with research and re-presentation has now, arguably, developed way beyond its past technical summits. The sheer amount of reinterpretation from within and without, the discography and bibliography, the teaching and professionalism, all now render it, effectively, a substantially new genre of 'folk'. Because it fulfils virtuoso potential, satisfaction of the artistic ego and commercial validity in the international marketplace[3] it is now a 'classical', international music in the manner of jazz.[4] But still, even as a free-standing genre it retains for sustenance much of its nineteenth-century romantic and nationalistic emotional legacy, which is often linked by many of its nationalist followers to similar aspirations in the present day. While not detracting from the underlying importance of the aesthetic, in this aspect the music's closest parallels are with popular political movements and Gaelic games, which share historical investment in idealism, and the thrilling feeling of being able to achieve something new or different; it is about being something worthwhile, having a value beyond the aesthetic and social pleasure of the actual pursuit.

Gaelic football

Political investment in Gaelic football has already been described; it is obvious and open, part and parcel of codification and organisation in the sport from the beginning: 'It is arguable that no organisation had done more for Irish nationalism than the GAA – not the IRB . . . not the Gaelic League, its linguistic counterpart, not the Irish Parliamentary Party . . . not even Sinn Féin which had broken apart under the impact of the Treaty. The Gaelic Athletic Association had fulfilled its mission – to revive the native games of Ireland and to awaken the National spirit.'[5] Such a belief in 'national' forms of cultural expression began in the Victorian era, and was strong all over Europe and is well-documented elsewhere.

> Ireland was by no means alone; elsewhere in Europe there were small nations struggling for independence and in that struggle trying to express their identity through the imagination. The progress of art in Norway, Sweden and Denmark offers remarkable parallels to that in Ireland: there too the mid-nineteenth century saw a vigorous interest in early medieval history (the period of the Vikings and the sagas) . . . Hungary is another example . . . in a sense, all these nationalist movements failed, because national styles are not created by acts of will. In another they all succeeded, for they expressed the nation's essence of continuity with its past. This in itself must assert its own influence on the future.[6]

So too with music, which as a powerful, non-elitist and democratic medium of aesthetic expression, *implicitly* became ideologically incorporated into nationalism. The strange thing about this, however, is that music was never *explicitly* defined as being of any key importance in the Irish movements. It wasn't until 1910 that a music collector articulated a clear view of music being vitally associated with the political ideal of 'nation', and this was done, significantly, from the US: 'Our national music is a treasure, in the possession of which we should be justly proud . . . there are very few labourers in the service of Ireland to whom we should feel more grateful than to those who have devoted their talents and their time to its preservation.'[7]

As the twentieth century progressed, Traditional music became increasingly politically identified, by outside ascription, but not as politicised as football. Because the music's revival after 1950 was taking shape within thirty years of the formalising of the new Irish state, and so close to the declaration of the Republic in 1948, it could not but have inherited some residual portion of the 'national' political force. Comhaltas Ceoltóirí Éireann entered the picture in 1951 carrying this national flag. It addresses itself, like many cultural bodies, to 'all of Ireland' but in the language it uses and statements it makes it is objectively addressing

An early banner of CCÉ's *Treoir* magazine.

nationalists and Catholics, and, above all, southerners. Northerners seem patronised by the rhetoric and considered not in terms of 'Irishness', but of religion: '... the simple magic of the Clare concertina player; the uniqueness of the Dublin piper; the native richness of the Connemara singer; the vitality of the traditional Kerry dancer; or the melodious and peaceful strains of the Northern *Presbyterian* [author's italics] fiddler ... they prefer the more stable and comforting sounds which have lulled generations of babies to sleep; exhorted Irishmen to strive for freedom, satisfied centuries of dancing feet ...'[8] [italics in original]. In this one hears striking echoes not only of the rhetoric of Eamon De Valera, but also of a similar statement from the conservative Catholic, Archbishop McQuaid, in the 1930s: 'Much remains yet to be done in utilising the vast resources of Irish music as a means of restoring the vernacular. In our enchanting cradle songs, pure love songs and vibrant martial airs lies buried a treasure too little explored.'[9]

Comhaltas Ceoltóirí Éireann

Through editorial in its magazine *Treoir*, and through its executive's actions, CCÉ, among other public stands it has taken, supported the Catholic Church's opposition to abortion in Ireland.[10] As an issue in the context of the filter-down effect CCÉ policy *may* exercise on uninvolved Protestant – particularly middle-class Protestant – opinion of Traditional music, it seems unlikely to be a factor in the designation 'Fenian music', which pre-dates CCÉ and which is applied mostly by the younger and urban loyalists who are unlikely to be perusing the pages of *Treoir*. In such editorialising CCÉ does no more than reflect the majority view held by its own (overwhelmingly Catholic) constituency, one which, on moral issues, concurs with Free Presbyterianism. By CCÉ's adoption of such a political leadership role, however, it diminishes its credibility with many musicians of both religions. The negative and highly significant fallout from this is that among the Protestant musicians who have had dealings with CCÉ, it encourages the vision of Traditional music as being institutionally incorporated into Catholicism and nationalism. It is a matter of debate whether or not the institutional national ingredient was critical in the gelling of the

---

TREOIR

Concern For Fellow Irishmen

THE FOLLOWING statement, issued by CCE, outlines the reasons for the postponement of Fleadh Cheoil na hEireann:

" Fleadh Cheoil na hEireann is a cultural festival of international repute. It attracts many thousands of people for the three-day programme. Comhaltas Ceoltoirí Eireann was anxious that a prolonged and extensive festival of this kind in one part of Ireland would not be used by the British media to detract from, minimise or ridicule the struggle which exists in another corner of our country.

" The decision to postpone the Fleadh Cheoil was taken as a result of the extenuating circumstances which exist in the six occupied counties. The introduction of internment without trial; the reported brutality by British soldiers; the non-recognition of the Stormont regime by the nationalist population have brought about unparalelled conditions in the North Eastern part of this country.

" Comhaltas Ceoltoirí Eireann could not divorce itself from the situation as it exists at the present time. We wish to demonstrate our solidarity with our fellow Irishmen in the North at this decisive hour; we wish to associate and involve ourselves with them and indicate our concern for their plight.

" We were fully aware when we made our decision, which was accepted and endorsed by the Fleadh Cheoil Committee in Listowel, that it would entail hardship, inconvenience and disappointment. These consequences are indicative of the magnitude of our decision and we hope that they will help to underline the seriousness and urgency of the present conflict. We are confident, also, that there are very few Irish people who would not willingly deny themselves the anticipated achievement or enjoyment at the Fleadh Cheoil in the hope that it would contribute to a lasting and just solution to the national problem.

" While CCE may not concern itself with party politics, it does not deny itself the right to national aspirations. Traditional music, song and dance are marks of nationhood and we view them in this context. As it is people who primarily constitute the nation and evolve its character, we cannot—and will not—in this time of emergency withhold our measure of support for the Northern population."

SEAMUS DE BRUN   LABHRAS O MURCHU
(Uachtaran),   (Stiurthoir).

Treoir editorial explaining the cancellation of the 1971 Fleadh.

revival; it does seem to be the case to this writer, as it certainly has parallels in other countries, for instance in the USA with jazz, which developed out of slavery. Yet CCÉ still retains Protestant members, even though many Protestant musicians who are not in the organisation hold critical opinions of it: 'Most of the musicians round here would be Protestants. One ran a Comhaltas [CCÉ] branch with a Catholic priest at Ballinahinch until Bloody Sunday. Then Comhaltas . . . cancelled the all-Ireland – said that they were supportin' their brothers in arms for freedom . . . the ones up here in the Comhaltas branch wrote down to Dublin sayin' that this wasn't acceptable at all. But they more or less were told "if yous don't like it – lump it". So en masse they all left the Comhaltas . . .'[11] The attitude is well-enshrined in popular consciousness: 'The famous line from Chairman Lao [Labhrás Ó Murchú, Director of CCÉ] of Comhaltas: "Isn't it great to hear *them* playing *our* music?"'[12] Protestant musicians did, and do, actually believe that the music should retain a non-sectarian ethos, and argue that political actions and opinions should remain outside the music, and private: 'Internment was the first real hurt, when Comhaltas cancelled the All-Ireland Fleadh. Protestant Ulster musicians and singers were up in arms at the time [1972]. We felt that the position which we had taken, that the limb which we had put ourselves on, had just been cut off by Comhaltas, who had made a political statement when no political statement should have been made in terms of the music. I had good friends interned, people with whom I never would agree with politically were, musically, firm friends.'[13] CCÉ had cancelled the All-Ireland Fleadh in 1971 following the initiation in August of that year of internment without trial of politically disruptive nationalists, socialists and republicans. By Catholic political standards CCÉ's action did not seem an unreasonable thing at the time; the majority of internees were Catholic, and it was within that community that the music was most widely practised and had most cultural meaning. But not all musicians, including Catholic musicians, believed that music is or should be viewed as a political agent. This incident, however, does align CCÉ within the music/politics cocktail clearly stated by its own editorial: 'The decision to postpone the Fleadh Cheoil was taken as a result of the extenuating circumstances which exist in the six occupied counties . . . We wish to demonstrate our solidarity with our fellow Irishmen in the North at this decisive hour . . . Traditional music, song and dance are marks of nationhood and we view them in this context. . .'[14]

CHAPTER FOURTEEN

The way it was?

John Rea of County Antrim playing hammer dulcimer. His repertoire was standard jigs, reels and hornpipes. The occasion here is a CCÉ session in Derryvolgie Avenue, Belfast c. 1964, where the religion of performers was not an issue.

Traditional music's roots in Northern Ireland are no longer totally rural. Its strongest presence is in Belfast and in the larger towns. Traditional Irish dancing is still evident in certain rural Protestant areas and in some urban contexts too. The 1996 award-winning BBC film, *Dance Lexie Dance*,[1] illustrates this. It demonstrates too the fact of cultural resistance to 'Irish' music and dance among Protestants, in the wake of the strong appeal of *Riverdance* to all versions of Irish identity. More generally, in the country areas of Northern Ireland the Orange halls have a tradition of organised dances (traditional dance is still performed in some), and older people remember dancing what are now called 'sets'[2] – lancers and quadrilles – at these. Once learnt, dancing becomes part of one's experiential make-up, is difficult to forget and impossible to suppress: 'I remember in the Watergate bar, Callaghan's bar, in Enniskillen, and there was a man up dancin', full. Plastered – he couldn't've pished in a straight line. He was absolutely langers, and we were playin' tunes and he started to dance. And you could see though he was fallin' all over the place he knew exactly what he was doin'. He was an Orangeman, in his late forties. He wasn't doin' any stage stuff – he was doin' *real* stuff [step dance] . . . So I say to a local woman, "What's he doin'?" She says, "That's what they do in the Orange hall up there"...'[3] So traditional was the Orange and other halls' Traditional dance style, that the Traditional revivalists couldn't understand it:

> I remember a set-dancing night at Queens and there were various demonstrations of sets. And a group of quite old people from Comber were discovered who danced a version of the Orange and Green set, very much old style, but from a strongly Protestant community, and they danced it in the local Orange Hall. Now they faced it totally differently. Very genteel-ly and very slowly, almost like the old military style of two-stepping. It was leisurely and very stylish with a lot of bowing, a nice kind of posing. But the difference suddenly was there – the onlookers were watching these people as if what they were doing was a piece of museum work. And then in turn when they watched the traditional set dancing – as danced by the Fenians if you like – I could see in their faces a sense of – not wonder – but bewilderment as if *'Sets aren't meant to be danced like this!'*[4]

In Protestant and mixed country areas it is an almost forgotten fact that Traditional dance music had considerable importance during the early part of the twentieth century:

> In the country those days [County Antrim, 1930s–1940s] you had old-time dances and you'd have played for the lancers and the quadrilles and of course old-time polkas and different other dances that would go along with it. My mother she came up in that atmosphere. There was quite a lot of girls in that family and they all went in for dancin' in a big way ... and then the brothers were good fiddle players. You see the grandfather and the four sons, four of my uncles, they were all fiddle players. That's how they passed the time on the winter nights. They lived in a wee stone-built house with just an earthen floor to it and then people would have come in to dance to them playin'. They had a fiddle each. It was a house of céilí-in'. It was full of music.[5]

Another musician recalls:

> Every year [County Antrim, 1940s] you always have a night round September, and you maybe had a dozen fiddle players, they come to our house now on a Friday night ... I was small at that time ... that was in Autumn and Springtime, before ploughin' started ... Well then I grew up and took an interest meself and I saw maybe forty fiddle players in our house ... so that was very different. My parents loved to hear music and all shades of opinion came to our house. There were no bars – if you could play a whistle, a fiddle, a banjo – the door was always on the latch.[6]

This tradition, however, was already on the wane in the 1950s, corresponding to post-war economic change: 'A brave lot of the fifers played the fiddle, played Irish dance music [in County Antrim], in the forties, fifties. Hughie Surgenor[7] I fifed with for thirty years. All them boys played, but it never was as much widespread as it would be at the minute [1992].'[8] Indeed, TV producers involved in the music in the 1960s and 1970s had, as mentioned earlier, difficulties with music 'standards': 'In those days [over the whole island north of the Dublin–Galway line, early 1960s] there didn't seem to be very many people in their thirties and forties playing – rather it seemed to be the young people at the fleadhs, or the very old people. The young people hadn't got the technical expertise; the old people maybe it was slipping away from.'[9] But music could still be found close to the heart of Belfast city centre, on occasion in the least expected venues:

> Away in the early days [1960s] there was a Police Barracks there in Brown Square. There was a buffer there Billy, he used to have a session up in the guards room up in the barracks. And I'll tell you, Seán Maguire [fiddler, a Catholic] as a young fella – that's where he started his playin'. . . I remember goin to a big festival 'do'[10] one time. This young fella was brought from Belfast by Billy McLean and Billy Montgomery – it was Seán Maguire, he was sixteen or seventeen at the time. Billy McLean was stationed in Rathfriland and Master Carson taught in Rathfriland. So Master Carson he came up to Brown Square to the sessions and Billy McLean brought him up in the car. He's from the Creggs. A Protestant. Billy Brown, stationed in Lisburn, came too – formerly stationed in Brown Square. And Sergeant Vincent, a very good fiddle player. And another boy McDermott, a very good fiddle player, and a couple of whistle players – played brass whistles. I was there too – in the late fifties this was. Must have been some of the police had made sandwiches and you got a feed and what have you, then headed up for home. That was a Friday night. Once a month there was another big man come from about Larne, he was a policeman, and there was a big policeman from Newtowncrommellin, he was stationed over in East Belfast.[11]

Despite sessions like these there was a gap, and younger Protestant musicians are aware of breaks in music continuity, even in County Down:

> There was never any music around Bangor [1970s], the Upper Ards, or even the Ards peninsula, that I heard of . . . I heard talk of one ould fiddler, but that's about it . . . there are quite a few playin' now. And there was quite a few twenty or thirty years ago . . . – between Bangor and Portaferry – the 'spit'. There's virtually no history of Traditional music that I know of down there. But on the inland coast between Killyleagh out . . . into Ballinahinch, Dromara, into Comber, that sort of semicircle there was full of it. I learnt from a fella there . . . and his

> son was the sixth generation of fiddle players handed down. But the family had no one to pass it on to . . . I suppose they passed it on outside the family . . .[12]

The revival altered that somewhat, and the 1960s saw a boom in music-making: '. . . in East Down [in the 1960s] there was absolutely no music about that we knew of or have heard of bar one well-known fiddler . . . And then the sessions come about here . . . all the rest of the people who played around the area were very new players, were sort of revivalists. I suppose I am too, it didn't come direct from the family.' This fresh burst of enthusiasm had apparently little to do with and cared little about religion:

> There were dozens of us . . . lots of Protestants . . . goin' up the Falls to the Felon's club which was a sort of a joke at the time – it was a drinking club – but those who were interested [Belfast, 1969] in songs could sing and get listened to . . . then I was going to predominantly Protestant sessions, a crowd centred to a large extent around one fiddler because he was a great repository of style and tunes . . . we were the end of, and the new beginning of what had been a continuous tradition in East Down. It was a Protestant tradition – very few Catholics. We didn't perceive ourselves as being a Protestant side of Traditional music, but as a branch of it which had a validity of its own but which was part of the whole Traditional music area.[13]

CHAPTER FIFTEEN

The bridge of glass – Scotland and Ireland

Historical population movement between Ireland and Scotland depicted in a wall hanging in the Burns cottage at Stephenson's Pond, County Louth.

> I can go over on a bridge of glass
> And I can come over on a bridge of glass
> And if the glass bridge breaks
> There's none in Ile[1] nor in Éirinn
> Who can mend the bridge of glass[2]

In a past geological era Scotland was connected to Ireland. More recently, the folklore riddle which is quoted above reflects that in the years AD 684 and 695 the North Channel between the two regions froze over, making it possible for herders in Antrim, Ireland, to drive stock to market at Campbelltown, Scotland. This dramatic image is a metaphor for both the intensity and fragility of the logistics of cultural interchange that has taken place between Ireland and Scotland over the centuries, and which continues to the present day. The only difference is the state of the water.

In all of its campaign the Provisional IRA does not appear to have planted bombs or shot at British soldiers in Scotland or Wales, even though regiments based in both areas were deployed in Northern Ireland (where, however, they became targets). The authorities knew this, and in this writer's memory of seeing both serving and off-duty soldiers in Scotland during the 1980s, they did not carry guns at the ready or take any particular precautions when travelling there (these were signs of not being 'on alert'). The reason for this is that the IRA saw itself as representing Ireland, a Celtic nation, and as having no quarrel with the other areas perceived as Celtic – Scotland and Wales.

Being connected by the sea in the age of the supremacy of boat travel, Ireland and Scotland were extremely close not only geographically but humanly. For this reason alone they could be assumed to have close cultural ties. While this is not borne out in any great cultural trafficking during the twentieth century, or by any particularly outstanding links established between the new Irish state and that region of the UK after 1921, there is much evidence in literature and history, and Gaelic scholars feel such bonds, shared through a common tongue. With the establishment of the Scottish assembly in 1999 formal structures have been set up, one of them being the initiation of a lavish poetry and art project, *Leabhar Mór na Gaeilge*,[3] formally launched at Dublin City Hall in February 2001. Long-established, shared linguistic associations are more important in the context of Traditional music. These are complex, and identify Scotland as originally:

> taking its name from the Irish who migrated from County Antrim between 300 and 400 AD to the west coast area known today as Argyll ('Earraghail', 'coastland of the Gaels'). By c. 500 AD the Kingdom of the Scots was established under Fergus Mór Mac Eirc of Ireland's royal dynasty, Dalriada. Their language was Gaelic and they adopted the Christian religion after the Irish missionary, Columba, had established the centre of Christianity in Iona in 563. In 843, Dalriada was united with its Celtic neighbours to the north and east, the Picts, under one king, Kenneth Mac Alpin, whose people, by that time, had also converted to Christianity. This new kingdom, which took the ancient name, Alba (Scotia, as the Romans called it), extended south to the Forth–Clyde [Edinburgh–Glasgow] line. The Latin designation for the people, *Scoti*, anglicised to *Scots*, ultimately gave the name Scotland to the entire country.[4]

Not all of Scotland was Gaelic. It is (roughly) the south-west region, down as far as Galloway (Gaelic-speaking until at least 1700,[5] the area opposite County Down), that is historically so. Since the Gaelic language remained a common Scottish-Irish tongue until the 1600s and survives still in both Scotland and Ireland, and because what is regarded as Scottish Traditional music is played in both Lowlands and Highlands, deductably both Scottish and Irish areas also share a music culture. Tune types, dance practices and singing styles are still closely related, for after the mid-1700s much Scottish repertoire was adopted in Ireland, adapted to local style, and still survives as a key part of Traditional music today,[6] though it is played with a different accentuation. It is considered that the north-west of Scotland, including Perthshire, and also the western islands, in language, songs, music and art has '... more in common with Ireland than with the rest of Scotland lying to the south and north-east of the demographic divide known as the "Highland line"'.[7] This, of course, applies mostly to non-Plantation Ireland. But from the time of the early English colonisation of Ireland, moving forward to the Ulster Plantation, there may have been no great distinction made between the then current, popular Irish and Scottish musics and languages. This supposition is suggested by the cultural links between the two countries arising out of well-documented common, historical origins.[8] It is also supported by the existence of extensive trading and population moves between the two areas since ancient times, and by recollections and records of the movements of pipers and harpers, from the Middle Ages on, between Scotland, Wales, northern England and Ireland.[9]

There were 6,520 Scots in settled areas of Ireland in 1622,[10] a significant number of people for a small place at this period in history. This number is indicated in later statistics as growing, and language is noted also:

> The population of Ulster then [1659 survey] was returned as 103,923, of whom 63,272 were Irish and 40,651 were listed as 'English and Scotch'. In every county the Irish outnumbered the others, though in Tyrone and Antrim the differences were not so great. Further, the survey shows that English (and Scots was then listed as English for the purposes of the survey) was the majority language in the following areas only: some towns, e.g. Derry, Carrickfergus and Coleraine; East Donegal; the barony of Coleraine and the area between Lisburn and Larne. Irish was the majority language everywhere else in Ulster.[11]

The mixture of settlers and natives suggests implications for language and accents, and thence for music. That such movement of people necessarily involved music can be deduced from sixteenth-century, music-related anecdote and literature from not only these islands but elsewhere in Europe as well. This demonstrates that music-making was widespread and, aside from being played on instruments, even for dance could be performed as mouth-music.[12] It also suggest that tunes were perhaps not melodically complex by today's standards, were of limited number, were easily transportable by any reasonable memory, and were absorbed voraciously by the curious and diversion-starved in an age of little change and slow communications.

Regardless of developments in the 'early', 'baroque', 'classical' or 'society' music scene, in an age of limited technological innovation, the instrumentation and hence the possible music of the ordinary rural and recently ex-rural folk up to the seventeenth century would have remained substantially the same and unchanged for several centuries. An assessment of the kind of music that was being played by the 'plain people' in late sixteenth- and early seventeenth-century Scotland must therefore consider the proximity of these areas, the music of their neighbours, and their likely instrumentation. The Highlands was associated with bagpipes,[13] and fiddle was popular in both Highlands and Lowlands during the seventeenth century, with folk music being the main focus of music life.[14] Were the tunes structured like 'modern' Traditional dance tunes? Unlikely, but since Northern English music shows similarity to both Scottish and Irish musics, it seems likely that Lowland Scotland would have exhibited characteristics of both Highland and Irish styles. The deduction is therefore made, that music among the Ulster Plantation settlers (where religious stricture approved, or turned a blind eye[15]) was much the same as that already played in Ireland, the Highlands and Northern England. Observation of how little fundamental difference those musics exhibit today suggests that there was probably no profound difference other than matters of accent. The big change in Scottish local music came about a century-and-a-half *after* the Plantation period. So it seems more likely that Scots and Northern English in Ulster would have retained the older music expression, which was closer to the Irish. Even though religion seems likely to have had some debilitating effect on the practice of recreational music, perhaps the nature and transmission of folk music makes the strongest argument that it thrived nevertheless. Folk music by definition is dependent on amateurs, is an unselfconscious part of life, can be accommodated by all classes, especially the poor, is reproducible both on voice and craft-made instruments, no formal education is needed and the repertoire is easily acculturated because it remains substantially unchanged.[16] The following chapter takes these points further by presenting examples of the crossing over of tunes and songs from island to island and culture to culture.

This Irish tune, 'Rakish Paddy', appears in early Scottish collections as 'Cabar Feigh' (The Deer's Horn), suggesting, as with many other tunes, Scottish origin and popularity in both Scotland and Ireland.

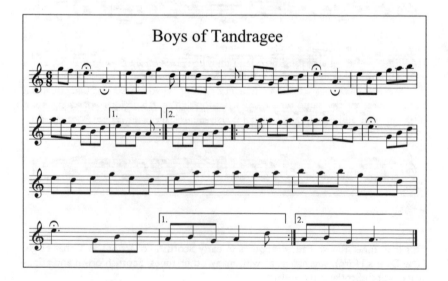

Three pieces of music which are essentially the same tune. The first is the Orange marching tune 'The Shanghai', which probably has British-army, Scottish origins. It is sung in Scotland also as a ballad entitled 'The Shearin'. The second piece is the Traditional music jig and song 'Boys of Tandragee', essentially the same air (but in a different time signature) as the first tune. The final piece is the Traditional music reel 'The Swallow's Tail', again the same tune in a different rhythmic setting. Overall, these pieces represent the same tune being used for different functions (marching, song entertainment and dance) and simultaneously being part of the cultures of different communities.

Chapter Sixteen

'Crossing over' of tunes and songs

Scotland and Ireland

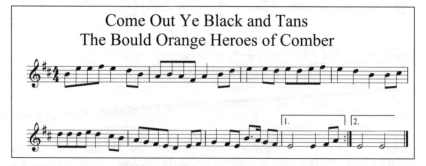

This air is shared by two contrasting political songs – one a Loyal anthem, 'The Bould Orange Heroes of Comber', (a.k.a. 'The Bright Orange Heroes of Comber'), the other a republican song, 'Come Out Ye Black and Tans' (a.k.a. 'Lanes of Killeshandra').

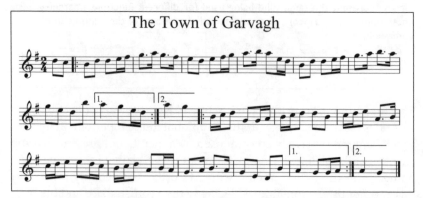

This tune, with the air of the Loyal anthem 'Battle of Garvagh', is a polka dance tune commonly played in Sligo. The original song is in political service still in Ulster, while the polka is played in 'listening' Traditional session music, but the melody is substantially the same. This example, and those above, suggests that the one body of popular melody served both religious/political communities, is likely to have originated with either, and has certainly been amended and brought forward by both.

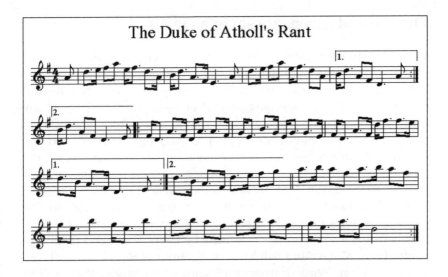

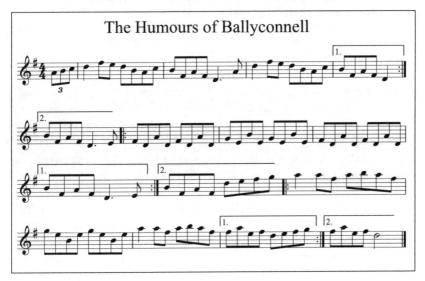

The first tune is from the 1765 Scottish Neil Stewart collection. The second is played commonly in the Traditional music repertoire in Ireland, and is reputed to have been composed by a member of the British army garrison at Ballyconnell, County Cavan. It is also claimed as a Sligo tune, named after the Ballyconnell townland north of the county town, and has another title 'Captain Rock'.[1] Clearly the Scottish piece and the Irish one are one and the same tune. The fact that they are in the Stewart collection – which is from a period of prolific dance-music composition in Scotland – suggests that this is the original, and that it came to Ireland with a regimental musician. A version of the same tune is also played by Orange bands.[2]

Orange and green crossover song airs

While this study has more to do with instrumental music, since it is uses of this which constitute the major defining difference in Ulster society, song and song airs are also intricately bound up with such tunes. It is not intended that this book should provide proof of genetic origins of any music or song, as it is taken as given that artistic cultural products are simultaneously a matter of creation, influence, adoption, selection and rejection. In this regard it is apt to mention two information sources which have been researched and published by others in the period since this study was begun. One of these is the excellent analytical discourse by David Cooper, head of music at the University of Leeds, England. The other is the exhilarating commentary selection provided for BBC Northern Ireland's information website by Derry singer and radio presenter Brian Mullen and Belfast-born flute player Rev. Gary Hastings, Church of Ireland Vicar of Westport, County Mayo. Each of these will be referenced here in their basic elements only.

David Cooper's analysis

In his article 'Lámh Dearg: Celtic Minstrels and Orange Songsters',[3] David Cooper, editor of the Cork University Press edition of *The Petrie Collection of Irish Music* (2003), analyses the Orange song repertoire in some detail with regard to evidence of local native-Irish structural influence. He notes that while there may seem to be a chasm between the emblematic Orange 'The Sash My Father Wore' and the deeply rebellious Munster 'Cath Chéim an Fhia', upon analysis of structure and period the difference is seen to be not so profound. He quotes Dick Mac Gabhann (University of Ulster), who had remarked at the 'Whose Music?' conference[4] that in many loyal ballads there were 'perfect examples of internal rhyming' as per the Ulster Gaelic verse tradition.[5] He reflects too that Cathal O'Boyle in his 1979 *Songs of County Down* also notes a 'kind of internal rhyme . . . a characteristic of Gaelic verse, in, for instance, the Orange ballad 'The Bright Orange Heroes of Comber':

> O'Connell he does Boast, of his great big rebel Host
> He says they are ten thousand in Number
> But half them you'll Find they are both lame and Blind
> But we're the Bright Orange Heroes of Comber[6]

Cooper notes that the issue of the influence of Gaelic poetry's metrics on English-language verse was a key factor in all Irish song, regardless of language, and quotes George Petrie from his seminal 1855 collection,[7] wherein he makes the observation that:

> Whether written in Irish, for the counties in which the native language still generally prevailed, or in English, for the counties where that language was becoming general, or, as often happened, in a compound of the two tongues, where both were still spoken, such songs had, to Irish ears, the important merit of a happy adaptation of words that would run concurrently with the notes and rhythm of the airs for which they were intended; and were, happily, thus the means of preserving the tunes in all their integrity.[8]

Cooper quotes other analyses concerning the absence of 'distinction between Scottish and Irish bardic poetry in the Gaelic language', the occurrence therein of 'key idiosyncratic characteristics of Gaelic verse'[9] such as the *ochtfhoclach mór* type with eight lines, consonance, 'rime', alliteration and internal rhyming. Most interesting for the Protestant–Catholic context is Cooper's quoted verse in Gaelic, from 1650, the work of the Church of Ireland Prebendary of Dunsfort in County Down who had to leave the Isle of Man on account of his disfavour for Cromwell.[10] Since the popular poets who composed the political songs tended to reflect high-art, bardic principles, Cooper can go on to deduce three principles about Ulster songs in English: 1. So similar is metre and music, that religion or political affiliation cannot be established for anything other than explicitly political song. 2. There is Gaelic song structure in the English-language verse of both Protestant and Catholic communities. 3. Some Orange songs are parodies of existing nationalist and recreational songs (and vice versa) and existing melodies would be adopted all the more easily (and eagerly?) if they were seen as part of a common legacy.

Cooper concludes that 'at least one third of the eighty items contained in the Ulster Society's two [song] collections show some influence of Gaelic metrics as filtered through English-language popular verse'.[11] He sees narrative content as its most significant distinguishing feature: 'what it signifies is certainly different, but the means by which it signifies is not'.[12] He gives key examples of Orange song, the older, seminal loyal repertoire, in the light of these observations, including 'The Defence of Crossgar – 17th March 1849', 'The Battle of Garvagh' and 'Arise, Arise, King James II' (1869). He holds that it is also likely that dance music has similar shared features,[13] particularly considering the occurrence of certain Orange tunes as the root of some polkas, and of some marches as dance tunes (see pp. 100). Most significantly he stresses that airs become political by association, not by inherent music characteristics.[14] In this context he notes that the hugely symbolic Irish anthem 'Wearin' of the Green' has, in fact, a Scottish composer (James Oswald), and that certain Orange anthems have Irish origins, notably the symbolic 'On The Relief of the City of Derry', which 'draws on Gaelic-inspired metrics filtered through the British operatic stage'. His conclusion is that the 'inhabitants of Ireland, whether Orange Flautists or Gaelic Pipers are inextricably connected by a series of entwining mythologies which reach back to Celtic Minstrelsy and spread across to the other peoples of the western seaboard of Europe'.[15]

Brian Mullen's song examples

The same territory is covered by Brian Mullen, both in his BBC website[16] commentary and at the 'Swinging Shoulders – Dancing Feet' seminar which was held in Derry in 2003. His approach is that of a singer, as seen in the song titles and snatches which follow: 'when it comes to music and song you can't talk in terms of two traditions. There's either one tradition or there's a million traditions – it's shared.'[17] He regards the period in which observation is made as critical:

> The differences between Orange song and, lets call it Fenian/nationalist/republican/separatist or just general song, are more apparent than real. When you take away the words of the song and just look at the tune . . . It can be *made* to have politics, like 'The Sash', because it's played on special occasions for a special purpose. But when you put words to it then the words convey a political or a social agenda . . . it's the same music that we're all using . . . the music of Ireland which itself is as mixed up as the people who live here . . . Three basic strands I think you can divide it into – native Irish music (whatever that might be), and Scottish and English which are coming to us from plantation or migration between the two islands, something that's been going on for a long time.[18]

Outside of the indigenous origins he points to the prevalence of borrowing popular song from other places:

> I'll give you an example of how far afield you can go for looking for a tune by singing you a verse from a Fenian song, and a verse from an Orange song but the tune is actually American . . . 'Tramp, Tramp, Tramp the Boys are Marching' . . . written in 1863 by George Root during the American Civil War. It became so popular that it was taken up by the Fenians. In 1867 T.D. Sullivan wrote 'God Save Ireland' to the same tune and the Orangemen made 'No Pope, Priest or Holy Water'.
>
> American original
>> Tramp, tramp tramp the boys are marching
>> Cheer up comrades they will come
>> And beneath the starry flag, we shall breath the air again
>> Of the free land in my own dear native home.

Nationalist version
> God save Ireland cried the heroes
> God save Ireland cried they all
> Whether on the scaffold high or battlefield we die,
> What's it matter if for Éireann dear we fall.

Orange version
> No Pope, priest or holy water
> No Home Rule for Ireland
> And if I had a gun I would shoot them everyone
> For walking on the Queen's highway.

Another major song Mullen cites is an indigenous air, a Jacobite lament for Bonnie Prince Charlie, but better known as a profound anthem in Munster, 'Mo Ghile Mhear'. Yet it is the same air as the Dublin street song 'The Spanish Lady' and the Protestant origin-myth anthem, 'Sons of Levi'. As with the previous example, the fundamental rhythmic similarity can be gauged from the patterning of the written words. 'Sons of Levi' is a lyric of major length, which has been sung in modern time by Antrim singers Joe Holmes and Len Graham in a more economical five verses.

'Mo Ghile Mhear'
> *Chorus:*
> Sé mo laoch mo Ghile Mear
> Sé mo Sheasar Ghile Mear
> Suan na sean ní bhfuaireas féin
> O chuaigh i gcéin mo Ghile Mear.

Changing the rhythm slightly gives 'The Spanish Lady':
> As I went down through Dublin city
> At the hour of twelve at night
> Who should I see but the Spanish Lady
> Washing her feet by the candlelight.

'Sons of Levi'
> Come all you brethren that do wish
> To propagate the grand design
> Come enter into our high temple
> And learn the art that is divine.

Many songs in both the nationalist and unionist traditions can be seen to have gone in both directions, as well as into popular music, but Mullen can point to items which are not easily identified. One is 'The Orange Maid of Sligo', written by William Archer in the 1850s:

> On Benbulben's high and lofty heights
> The evening sun was setting bright
> It cast a ray of golden light
> Around the bay of Sligo

Almost a century later Dublin singer, Dominic Behan, wrote the parallel lyric 'Avondale' celebrating Charles Stewart Parnell, Protestant landowner and Irish nationalist:

> O have you been to Avondale
> And wandered in her lovely vales
> The tall trees whisper lo the tale
> Of Avondale's proud eagle.

Mullen also demonstrates tunes which jump both the political and linguistic barriers, one significant piece being 'Ólaim Punch', a drinking song:

> Ólaim Punch is ólaim tae
> Is ólaim whisky, ale and brandy

The same tune is used for the Orange song, 'Lurgan Town', about a banned Orange march through Lurgan in the 1840s:

> Lurgan town's an altered town
> Since Papish Hancock he came to it.

Even the primary anthem of Orangeism, 'The Sash my Father Wore', is not exempt. Mullen notes that it dates perhaps to the beginning of the twentieth century, and is pre-dated by a (popular music) love song, 'My Irish Molly O'.[19]

> *Chorus:*
> She is young and she is beautiful
> And her likes I've never known
> The lily of old Ireland
> And the primrose of Tyrone
> She's the lily of old Ireland
> And no matter where I go
> My heart will always hunger for
> My Irish Molly O

'The Sash My Father Wore'
> *Chorus:*
> It is old but it is beautiful
> And its colours they are fine
> It was worn at Derry, Aughrim
> Enniskillen and the Boyne
> My father wore it as a youth
> In the bygone days of yore
> And it's on the Twelfth I love to wear
> The sash my father wore.

The tune and song examples shown[20] illustrate general principles of the use of shared melodies by otherwise (or occasionally so) antagonistic communities. Rev. Gary Hastings' comments on a BBC website support Mullen's observations and provide a fitting coda:

> Music and song traditions are living things, constantly changing to suit the context they exist in. To survive they adapt and alter themselves, take on some new aspects and drop some old. As living things they are complicated and messy, and can't be simply divided up into this or that, Orange and green, ours and theirs. They might comfortably and often be both.[21]

A reading of both Mullen and Hastings on the BBC website gives a much more solid picture than the brief review here, and Hastings' ideas are additionally thoroughly developed with a tunes repertoire in his 2003 study, *With Fife and Drum*.

CHAPTER SEVENTEEN

A music- and song-transmission cornucopia

Douglas Hyde, son of a Church of Ireland rector, founder of the Gaelic League, and first President of Ireland after Partition, was from a Glens of Antrim family.

Much information must be drawn together in order to get a clear picture of Traditional music in present-day Northern Ireland. Issues of identity, cultural practice, geographical location, history, political identification and religion have been presented already. Some conclusions drawn from consideration of these post-Plantation issues include:

- The Gaelic languages, as still presently spoken in Scotland and Ireland respectively, are the same tongue and are (allowing for regional accents and dialect) reasonably mutually understandable. This would always have been the case.
- Gaelic was spoken by some 50 per cent of Scottish settlers in Ulster, and by some of their Presbyterian clergy.[1]
- Evidence of similarities between Irish and Scottish musics is found in the early period of documentation of Scottish folk music from the Culloden period (1745) onwards. Collections such as that of Neil Stewart[2] include pieces that can be played with either a distinctly Scottish 'sound'[3] (as defined by present-day standards), or with an Irish 'sound' (this is more difficult to achieve with Scottish music from a century later).
- Present-day Traditional music on Cape Breton Island, Nova Scotia (which could be approximated to eighteenth- and nineteenth-century Scottish music in exile), exhibits accentual similarity to Irish Traditional music, features which are not typical of present-day Scottish music.[4]

- The repertoire of Irish tunes still played in Ireland by the 1960s included very many tunes that had never appeared in print, in addition to the popular 'recycled' items which had been assembled in the earliest printed collections. The overall 1960s repertoire included many pieces which had earlier been noted or 'collected' from Irish emigrants who arrived in America between the middle and the end of the nineteenth century.[5] Since significant changes in other aspects of Irish rural culture and lifestyle did not occur until almost the 1950s, this suggests that the dance-music repertoire had been fairly static for a long time.
- There are many tunes common to both Scottish and Irish (north and south) repertoires.[6]
- Scots Lowland singing influenced Northern Irish singing style and repertoire. In Lowland Scotland (from where a major section of the Ulster Plantation settlers were drawn) the Gaelic, Highland music and style are likely to have been (by dint of migration, military activity and job-searching) familiar to all who were interested in the playing or enjoyment of music.[7]

Indeed, the Gaelic language itself survived in the Antrim Glens into modern time.[8] Communication and local trade with Scotland continued, post-Plantation, in any case, and in one view: '. . . there's a continuity between here [Northern Ireland] and Scotland. But it's just exactly the same culture. The language started to change in the 1600s when everything fell apart, so Gaelic was spoken in Rathlin and round the edges of the Glens . . . it was just exactly the same . . . boys from the Glens used go to Scotland for the fairs – it was easier to do than to get to Ballymena . . .'[9] Two decades prior to the Ulster-Scots identity manifestation, approaching the turn of the twenty-first century (which coincides with the formal ending of Ulster Catholic–Protestant hostility after 390 years), even strongly Unionist opinion conceded that there was shared cultural lineage which long pre-dated the actual Plantation: '. . . the alleged racial difference is a mere fiction without warrant in history. The vast majority of colonists . . . were Scots descended from the Irish colonists of Scotland in the third and fourth centuries . . . it is on record that many of the planters spoke Gaelic hardly distinguishable from that on the lips of the old Irish[10] . . . there had been comings and goings between Scotland and [geographical] northern Ireland since time immemorial; the Planters were distinctive in their religious convictions, but indistinguishable in every other respect from the numerous Scottish families who had settled in Ulster prior to the seventeenth century.'[11] All of this suggests that the ordinary folk in seventeenth-century rural, Gaelic, Scotland and eventually those of them in the Lowland centres to which they migrated in response to industrialisation, probably enjoyed for recreation much the same music as that in vogue in rural Ulster, if not all of Ireland, at that time. Therefore, the original recreational music of all the inhabitants of Ulster, native and settler, Catholic and Protestant alike, had more similarity than difference. Scotland is not a monolith, of course, and there were differences existing within even its seventeenth- and eighteenth-century music. Lowland ('Lallans') culture – the 'Ulster-Scots' connection – contains much that is unique, particularly in English-language song. But dance music (the area this study is mostly concerned with) appears to be, simply, 'Scottish'.[12] As far back as the seventeenth century, dance music structures in England too were similar to what was practised in Scotland and Ireland. Lallans culture may have been more of a hybrid, but its basic music 'sound' most likely varied only according to preferred local music *accent*, as is the case within all Traditional musics.

This constant human contact between the northern Irish counties and Scotland is so well established in history and folklore that it can, in fact, be cherry-picked to suit any political agenda. For instance, in defence of Plantation as a territorial re-annexation: 'A great deal too much nonsense has been talked about Ulster being Scottish. For, as a matter of fact, the Lowlands of Scotland were first peopled by Ulstermen!'[13] In more recent times it can still be quoted as the opposite, in defence of British identity: '. . . the Scottish connection is the Scottish connection – because of most of our ancestors three or four hundred years ago . . .'[14] In any case, even if regional differences, accents or preferences were obvious in cultural matters, absorption, amelioration, exchange and borrowing still held sway in the process of adaptation to new terrain and new associations. This was probably an easy process (apart from the danger of sporadic attack by the native Irish). It seemed logical enough too, even in the crudely Darwinian logic of loyalist writings from the turn of the twentieth century:

> . . . a great deal too much has been derived from the much-discussed 'plantation' of James 1, and from the subsequent passage of English and Scottish families into Ulster, as an explanation of Ulster's character and the religion of the majority in Ulster. The new arrivals were soon absorbed; and those families which held themselves aloof from the Ulster people, in many cases died out as a result of intermarriage. The original Ulster stock persisted.[15]

But such enculturation is also cited more scientifically in relation to song:

> Ulster and Scotland can be said with some confidence to be one ballad region . . . Being Celtic and contiguous, Ireland and Scotland were culturally identifiable to the extent that Roman historians in the fourth century and Continental writers up to the fifteenth century referred to the natives of Ireland as 'Scots', and fourth-century references to 'lesser Scotia' mean in fact Scotland.[16] Up to the eighteenth

century there was continuing interchange between the itinerant harpers of both countries[17] ... the twilight for the harpers, who functioned within the Gaelic tradition, was accelerated by the introduction of alien musical forms ... One such alien form much strengthened by the Scots planter was ballad singing.[18]

In any case, an awareness of the music significance of this Scottish connection was well established on the ground among Protestants. In the words of a late twentieth-century political activist: 'Plantation times had brought the music ...'[19]

With regard to the desirability of figuring out possible implications for Traditional music in the earlier, Gaelic, era, interfaces had already been noted in Scotland by military fiddler and collector Simon Fraser at the beginning of the 1800s:

> ... it may become a matter of very interesting research, to trace the Analogy and Similitude betwixt the Ancient Music of the Highlands of Scotland ... and that of Ireland, or if they bear the affinity which their native languages do: when their languages appear to have been the same at one period, it will not seem surprising that a few of the melodies sung in that language are common to both countries, with little variation ... their own delightful jigs and country dances electrify the Irish, just in the same manner as our strathspeys and reels so irresistibly affect our countrymen ...[20]

Title page of 'the Fraser collection'.

Fraser here is referring to Gaelic – *Highland* – music, the same strains which today dominate the Scottish instrumental repertoire which is presently played by the Ulster-Scots Fowk Orchestra. The same process in song in the English language has been documented by Tom Munnelly and Hugh Shields and leaves an even clearer trail:

> The implantation of the ballad genre in Ireland was begun through immigration from Britain and has continued through two-way traffic. The Scots contribution as we know it today reached Ireland through two main types of migration: 1. British colonisation of Ulster from the seventeenth century onwards, a movement in which Scots settlers participated massively; 2. seasonal or periodic migration between Britain and Ireland, a movement involving Irish workers mainly and one which first became economically significant after the Napoleonic wars . . .[21]

The consequences of this are particularly relevant in Lowland – *popular* – song which was in Scots English rather than in Gaelic:

> Scots ballads were current in the Midlands if not the most southern parts of Ireland already in the eighteenth century . . . soon they were serving as models for new Anglo-Irish compositions . . . For Scots ballads the Plantation of Ulster opened up access not simply to a North Ulster colony but to the new Irish public at large . . . Soon Ireland was sending over new ballads in broadside style. We have recently found the most famous Irish Protestant political ballad, 'The Boyne Water', in a Scottish chapbook appreciably older than any Irish source (1766) and printed in Edinburgh.[22]

More modern movements of people carried on this process, in particular seasonal workers who migrated for the harvest:

> First are the tatty-howkers . . . from Donegal but also extended as far south as Mayo and even Galway . . . Second are the tinkers or travelling families . . . Without sustained school education, the travelling tinkers make up the last surviving pre-literate group in British and Irish society. Scots ballads and ballad types circulated through the whole of English-speaking Ireland, with greater concentration in the North . . .[23]

Scottish Gaelic associations had most relevance for north-coast Antrim, where the ease of travelling to and fro pre-dates the Plantation. This suggests there should be a corpus of Scottish Gaelic influence in this area, one which had already been sharing with and contributing to Irish music from 1,300 years before the Plantation. Nevertheless, there is a suggestion in the recollections of present-day older Protestant musicians that this original connection may have become considerably diluted, but it was eventually either overwhelmed by, or enriched by, more modern associations:

> ... the older two uncles, they went out to look for work in Scotland and worked in the pits ... then World War 1 started and they joined up. They were both killed and there was only a day between them ... they'd learnt the pipes when they were over in Scotland with the Royal Scots. When they came home [to County Antrim] they just paraded right from the home down to the little village and way back up again playin' the pipes ... they were also good fiddle players. They learnt a lot of Scottish music when they were over there – they *brought home* strathspeys and all with them ... Antrim was the same as Donegal. They had to go to Scotland to work in the harvest time and they spent a long time in Scotland during the harvest and then they *came home with their tunes* and *taught* them to other ones at home [editor's emphasis]. That's how that came about ... I think it would be the Lowlands of Scotland. But there was shortage of work. They couldn't make ends meet any other way. Before the 1900s it would have been, and up to the twenties they'd still have been doin' the same thing. That's why the Donegal people have a different style of playin' from further down and that's how it comes into Antrim too, and that's how you get that Scottish touch in the music.[24]

This is similar to the situation existing in Cape Breton Island, Nova Scotia. There there was indeed already an overwhelming eighteenth-century Scottish ingredient in the music. But first, Scottish recording and tune books were introduced in the post-WWII period, and then a fiddle revival followed in the 1970s.[25] While such a cultural reconfiguration and assembly of tradition does make surviving oral practice difficult to assess, it nevertheless confirms that a cultural appreciation of and viable need for the music had remained consistent.

In Northern Ireland, in 1992 however, Protestant Traditional musicians appeared to have little interest in these kinds of past shreds of identity with Scotland; they were clear about what music they were playing regardless of origins theorising and the intermixing of communities. No matter what it might be called, they had a music familiar to them, which was decidedly NOT Scottish. Most expressed little enthusiasm for Scottish identity, and demonstrated this objectively in their music: 'This was [in north Antrim] Traditional Irish music, not Scottish. Old Irish hornpipes, passed down through generations.'[26] It cannot be concluded that players who held that opinion did not hold the past in high regard, but pragmatically, people can only be comfortable about one identity; most live in one place and become of it:

> If you remember the sixties, the White Heather Club used be on UTV. That was something to do with it and there were Scottish programmes from Scottish TV on here and not no more ... I don't think the interest was there, strangely enough. I know boys here speak about Ulster-Scots and some of them have relatives in Scotland. But boys in Donegal have more in common with Scotland because they

all went there. I think we're cut off now. We're sort of British rather than anything else ... The [bagpipe] band culture is band culture – not Scots culture. It's a sport like football. They do it in Canada as well. More of the bands aren't pipe bands – which is surprisin' us bein' so close to Scotland ... If the Protestants are so interested in bein' Scottish,[27] why aren't they more Scottish than they are? *And they aren't!*[28]

CHAPTER EIGHTEEN

Migration, movements and music

Political history writing of the last three centuries is not a great source for music references. One could conclude that either there was little music around (life being tougher in the past than after the middle of the twentieth century) or that, since the historians were of the wealthier classes, they considered the music of the masses beneath mention. But, if the popularity and demand for all forms of modern-day musics are anything to go by, it is in fact most likely that music in the past was highly regarded, but was so ubiquitous that it was simply a 'given'. It was taken for granted, and it was assumed that it would always just be there and, relatively, unchanging. Like fresh air it must have been in abundance in one form or another: the most democratic and versatile of the arts, it could be practised in a palace or a prison cell, a tavern or a mountain top. What early-nineteenth-century historian could have predicted the miracle – the sheer magic – of sound recording, coming as it did so late in the evolution of technology? Therefore, before the inconceivability of rendering music portable by recording sound, or dispersing it by broadcasting on radio, music was an ephemeral commodity that had to be created *in situ*. Surely there was plenty of it, in all situations? History has been much more concerned with religions, the vision of improvement of worldly comforts, exploration, conquest, technological innovation, trade and acquisition of power and wealth. Since historians cannot universally have been Philistines, it really must have seemed to them that there was no pressing need to document music's existence in economic and political tracts: it would always be there.

Some guesses must therefore be made from music-related historical material. For instance, documentary evidence records the establishment of breweries in several Plantation centres by the 1630s.[1] Allowing for the fact that beer was an important social beverage in the pre-tea age, that substance must have inspired revelry on at least the odd occasion. This would have been expressed in music, song and dance that travelled to Ulster with the settlers as ritual and recreational diversion. Religious affiliation to strict Presbyterianism might have tended to suppress such levity, but still, there seemed to be plenty of it back home in Scotland, for even then the established church, the General Assembly of the Church of Scotland, in 1649, had been obliged to pass an act prohibiting 'promiscuous dancing' (mixed-sex dances), affirming this again in 1701.[2] By 1680 a craze of dancing to indigenous music and imported steps was beginning in Scottish high society[3] and it is unlikely that some didn't spill across to Ireland. In the English-settled areas of Ireland the predisposition to music and dance is unlikely to have been much different. Project this up to the later nineteenth century, when popular music culture was well developed as a norm on stage. This included 'music hall', a mass-audience form of entertainment complete with cultism and stardom,[4] which thrived in response to the industry-fuelled increase in population density of urban centres. A national Irish picture gradually emerges of a people, regardless of religion, by the end of the 1800s all regarding themselves as Irish, while living under the control of the British crown, whether they were loyal or disloyal. Where the strictures of their faiths so predisposed, tolerated or permitted, these people participated in, or at least had first-hand experience of, similar forms (and perhaps on occasions in the same venue) of, musical diversion, all as part of a continuum dating to the original Plantation.

In the early days of the Plantation there had been a constant movement of Scots and Northern English within Ulster, and to and from Scotland[5] and England. Leases and tenants changed but, eventually, the Scottish settlers stabilised nearest to Scotland (the north and north-east, a still predominantly Presbyterian area); the English settled in the Lagan valley back to Armagh and west and north to Derry and Enniskillen (still predominantly Anglican):

> A consensus of the surname, religious and dialect evidence strongly suggests that the present-day 'British' settlement in Ulster is comprised of two major components: an outer area to the north-east, north and north-west where the non-Irish population is primarily of Scottish origin, and an area in mid- and south Ulster where it is predominantly of English origin.[6]

This is of interest music-wise, for it is in these 'Scottish' areas that Traditional music still appears strongest in recollections from the early twentieth century. It is there too that one Antrim fiddler vividly recalls its intensity during his childhood, and interest in its revival seems to have been most effective among the Protestant population, where the fiddle was the dominant instrument. In summary, there are three main points:

- The pre-Plantation period saw much trade and cultural exchange with Scotland; this has implications for the introduction of and exchange of music.
- Historical research places Scottish Protestant Plantation settlement

in areas of Ulster where Traditional music is strong today, and which have a living memory of its more widespread practice.
- The main instrument appears to have been the fiddle, which, significantly, was popular in post-seventeenth-century Scotland; in addition to Irish music there had to be some Scottish music being played in Scots-settled areas.

Much of the folk instrumentation and popular tastes in music in these islands spread through diffusion from European centres of cultural influence to both Ireland and Scotland (in the manner of the bagpipe and court music).[7] Such movement was both direct (from Europe) and indirect (through England). The life of the poor and the peasant throughout pre-eighteenth century Europe involved rude accommodation, clothing and technology. Work was tough and unrelenting, there was a low life expectancy because of poverty, starvation, disease and climate, and great uncertainty caused by the proliferation of wars. Among all of this, it was the people with leisure time who could invent and indulge in music: those who were better-off, many of them 'at court'.

The idealised 'folk' certainly composed music, but, if the present-day diffusion of popular music is anything to go by, they are also likely to have made great use of what arrived by osmosis from the centres of leisure,[8] through servants, etc., in the same way that modern forms of flute and fiddle entered into the folk realm in these islands. Much can be learnt too from the travel of the bagpipes. Once a popular instrument for professional and casual diversion, particularly at the French court, they moved north to England, where Henry VIII had five sets, and where James I was also familiar with them. Pipes have since been played in unbroken succession in England, Ireland, France, Italy, Spain, the countries of the former Yugoslavia, Poland, Russia and Czechoslovakia. Their use ceased in the last hundred years in Scandinavia, Germany, Belgium and Holland, and there was severe cultural pressure against pipes in all of these countries with the movement of entertainment indoors in the late Middle Ages. By then, a middle class had developed that had tired of the novelty and now considered the sound of pipes too loud, unfashionable, or coarse. After the 1700s people no longer lived in rude shelters, and new, modern instruments had been developed with a wider tone range.[9] Traditional Scottish dance music appears to have always utilised tunes and instrumentation which did not differ greatly between Highlands and Lowlands. Seventeenth-century Scottish and Irish musics are most likely to have also been mutually meaningful in dance-tune, song and air structure and style. This certainly appears to be the case in Scottish and Irish tune collections, which show, from the eighteenth century onward, much similarity. Such points reinforce the idea of Scotland–Ulster – if not Scotland–Ireland – as being the one music-culture area.

The intervening years

The Plantation in Ulster gelled, aided by Protestant migration from Scotland to Antrim and Down. The linen industry became a major source of income to supplement farming. In the early eighteenth century song and music – particularly song among the weaving trade in County Antrim – thrived in a period of comparative calm, up to the events that led to the formation of the Orange Order in 1795. The 1798 rebellion divided Protestants – Presbyterians being, on the whole, republican, Anglicans supporting the status quo and crystallising as the Orange Order:

> The conflict in Ulster with the United Irishmen was essentially a sectarian war between Presbyterian and Anglican. All of the battles took place along the frontier of those two cultural zones – Rathfriland, Saintfield, Templepatrick, Randalstown – whether in Antrim or Down, always on the boundaries of where the orange yeomanry based their peasant recruitment. It was like the border warfare between the Scots and the English ... The end of the eighteenth century saw the Masonic order in English areas become the Orange Order, and in Scottish/Presbyterian areas become republican ...[10]

The late eighteenth century was the beginning of a heyday for ideologically motivated fife and drum bands. Initiated by the military, strong during the Napoleonic wars (1805–15), music and marching became popular in civilian political manoeuvres. The peak of this was the 1840s Temperance movement, which had more than 300 bands, mostly in the southern part of Ireland. Ulster was poorly represented in that movement, but had its own band structures in the Orange movement. Therein, fife[11] and drum bands were popular in the later eighteenth and early nineteenth centuries, with flute[12] bands taking over by the turn of the twentieth. Where there is marching band music there are musicians, and where there are musicians there are a talented few who are adept at the dance music that was so vital to social recreation in the pre-recording/broadcasting age. In the middle of the twentieth century things were no different for Orange band musicians:

> ... they weren't just playin' four or five party tunes all day on the Twelfth day ... them boys learnt from boys who date back to the late 1800s. John Kennedy says that he was fifin' the same tunes as his grandfather. Because it's a conservative tradition, there's no reason for that to change. So you can say that they played whatever music they knew and the only music in Ireland for punters was the jigs, reels and hornpipes ...[13]

The end of the seventeenth century onward was the developmental period too for the bulk of the music which is still played in Traditional circles in Ireland and Scotland today.[14] Communication with Scotland continued, but now differently; it developed most strongly in the Catholic community, particularly in Donegal, where seasonal and permanent emigration had established an Irish cultural niche in Glasgow in the early nineteenth century. These economic associations provided a productive culture-mix interface, which is still reflected in a Donegal repertoire of dance music that represents both Scotland and Ireland.[15] Traditional music in Ireland and Scotland consistently pushed as far as available technology and leisure time would allow. Today it has a considerable surviving and documented, popular legacy in both regions. Indeed, since Donegal music is strongly modern-Scottish in character, for a long time in the twentieth century it was considered, in the best of fashionable 'tradition', as the pariah of Irish Traditional music.

CHAPTER NINETEEN

The fluidity of change

The Traditional music of Ireland has certain well-attested visual associations, some of them internationally known. Among these is now not only the harp, but also the bodhrán drum and the uilleann pipes. Similarly, the general sound of the music is internationally distinctive. Within the island, however, there are many senses of identity associated with it, not least regionalism and regional accent or 'style'. As for the idea of authenticity, one's 'real thing' is a personal choice, or set of choices, rooted in musicianship and/or taste, but defined by region, era of origin, nostalgic associations and, sometimes, rural life. It is often influenced by particularly brilliant or charismatic players. The oldest accurate historical record of what Traditional music actually was, or sounded like, in the past is contained in scarce 1890s and early-twentieth-century Ediphone cylinders, and in the early-twentieth-century 78 RPM records. Beyond that, the 'truth' can be found in some shape in manuscripts, even if there is no reliable evidence of how tunes might have actually been played. Popular belief has it, however, that outside of these, the oral tradition has preserved much of 'the way it was'. This may or may not be true, for probably everyone in the post-recording past has been influenced by recordings (whose artistes themselves may have been influenced by other music styles in the US). Often, the oldest person in the most remote spot in Ireland turns out to have been influenced by 'the 78s' sent over by relatives in America, or may even have lived in the USA for half a century themselves. Again, it is difficult to estimate the directive power of radio broadcasting of Traditional music in Ireland from 1926 onwards.

Earlier again, certain players would have been subject to moulding by manuscript sources via the odd musically literate player who passed on written material orally. Beyond that, music-hall and other popular music and song styles exerted some outside influence – in response to musical challenge, curiosity and fashion – as part of the natural, logical, slow development and change. However, arguing against that slow drip of inevitability, there is the absolute certainty which language offers, namely that local accents do not substantially change over time. If inside

Ediphone. The oldest evidence of the 'sound' of Traditional music from Ireland is on wax cylinder recordings made on the first recording machine, the Edison Phonograph.

fifty years of middle-ground presentation voices amid the mass popularity of radio, television and latter-day global broadcasting, local accents remain solidly distinctive, then it is most likely that music's accents and styles, being also aurally transmitted, entered the pre-tech age in great variety. Even so, while there may be such a core stylistic bible and repertoire in Traditional music, there is unlikely to be absolute 'authenticity'. There can only be individuals with different emotional make-ups, opinions, sociability, tastes, technical and interpretative abilities and retentive powers. One plays a 'Traditional' instrument (one for which the music was made) and applies the acculturated 'Irish' (or Irish regional) Traditional intonation (like accent in language and, like it, an accident of birth and only acquired by enculturation). This may happen by early-life osmosis, but today is more likely to be achieved by studying or intensive listening to renowned players' personal attributes, and choosing one's particular fountainhead of truth. Then 'rules' are laid down. Every age group has different standards, and players of particular instruments have their own police and gurus, many of whose opinions are repugnant to players on other instruments, or to singers. But varied or not, those who produce the stuff remain talented and expressive musicians. It is likely that it is just their admirable passion and interpretative ability which, being admired and respected or held in awe, is simply described as (or confused with the idea of?) 'authenticity'. Even so, it must still be said that people within Traditional music consider themselves with reasonable certainty to be able to know the real thing (or the most real thing) when they hear it. Colloquially, this is sometimes referred to as the 'nya', or rhythmically, the 'gimp'.

Irish Traditional music, like folk music in all of Europe, has been both sidelined and changed in tandem with technological developments, industrial lifestyle and availability of other choices in musics and entertainment forms. This process has been strongest since the introduction of 'take-away', everlasting entertainment (cinema, and mechanical and electronic recording) at the end of the nineteenth century. Such relentless pressure to change has had the greatest effect in cities, less so in peripheral regions. It has not influenced Ireland as much as it has the neighbouring island, and within Britain it has not impacted as much on remote (from London) north-west Scotland as on easily accessible Wales. Pressure to change and conform is also resisted more in a country which is occupied by, is economically and politically controlled by, or is aggressively culturally dominated by, another. In these situations, items of cultural expression from the past are retained by the dominated people as valued, hereditary identity markers, their importance being related directly to political pressure and strife. For instance, folk music in Bulgaria is said to have been dearly treasured as a motif of cultural resistance during the 500-year Ottoman (Turkish) occupation, and even though the influence of Turkey may appear obvious in Bulgaria's music today, Bulgarians are adamant that it is uniquely Bulgarian. Absolute 'Bulgarian-ness' in the music, therefore, leans more towards aspiration than fact, making it likely – as with the definition of what 'Irish' music is – that such a desire for 'purity' is a recent product, an anti-imperial political expediency of the nineteenth century.

What is of significance in Ireland is that by the early part of the twentieth century, folk music was a well-established feature of Ireland's cultural life, as indeed it was in similar-style pockets throughout the western-dominated world. And while, perhaps ironically, typically it had been documented by representatives of the Protestant upper classes, nevertheless by now it had a political charge and was defending not only its existence, but an integrity for itself. Even so, such folk musics are constantly 'undermined' by the relentless, collective need for change within their societies, expressed through people's compulsion to follow fashions in pursuit of a better quality of life. The first major non-ideological diluting effect on Irish 'folk' music (what we know today as Irish 'Traditional' music) may indeed have come from religious and classical sheet music, but this initially would have only affected the upper classes, who sought British and European society music as their entertainment. Since this stratum had élite status and thereby influence, its music choice became a measure of social standing. So were planted the seeds of doubt and inferiority – manifested as a sense of deprivation – in the minds of the 'plain people'. Such a devaluation occurred among all religions as a class issue. In this way was instilled the foundation of the lower classes' lack of confidence in their own indigenous, accessible entertainment.[1]

Despite all this, however, in rural areas all over the island of Ireland and among the urban ex-rural poor in towns, the dominant music for leisure would have remained the dance tunes and songs from the Irish/Scottish/English mix until the arrival of the gramophone. This device froze performances in a mass-reproducible, durable, saleable plastic, and for such limited leisure time as people had, it brought other music 'live', so to speak, into less-well-off homes after the opening 1900s, and reaching out to all parts of the island by the 1930s, with the availability of cheap phonographs and emigrants' money. The gramophone had two simultaneous effects, one regenerative, the other destructive. In rural areas – Sligo, for instance – where big-name USA recording artiste, Michael Coleman, hailed from, people would gather round a gramophone to hear the local exile 'perform' over and over. This was also the case in far-off Cape Breton, Nova Scotia, where the tale is told of the fabled fiddler, Winston Scotty Fitzgerald, putting dime after dime in the juke box in order to learn Coleman's version of the Scottish tune 'Bonnie Kate'. In rural Antrim too it was just the same, and tunes and style were passed on via the machines right up to the 1960s:

> In the Creggs there was a man they called Thomas Hugh Wright, and he had the greatest variety of traditional records in Britain. He was a funny man, he loved music but he couldn't play it and he got the records catalogue and every traditional record in that catalogue he got it. Whenever the modern LPs came out he already had 7,000 78s and he had them in a room shelved right round. He had all the records ever Morrison made, Coleman made. There was never a flute player ever made a record he hadn't got him. Accordion players, fiddle players and all and you'd say: 'Thomas Hugh, I want to hear so and so – he's a tin whistle player.' 'Well just give me a minute.' And down he went and up he come with all the tin whistle players: 'Now is that what you were lookin' for there?' . . . he brought me out every record in them days that Leo Rowsome has made and the Pipes Quartet and

> all his single records . . . and he played me flute players and he played me fiddle players and let me tell you they were magic.²

On the destructive side, however (for Traditional music), the majority of people had a more practical interest in the gramophone – as diversion, as entertainment for entertainment's sake. Untroubled by burdens of authenticity, the machine was simply seen as providing something exciting, possibly different, especially new. Used widely as a substitute for live music for dancing to, it also became the vehicle for the introduction of other dance forms. This was as much the case in Protestant Antrim as Catholic Sligo (allowing for the effects of political issues), right up to the 1960s, and had a progressively debilitating effect on the older, long-standing forms of entertainment and music-making:

> Yankee Truesdale – they called him the Yankee because they thought he had money – he was a high-class painter and decorator, painted pubs, and he had a big radiogram³ and immediately before the war the big pop songs were 'South of the Border' and Maxi, and on a festive occasion he would've pulled the radio[gram] next the door and turned the volume up high and before you knew it there was couples out dancin' about the street. We were all kids sittin' on the cribby, all enjoyin' the crack . . .⁴

The cinema was initiated as a form of mass entertainment in Ireland in 1896. In the same period as the gramophone it provided another major popular recreational diversion. Radio followed it, and, eventually, television and the home-focused, electronic products of today which, paradoxically, return entertainment to the privacy of the home and fireside. Through them one can access unlimited choice of subject and medium from the armchair. Music, like everything else, moves with the times. Fashions change relentlessly, and what once was terribly up-to-date, at a later time seems tackily cheap. Attitudes to the music of the past are also often imbued with memories of the associated hardship of poor rural life and lack of education and opportunity. Those who have escaped that existence through a job (or the dream of one, or of a better one) have generally not thought much of it. And so, the old (now called the 'Traditional') music was always destined to be constantly on the wane, most rapidly in the middle of the twentieth century, a victim of improved lives and increasing prosperity. The impact of such undermining should have been equal in both Catholic and Protestant areas in the North of Ireland, but industrial work – and its associated values critical of things associated with the tougher rural life of the past – was, by dint of Northern Ireland employment policy and opportunities, more the territory of Protestants. Therefore, the undermining of the Traditional would have been more thorough in Protestant communities. In rural areas change was slower, and things seem to have been much the same for Protestant and Catholic. There were other reasons, even in a tightly knit but remote industrial area like the environs of Ballymena, for slower rates of change:

> The music . . . survives in the Glens because the Glens are a cut off area. It survives in mid-Antrim because there was industry in mid-Antrim. Boys didn't have to leave it, didn't have to go into it . . . There was a linen industry there . . . Draw a line around Ballymena – alright there was a train line – but you didn't have to go to Scotland, you didn't have to go to America. Nobody was comin' into the area because the population would sit there and work. So basically it was cut off . . . If you think of the fact too that their accent is considered unintelligible in the day and age of radio and TV – while everyone in Belfast is tryin to talk 'proper'. . .[5]

By the 1950s, overlaps of occasions of music and socialising among Protestants and Catholics involved either non-indigenous music, or the levelled-out, 'general' sound of the available or surviving music (subject to regional styles, or accents), as found in all of the island of Ireland. Ignoring political factors, at that time the picture showed a common 'Irish' music that was generally on the wane but still more practised in Catholic society than in Protestant, because fewer Catholics were in industrial employment, with its associated undermining of older entertainment traditions. The next chapter looks at the emergence of the revival phase of Traditional music.

CHAPTER TWENTY

New nations, new times, new cultures

In addition to the allusion to authentic Irishness in music contained in this poster from the post-famine year of 1849, harper Byrne also tips his hat to the gentry and the establishment by including references to his having played for 'Prince Albert, Queen Victoria and the Queen dowager'. While at face value both of these amount to no more than a musician maximising his audience, as a document of history this, and the concert's location in the 'hall of the Literary society', indicates an active middle-class interest in the cultural/identity value of indigenous harp music to local society. (*National Library of Ireland*)

The rise of European nationalisms from the eighteenth century onwards marked the beginning of political consciousness being invested in, or ascribed to, folk musics. Irish political movements – from the United Irishmen through to the 1840s Repeal movement – cemented the associations in the political imagination. This has had separate but distinctive effects on both the decline of Traditional music among Protestants and its regeneration among Catholics. For instance, in the mid-nineteenth century the largely Catholic Temperance movement rose to enormous significance just prior to the famine, peaking at the same time, and in substantially the same space, as Daniel O'Connell's movement in pursuit of the repeal of the 1801 Act of Union. Such a concurrence of moral/social and political agendas is not unique; it is a phenomenon common to other

Edward Bunting (1773–1843), the first major collector of the music of the old Irish harpers, made publication of this music a major part of his life's work. A Protestant raised in Armagh, he was an associate of the McCracken family in Belfast and leading figures in the Society of United Irishmen.[1]

historical periods and other countries. At that point in Ireland, however, Irish language and song became inscribed on the consciousness of a large body of co-religionists for whom it came to be part of the representation of their political identity. This of course applies to Protestant organisations also, but with all of these, loyalty to the crown as a form of hierarchical servility seems to have always dominated the agenda.

Engraving of Edward Bunting by William Brocas, 1811.

As in every other European country, retrospective nationhood was conferred in Ireland, with a consequent effect on music. County Antrim had a stronger indigenous music, Gaelic language and games culture than more inland areas of Ulster, dating to ancient associations with Gaelic Scotland. There the new 1880s process of 'identification' of these forms of culture with Irish nationalism and Home Rule may indeed have caused particular annoyance:

> Nationalism grew in Ireland, from about 1870 on – the Society for the Preservation of the Irish Language, Gaelic League and so on, GAA, and all that. Protestants were alienated from Irish culture because they had to call it Irish. Up to that it was just what you did . . . Up to the 1790s you get Protestant boys and all them boys in the Belfast Harp Society, and they were *interested*. It was happenin' all round them . . . it wasn't Irish, it was just *happenin'* – and it seemed that: 'we have to preserve what's bein lost all over Europe'. Then you go a hundred years on to the 1890s and 'it's Irish' and you have to preserve it because it's *Irish* – not because its dyin' out and important all over Europe – but because it's *Irish* and it's *'ours'*. There's a big hockey thing up round here [North Antrim] because the Protestants used to play shinty. But then when they [the GAA] called it 'hurley'

Protestants changed over and played hockey. Because it couldn't be hurlin' – you have to do something else because you can't be seen to be doin' their thing . . .[2]

How significant this kind of logic was in causing rejection of recreational dance music is difficult to establish, but it is somewhat challenged by the fact that the early collectors were very often Protestant,[3] and indeed titled their works *Ancient music of Ireland, Ancient Irish music*, and so on. There seems to have been no particular problem about loyal unionists also regarding themselves as 'Irish', or about identifying things around them as 'Irish'. On its own, therefore, and in its own time, the Gaelic League's implied policy on the music of Ireland could not have discouraged 'Protestants' *per se* out of music, but the organisation was associated with national movements that culminated in the War of Independence and the setting up of the Irish Republic. So, retrospectively, it certainly would have been a disincentive to Protestant interest in Traditional music. So too, of course, would have been the obvious association between popular indigenous music of the nineteenth century and nationalist identity in Ireland at large, an inevitable interdependence that is documented widely and is too specific a subject to expand on here.[4]

This factor constitutes another predisposition amongst (mostly nationally-minded) Catholics to favour the retention of the indigenous music in the face of its 'natural' evolutionary decline. It has a similar – but possibly much greater – effect as a disincentive to Protestants. The post-Republic period of the twentieth century inherited a legacy of association between antiquarianism and nationalism, the secular and the political, music and politics, and the era also marks the most emphatic 'them and us' separation of Protestants and Catholics in Traditional music. In the 1950s, Traditional music was espoused as a widespread, but politically flavoured, form of entertainment in Catholic rural Ireland, played for dancing by the céilí bands. Protestant rural entertainment was expressed as the Orange and other 'hall' dances, which still used the jigs and reels and the like, but also modern musics as well, and probably favoured touring Scottish bands. Among these was Fifeshire accordionist Jimmy Shand (1908–2000), whose Scottish 'sound' was hugely popular among Catholics; also it was part of the then-available popular music and indeed was liked all over the Republic,[5] where it affected public taste and the céilí bands as well. In both Protestant and Catholic communities of Northern Ireland, classical and church musics were acceptable alternative or competitive choices too. But it was the emerging modern, popular-dance music on records, via radio and from bands, that after the 1930s came to be the biggest disincentive to the Traditional. Universally frowned upon by parents, colloquially known as 'jazz', and with a universal language of criticism that embodied fear of African-Americans, this modern music was considered as being of little economic value, encouraging of slothfulness, wasteful of time and of God's given energy and vitality – neither a proper job, nor a decent thing for children to be indulging in at any level. Such taboos would appear to have been held by both Catholics and Protestants, for the work ethic was the common code of life. The music to loathe was 'jazz' and at its door the blame for all cultural and moral decline came to be laid. Donegal fiddler Néillidh Boyle, composer of 'The Moving Cloud' and other pieces, denounced it in an interview as 'jungle music',[6] the common racist term of abuse throughout developing Irish, British and US societies at the time. But while Protestants had less 'traditional' baggage to hinder them in enthusing about such new, life-enhancing music, Catholics had many absolute 'culture' hurdles to negotiate. In Catholic homes particularly it was still considered to be 'a good thing' to have Traditional music taught to children; it was an identity marker of Irishness, something that needed nurturing as a matter of survival in what was now a legislatively oppressive, Protestant- and British-identifying[7] state. Hence many young, middle-class Catholics were taught to play instruments and to sing. The fare then wasn't the 'heavy', dedicated end of the music that we are familiar with as Traditional music today. It was mostly the respectable: Moore's melodies, some lighter dance tunes, songs in Irish from the

New settings and prestige for Traditional music – here Frankie Gavin plays with Malachy and Brian Bourke (fiddle and bodhrán) at Brian's art exhibition launch in the Caldwell Gallery, Dublin, 2003.

Gaeltacht, the 'grand' patriotic songs relating to 1798 and the War of Independence, and the sentimental, American-exile music-hall ballads. Related to the music, but practised separately, artistic step dance ('Irish' dancing) remained a strong, visible expression of indigenous art and cultural identity. This continues to be practised all over the island, with a significant international dimension and continued practice in some parts of Antrim by both Protestants and Catholics.

Development in the revival period

The major changes in society that resulted from the economic growth of the 1950s and 1960s undermined Traditional music hugely. Paradoxically, however, in improving leisure time and providing disposable income, it also aided the revival process, which was under way by 1951, reached a dizzy headiness by the 1970s, and a peak of mainstream popularity by the mid-1990s. Revivals were also happening in other European countries, and indeed in former European colonies abroad. In the English-speaking world the process was not unique to Ireland, as folk revival was a huge movement in England, Scotland and the USA. Its main organisation in Ireland, north and south, was Comhaltas Ceoltóirí Éireann, predominantly Catholic, but with some Protestant members and officials in the North. The revival caused a rapid growth in Traditional music, blossoming in tandem with all the technological advances of the 1960s: 45s, EP and LP vinyl records, cassette tapes and minute 'transistor' radios, better roads and cheap transport, the availability of sleeping bags and damp-free tents, and the withering away of taboos on mixed-company socialising and drinking. Many late-teen to thirty-year-old Catholics and Protestants began playing or listening to Traditional music in this climate, some developing a passionate interest in it; they travelled to the endless number of *fleadhanna ceoil* 'down south' to pursue what can only be described as an addiction.

This was a considerable turnaround for the music. Previously its star had been waning in the manner of all things of the past. It had suffered from the development of other musics as a result of changes wrought by 'progressive' thinking in all things, particularly the remarkable spate of technological development after the turn of the twentieth century. In the climate of 'revival' the Traditional was no longer a music played simply for private, local and fair-day entertainment. It gradually took on all the other trappings of the age of technology and mass communication. Standards improved and instruments were freely available and in great variety. Radio-performance opportunities created figureheads and there was a market for music talent; ego entered what had previously been a mostly humble picture. Criticism – of youth, and of playing practice, performance demeanour and social behaviour – formerly reserved for 'popular' musics, began to be applied to Traditional music:

> In bygone days now I think maybe you've . . . probably a better sort of person'd play Traditional music. The people who played Traditional music in my time . . . they'd like a good fiddler and they'd be interested in learnin' a good musician . . . Goin' back a long time when you went to a session, I remember in Portglenone (Portglenone is sort of half-and-half you know) the hall was jammed to capacity. There was roughly about twenty musicians jammed on to the stage and that whole night you'd a had to put on the lights to see if there were people in the hall . . . and of course they were playin' music at the proper tempo then. That was a mixed hall in them days and you see them musicians – they werenae getting' sloshed . . . they don't want to know you now unless you're just a real *druth*.[8]

By comparison with the new age, the past could be looked back to as a golden age of innocence:

> I think it's terribly commercialised now. A lot of them are not in it for the playing, for pastime. It seems as though they're playing it for what they can get out of it. We played for the pleasure of playing it . . . I wouldn't think a thing of playin' somewhere and never get a bean . . . The system of playin' has changed totally. You see these 'sets' that they're goin mad about? Well, it has increased the speed of the music and its takin' away from the qualities of the music because they're playing to suit set dancers, and set dancers about the city can't get the music played fast enough.[9]

All advanced rapidly to create the commercial international practice and ethos which fodder Traditional music consumption today. This includes a distinctive set of vocal, physical and instrumental dimensions, social and artistic expressiveness, standards, orally transmitted stylistics, and graphically, mechanically and electronically presented repertoire as well as large professional and amateur practices, definitive media with review, feature and documentary interest. The music is inspired and catered for by ideological, teaching and competitive structures. It has ad hoc, dedicated and general organisational bodies which draw on state and local arts funding, and has such recognition *as itself* at all state levels that there have even been scandals.[10] The music also has both aural and formal standards of assessment, a professional and quasi-professional academia, including collectors. It is included in second- and third-level education, with ongoing postgraduate research and teaching overseen by specialised persons and institutions. There is too a substantial analytical and documentary literature, and a state–funded archive of all Traditional music material productions and representations over some

An international dimension to Traditional music is seen here in the context of the life and livelihood of Castlemaine, Melbourne flute-maker, Mike Grinter, here seen playing with his famiy. He supplies flutes at the highest levels of talent in Traditional music.

three centuries. Perhaps then 'revival' could more objectively be seen as a new beginning? It has developed and built on the old foundation, but as well as recycling the old, it also reinterpreted and created anew out of its exile and international experiences. This gives it a 'classical' or 'art' status, but in any case makes a *new* music of it, a modern folk music – what we know today as 'Traditional Irish music'.

Early music and song revivalists had operated with the notion that there was a fixed form of older music which could be reinstated as the core of artistic and cultural life. Their concept was that 'revival is an overt and explicit act of authentication'. But Traditional music is *not* just like a preserved, calf-leaved tome, or an iconically symbolic marble bust. It is played actively, explored in many differing interpretations, sometimes using borrowed concepts of rhythm and harmony, a new backing instrumentarium. More accurately, it can be described as a new sub-genre.[11] The music has roots common to both native and settler traditions and its older repertoire was from both of those. But as a new music it is now the territory simply of those who play it, of those who like it, or who like it and want to play it, whether or not they have been (by accident of birth) predisposed to do so or not.

Modern-day political associations

The germination of the revival of Traditional music also overlaps with political movements. In the early days of the revival a lot of people who were totally new to the music had developed such an interest that they took up playing. Student bodies perceived the music as radical, trendy, stimulating and so on:

> When I was at Queen's [University, Belfast] I met Harry O'Prey and 'The Pride of Erin' band. They went to play in the Gorey fleadh in 1962. Out of this fleadh traffic came a group of people who began to get to know one another ... definitely revival musicians. Everybody went to the fleadhs. The Traditional music scene broadened to include people like Andy Irvine – [nineteen] sixties differentiation between

New nations, new times, new cultures 133

Sandino's Bar. The association of Traditional music with the avant-garde or non-conventional and socialist-leaning dimensions of society is real, and while it can be curious or off-putting to a drop-in stranger at a session, it nevertheless neither improves nor dis-improves the music beyond underlining its perceived ethos as 'music of the people'.

> the 'balladeers' (nasty term) and the 'real' tradition has now changed. The edges now have become properly blurred.[12]

The Belfast Folksong Club, for instance, later to develop into the Belfast Folk Festival, was a mecca for the liberal students of both persuasions, and for Marxists and republicans too:

> ... it was the start of the revival really ... Derek Peters was there – he was a Communist Party man, and he formed a club called Unity in Castle Street and there'd be a few tunes and a few songs in it ... I didn't realise it at the time – it was years later – but it was all completely left-wing. Even after you'd learnt a lot of tunes and you went up to the Ould House – it was sort of left-wing before the troubles even – it was all a sort of socialism in those years.[13]

Marxism as a philosophy could appeal to anyone – it was universally held in terror by all religions because of its godlessness. Republicanism was more specific to Catholics, but it could also be supported by Protestants who, for historical, family or ideological reasons, admired the 1798 rebellion, or who were staunch in the trade union movement and the Northern Ireland Labour Party. So, within those groupings, among people of Protestant background who had no Traditional musical experience in their families or locality, there was a new leftist predisposition potentially conditioned by, and certainly reflecting, what was happening on the folk scene in Britain: 'As far as Europe is concerned, Britain is probably unique in the degree in which it depends on folk melody for its present-day political songs ... as a whole, the present revival in folk music shows some left-wing political colouring.'[14] Although the 'folk' movement in England had been started in the late nineteenth century as part of a growing desire to establish individuality among European nations,[15] the later folk consciousness had a blue-collar, CND, or at least liberal politics. This too affected Belfast and represented a new constituency of favour for the reviving Traditional music, which at this time was perceived to be 'Irish Traditional music'. Among formerly uninterested Catholics this new predisposition would have built productively on the already-existing folk memory of the music in the Catholic community at large.

The beginnings of Civil Rights agitation in 1966 impacted on the music too. That movement involved Catholics, Catholic nationalists, republicans, liberals, leftists and trade unionists. It also involved Protestant leftists, liberals, trade unionists and republicans. As that issue rapidly transformed into the 'Troubles', the Catholic community went behind barricades and dusted off the surviving Gaelic cultural

Children at the village of Tocane St Apre in Southern France playing, following a summer school in Traditional Irish music. The music is a common feature of cultural life in Europe. Today there are probably as many people playing it abroad – in environments where religion is of no consequence – as in Ireland itself.

programme of the early part of the twentieth century. This doctrine accommodated the new interpretation of the old struggle, and the reviving Traditional music was, conveniently, on hand; it was, nominally at least, part of the process, as a very definite *sound*.

Chapter Twenty-one

The creation of modern style

A typical session venue, the Dungloe Bar in Derry city. Herein the publican becomes the sponsor of the music, the community gains a cultural venue or reputation, while the performer carries on a music tradition, gets the chance to play, the possibility of developing a career and, at least, minor fame.

The scientific-minded do not see just a wasp or a helicopter, but find themselves considering mass, dimension, proportion, density, capacity, stability and methods of suspension and propulsion. Sociologists and ethnomusicologists look at musics and ask 'which?', 'where?', 'how?', 'on what?' and indeed, 'why?' With folk music, the most obvious consideration is 'context': where is it played?, for what reason? and how important is it to those listening, the event to which it contributes, the locality, the region, the 'nation' or out-of-state community? Music performance has been so viewed as: 'situated behaviour, situated within and rendered meaningful with reference to relevant contexts. Context is another way that performance is patterned in communities . . . Contexts, whether formal or informal are defined by each society and isolated in time, space and degree of public evaluation.'[1]

Pathways and associations

Irish music has always been one of many 'music pathways'[2] through life in Northern Irish society. Other such melodic routes are band, church, choral, popular, jazz, country, bluegrass, and rock. For Protestant society, the Traditional music path inevitably leads into a significant 'no-go' area, and so the Protestant aficionado or player has, in the end of the twentieth century, been obliged to consider the possibility of danger. There have been no instances of Protestant musicians being attacked while engaged in the pursuit of Traditional music in predominantly Catholic areas, but this does not mean that individual Protestant musicians do not feel apprehensive; they will choose quite carefully the area they enter, and the time or occasion that they enter it. The identification of the music with Catholicism, or 'Irishness', is not the only problem; within the Irish-identifying nationalist community itself the stylistic changes that the music has undergone since the 1960s have generated a whole other set of reasons for rejection and unpopularity, especially among older people. The political considerations, however, remain dominant, and foremost among these are the changes in the uses, functions and very performance styles of Irish Traditional music since the 1920s.

Particularly significant is the music revival's overlapping with Civil Rights agitation and the Troubles. This parallel association – in time and space – has rendered the music strongly affirmative of identity, this almost exclusively for Catholic society. Within Protestant society the music by the early 1990s still persisted at several levels: as personal or minority-group expression, as older people's expressive culture in North Antrim and in East Down, where old, local tunes and dance forms survive; for instance as seen at the 1990 'Whose Music?' conference, or the Ballycastle '*Festal*'.[3] In other areas and on other occasions it can also struggle, often uncomfortably and self-consciously, if not tokenistically,[4] as a bridging device to mend disconnections in the present political infrastructure but, in general, Traditional music is viewed by Protestants as alien, if not potentially subversive.[5]

South of the border things have been different. There Traditional music revival and change happened within an independent state that recognised it (however superficially and casually at times) as indigenous music, within a different set of social forces. In the years after indigenous music had declined for societally regenerative dancing, or had become redundant, career musicians were mostly playing modern musics. 'Traditional' music had little widespread function and, deprived of its use value, was in danger of being consigned to artistic pedantry, to symbolism and the tourist brochure, on the way to the display case. Seán Ó Riada came into this early revival period with an experimental approach that he presented on radio. By focusing on the melodic in Traditional music he emphasised the *individualistic* in its performance, as opposed to the *communal*,[6] which had been a key part of its role in earlier social dance. Effectively, he refashioned indigenous dance music as a 'classical' genre for listening and aesthetic appreciation, and promoted players as *performers*, to be observed and studied, while also shining a spotlight on the previously invisible category of *listeners*. Key to this are recognition and acknowledgement by performers, aficionados and audiences alike of the concept of quality, of differing levels of physical music ability and aesthetic expressiveness, factors inimical to any genre. Seminal influences in the same period were Séamus Ennis[7] and Breandán Breathnach.[8] Later, other commentators, like Tony MacMahon, took up Ó Riada's assertion that the music is most expressive as 'a solo art'. Even if nothing can be absolute in music (and these attitudes maybe are best regarded as time-bound taste or fashion), such thinking nevertheless shifted Traditional music all over Ireland out of the céilí bands' lack of specialisation and (comparative) muddle of sound (which the session format re-enacts) to crisp, clean, perfectly matched playing. They moved it from a music to participate in with dance, to one that can be observed, savoured, compared and commented upon. Traditional music these days has its thinking musicians, who through public utterance and halo-polishings consistently defend the absolutism of such new and re-worked visions. The cognitive has taken over from the social, regardless of whether the new self-consciousness is received by an intelligent, otherwise-informed audience as patronising (even if well-intentioned) wishfulness, and runs the risk of making a casualty of the actual music.

Sponsorship

Beyond the notion of solo performance, the most obvious development since the 1950s is the new 'music-pub' scene. This amounts to 'sponsorship' influencing music performance.[9] In the past the bar proprietor merely made the space available, or maybe provided the musicians with some drinks (which in poorer times were not insignificant gestures). At present the publican hires two or three players to simply be there for specified hours each night, effectively to act as catalysts to encourage and/or a bait to attract other players and particularly drink-consumers. This provides the opportunity of freeing the contracted musicians from other dreary professions and gives them space to concentrate on music as a profession and to contribute generally to the improvement of music quality.[10] Since the vast majority of such paying music-hosts in Northern Ireland are Catholic, this creates Protestant distance from what is arguably the greatest site of playing in the present day.[11] The idea of 'sponsorship', however, can be recruited more subtly in an account of the overriding political situation: with nationalist culture favouring Traditional music and unionist culture rejecting it, the music's fortunes should be affected by political upheaval in which those philosophies are instrumental. The post-1969 period is one of assertive nationalism, and that in fact is the era of the flowering of Traditional music. Its cultural climate has been one in which the best music opportunities were open to perceived nationalist genres; popular ballads – political and otherwise, Republican and Orange – have benefited most (the latter as by-product), with bands too getting a great boost in functional popularity. Traditional music's integrity as an art form was also thrashed out and definitively moulded in the course of these years. Such a development might be expected, of course, and has been explained already. One recalls John Blacking's observation that 'little musical variety and originality is to be expected in a society with a unified, hierarchical political system, but considerable variety can be expected in a segmented society'.[12]

While this exploration is useful in appreciating Irish music revival in the north of Ireland, it is perhaps secondary in importance to actual boundaries between Catholic and Protestant societies. The Reformation and the impact of its moral strictures in the politics of British governments of the seventeenth to nineteenth centuries, laid the foundation for these. Present-day religious observances and practices, their powerful transmission of attitudes to social and political life, build on this to condition separate expressive cultures on either side of a wall. This 'boundary' is the ultimate controlling force in religious, educational, recreational and working life, and is reflected in the attitudes of the people involved in different kinds of music. Understanding the boundary necessitates exploring the development of the music to its present-day pitch, in the light of political events, religious division, economic disadvantage, ancient and modern history, and Northern Irish mythologies.

> We held a dance in ould Kilmore,
> The Fenian bulldogs they came to it.
> They danced our maids right round the floor,
> And ordered Patrick's Day to play it.
> Garryowen and the White Cockade,
> These were the tunes that they did want sirs,
> As round the floor they danced our maids,
> Sayin' 'You never stood before such dancers'.
> *From the song 'Lurgan Town'*

CHAPTER TWENTY-TWO

Tonal boundary-marking: prejudice, politics and ethnicity

'Catholics dance, Protestants march'

This slogan is a well-ingrained Ulster notion. That both communities do both, on appropriate occasions, is not important. Dancing and marching are, of course, closely related pursuits, in that each involves body movement choreographed by music that has been invested with particular meaning. Both dancing and marching are also symbols of political universals that have been conditioned by religion-bound cultures. George Patton, the former Director of the Orange Order and now chief executive of the Ulster-Scots Agency, has earlier described how, because band music and Orange song are iconic for Protestants, they simply *assume* that there is an equivalent equation of Catholics and Traditional music (see Chapter 13). Protestants' view of their own political music is that it is part of a symbol process,[1] which involves bowler hats, lavish banners, stoic demeanour and allegorical, biblical speechifying, all of which denote assertion of Protestant political power. While appreciating that the majority of Protestant marching-band musicians are as likely to be as obsessed with their art as most Traditional musicians (including Protestant Traditional musicians), *participation* in 'Orange' band marches is unlikely to be a totally benign process. But since not all Protestants belong or want to belong to loyal organisations, *observation* of the marching-band music and parades can easily be benign.

So within the Protestant community there are different levels of certainty: the Orange parade actors are definitely making a declaration; the spectators (and the people who don't attend) *may* be making a declaration. Within Traditional music, however, both actors and spectators at a session *may* be experiencing an occasion politically – investing it with political symbolism – but if this is done, it is done *privately* (excepting cryptic and direct declarations of nationalism or Catholic ideology in the form of explicit song lyrics, and on occasion statements from CCÉ). By contrast, the Orange marching bands (outside of investment of artistic energy) are making an *unambiguous* political statement that commandeers open public space for the approval of supporters and heeding by opponents. Traditional musicians *may* be making a political statement, but even if they are, it is in a confined public space to which there is optional access/egress for those who don't like the music, or don't want to be there. Indeed, the sound of their music is contained by the room and, in addition, whatever the process means to an individual is private and need not be communicated to or shared by the person beside them.

Orangemen wish and need to have political space tonally defined. It is not difficult, therefore, to reach the conclusion that it is convenient for them (in either ignorance or awareness of the information in this book relating to common Catholic/Protestant practice and origins of Traditional music) to mis-assign Traditional music to nationalism, and to ascribe it 'Fenian'. Whatever way the conclusion is reached, this is the case currently in the urban areas of Northern Ireland. It is simple and convenient, and it adds a strong reinforcement to boundaries, which otherwise seem to the outsider to be barely there. Actual cultural differences between Catholic and Protestant have been initiated in school and church culture in formative years. Church culture is particularly significant: many of those interviewed for this work heard their first songs and music there, played their first instrument in the Boys' Brigade, Sunday School, YMCA, Sea Scouts and Orange bands: Protestant organisations that are a mystery area to Catholics. This culture gap is illustrated first by a Protestant, then by a Catholic:

> In one sense the Orange culture equates to Protestant culture in Northern Ireland. It's through our parades and things that most Protestants give expression to culture. Through that we've been involved in music, and increasingly in art and drama. Art . . . maybe that's a bit of a euphemism – we're talking about the wall murals and the arches . . . folk-art, I suppose that's really what it is.[2]

> As deputy mayor I go to some functions and – it's goin' into a new world in that their values aren't my values, whether it's real or whether it's something they're tryin' to hold on to (Britishness?) – that's foreign and strange to me. You go to an RAF thing, ex-servicemen's groups, say on Poppy day – it's a weird experience, you're an outsider.[3]

This only affirms that culture is learned behaviour, marking what is otherwise obvious: the polarisation of Protestants and Catholics as a result of religious and political upbringing. It suggests the use of the term 'ethnicity' to describe Protestant and Catholic identities: 'People become aware of their culture when they stand at its boundaries. . .'.[4] The ascription of Traditional music to Catholics by Protestants who are not involved in it poses a problem for the Protestant musicians. If indeed 'man is a cultural animal suspended in webs of significance he himself has spun',[5] and if 'culture is taken to be those webs . . . the analysis of it to be . . . an interpretative one in search of meaning',[6] then they are obliged to live double lives.

This is borne out by several musicians' comments. Here the dawning of insecurity is described at a session:

> The room was full of boys swinging off the lights and everything. I looked round the entire room and I was the only Protestant in the room. And it was the first time it actually struck me. I says to a Catholic friend, 'I'm the only Protestant in this room!' 'Shut up!' says he. I mean it was terrifying, you know. It was very strange . . . because up to that you'd never been in that situation . . . Not that anybody gave a haet[7] about it because that was before the students were touched by the Troubles.[8]

The bomb threat to musicians in Newtownards in 1993 (outlined in the introduction to this book) was a most significant and frightening consequence of this conundrum. The other side to the duality of attitudes relating to Traditional music in the Newtownards case is that on that occasion cultural and/or artistic concern within the Protestant community resulted in a withdrawal of the threat to musicians. The lifting of the threat was not made simply because it was discovered that the bulk of musicians playing at the venue were, in fact, Protestant. It arose out of a genuine goodwill towards music, *as music*, from leadership within the local Protestant community. Even still, such an incident illustrates that there is a difficulty in drawing the lines clearly between Protestant and Catholic, suggesting that perhaps the boundaries are not so distinct as to merit the use of the concept of ethnicity, and are closer in fact to the divisions between political parties. However, as was argued in the 1960s in an attempt at descriptive clarity:

> In analytical terms 'Catholic' and 'Protestant' can be regarded as imperative statuses, and the two conflicting groups can be analysed as ethnic groups . . . the critical focus of investigation . . . becomes the expression and maintenance of ethnic boundaries, 'the social organisation of ethnic difference'.[9]

Such a stand presupposes, however, a degree of independence of ethnicities – particularly a separateness in economic life – which is, in fact, disappearing in Northern Ireland. It does, however, help clarify the problems for Traditional musicians:

> The ethnic boundary canalises social life – it entails a frequently quite complex organisation of behaviour and social relations. The identification of another person as a fellow member of an ethnic group

implies a sharing of criteria for evaluation and judgment. It thus entails the assumption that the two are fundamentally 'playing the same game'... On the other hand, a dichotomisation of others as strangers, as members of another ethnic group, implies a recognition of limitations on shared understandings, differences in criteria for judgment of value and performance, and a restriction of interaction to sectors of assumed common understanding and mutual interest.[10.]

Following that logic it is necessary to keep the potentially disloyal out. The term 'ethnic' is therefore – for analytical purposes – applied here to Northern Ireland. This is done in consideration of several characteristics, which Barth indicates as delineating an ethnic group.[11] These seek to establish if such a group:

- is biologically self-perpetuating
- shares fundamental central values
- makes up a field of communication and interaction
- has a membership identifying itself, and being identified by others as distinct.

All of these can be clearly observed where there are rigid racial and sociopolitical characteristics and conditions, as for instance with the black, Surinam-origin section of the population of the Netherlands. But the points appear considerably weaker in the Northern Irish context, where all people have the same skin colour and range of physiological features. In Barth's analysis the critical focus 'becomes the ethnic Boundary that defines the group, not the cultural stuff that it encloses'.[12] Yet, it might still seem that it *should* be possible for Protestantism to contain Traditional music in the way that all groups contain various popular, country and classical musics, but the religious umbrella does not do this comfortably. The reason it doesn't, as suggested by Des Bell,[13] is because control of the boundaries is in radical hands. He argues that loyalist ethnicity, while validating itself through ritual (the purpose of which is boundary maintenance), does so by means of its cutting edge: the alienated subculture of loyalist youth. Since hostility to Traditional music is found mostly in urban areas, it is helpful to look at parallel studies of other aspects of Protestant culture.

In relation to loyalist murals, for instance, it is argued[14] that, though constant relocation and defending of boundaries has been a feature of working-class life in Belfast ever since the early nineteenth century, the parading and mural-painting are nevertheless part of an *internal* debate concerning power.[15] If this is so, the significance of Traditional music being viewed as 'Fenian', especially where Protestants play it, explains the persistent loyalist need to banish it as part of a drive for 'purity', a removal of any taint of the 'pan-nationalist conspiracy' (see Chapter 6).

That is, the 'cultural stuff' – which is being kept out of Protestant life by the boundary – is seen to be potentially pathogenic, particularly if the rest of the culture it is obliged to be part of is not in good health.

Northern Ireland societal organisation had always been a demonstration of unionists' emphasis on separateness: after the foundation of the border they actively shunned the concept of Irishness, since this was already claimed as the territory of nationalists and would have undermined the solidarity of unionist 'Britishness'.[16] However, that did not always have such a great effect on Protestant perception of Irish music, until the music became important in the period of a revival – which was paralleled by the troubles. It is only since then that the issue of the music has become so thorny for many Protestants. The easiest option – in the city at any rate – has been to throw in that particular cultural towel, implicitly abandoning the Protestant Traditional music lovers. The derogation leads Catholics into the complacency expressed in the common (outside) perception 'Traditional music is Catholic music'. In a comparatively short space of time, many in both the Protestant and Catholic populations have forgotten what has just gone before, in the manner of all Folk traditions of course. The younger generations simply don't know.

Public expressions of all of this are commonplace in the political life of Ireland, particularly in that of Northern Ireland. Though rarer in the society of those who actually play the music, the absence of information does now appear to be conditioning even *their* collective subconscious. Especially vulnerable to this particular revisionism are those who have been born since, or were very young during, the late 1960s (those born into the Troubles, so to speak). Commenting on first hearing of the existence of Protestant Traditional musicians, a Catholic university music student shows how little in fact was known about Traditional music among the under-thirty age group in 1991: '. . . but *they* don't play *our* music – *do* they?'[17] In the beginning some 'revival' Protestant musicians were none the wiser, and some of those who learnt in what they felt had been Catholic contexts were surprised and gratified to eventually learn that older Protestants played: 'I had to think about it because I was doing this fife book . . . when I found out the Protestants were doin' it amazed me . . .'[18] The logical crystallisation of this way of thinking is the 'Protestants march, Catholics dance' cliché – a convenient expression of the concept of two musical traditions. One may have Orange bands and songs, be militant and political, and the other have only fiddles and flutes, yet regardless of acoustic or recreational intent, the (perceived) Catholic practice is essentially viewed from the outside as merely *posturing* as entertainment – but in reality it is thought to be subversively, privately political. Such conferral of political status and significance on music is not unusual, has happened before in Ireland (for example, during the Temperance crusade years, 1838–43), and has been identified as a curious universal: the way in which 'materials from "folk" sources . . . can bring with them, or are conferred with, the capacity to symbolise the cultural values of a "folk" or sub cultural group . . .'[19]

John Blacking has documented that same process in South Africa during the 1970s, describing the relationships between political aspirations and musical performance. He argued that the music of the Black churches there expressed and enhanced a Black collective consciousness that members were not able to express in words. In the Northern Irish context, in the process of Catholics taking to Traditional music in its revival phase and Protestants not identifying with it during the same period, the parallel existence of, first, Civil Rights and then the Troubles cannot be ignored. Blacking interprets music as:

> . . . non-referential and sensuous, and no claim can be made that it is directly political . . . some music can become and be used as a symbol of group identity, regardless of its structure; and the structure of music can be such that the conditions required for its performance generate feelings and relationships between people that enable positive thinking and action in fields that are not musical . . .[20]

This observation sheds light also on present-day Southern-Irish Catholic perception of Traditional music as 'nationalist'. Such an attitude is an easily understood consequence of the process of the development of the Irish nation state, but also, considering CCÉ's Southern/nationalist focus, the analysis can offer some non-polemical explanation for that organisation's political actions. Inversely, it also contributes to making the Protestant rejection of Traditional music clearer still.

CHAPTER TWENTY-THREE

Withering and blooming in the seventies

Something of the classlessness of Traditional music, yet of its moving into an artistic, academic and social stratum different to its perceived 'proper' territory is gleaned from this picture, in which all the highly talented players are, variously, in the medical profession and third-level education.

Musics of the world buzz in relation to outside factors – international fashion, movements in art, consumerism and economics. They respond particularly well to political ferment. Yet politically motivated people do not generally have an interest in music that is even remotely similar to that of the actual musicians and music communities. Typically they see it as part of a wholeness, the cultural/political 'package'. In any case, throughout the 1970s whether 'it' liked it or not, Traditional music found itself sustained by, and itself sustaining, political energy, a mutually beneficial synergy.

One of the manifestations of this was CCÉ's All-Ireland fleadh cancellation in 1971. Benefit gigs for internees and republican prisoners often used Traditional and folk musicians; so too did many of those for socialist and trades union issues, both of which were often mixed-religion by origins of birth. The strains of Traditional music became for many

Northerners synonymous with the nationalist, left and liberal political environments. For sympathetic Southerners the music would therefore become, in the headiness of the revival and in the intensity of the political upheaval, their *solidarity*, what they were doing to help – their Irishness in fact. 'The music is what will unite Catholics and Protestants and get rid of the border; we should be all getting together through the music'[1] became a typical altruistic, Southern, Catholic, music-insider opinion of the day; genuine in intent, but loaded with pre- and mis-conception. The actual political power wished for the music in this statement is no different to the nationalist overview of the one indissoluble island nation.

Incentives and disincentives

Older Protestant musicians who loved the music they played were faced with a world in which their art had all the appearances of becoming redundant. Some did have an interest in passing it on to their next generation, and they managed to do so. In order to interest youth in music, however, there must be a reason: an occasion for its use, a stage, somewhere to show off, and a feeling of being loved and 'thought-well-of' for playing it. The Protestant young after the 1950s could see their parents and neighbours dancing mostly to pop cover-bands, country and western and country and old-time, rather than céilí or céilí and old-time. In homes where Traditional music or song had been an actual part of cultural experience, the music came to have little function for the children there other than the pleasing of musical parents and older people, or else the isolated (in the context of Northern Ireland political life) pleasing of one's self. That was not enough incentive to get anything more than a handful of young Protestants to carry on playing or singing. It isn't difficult to see why the next generation of Protestants might not be taught the music and song. And so a gap developed.

In contrast, by the 1960s the Catholic community had the psychological comfort of nineteenth-century association of Irish music with Irish identity. They had been in touch with the music ideologically (no matter how superficially) for all the years after the formation of the Gaelic League, and many had learned it courtesy of the opportunity of its political complementarity. There was a revival going on, which was particularly identified with and also mainly located in the South, towards which Catholics were generally well disposed. There was also a full-blown political struggle in progress in which there was kudos for playing the music, ready platforms and heady, enthusiastic listeners ready to clap players on the back for what was perceived as 'great work'. This constituted a significant boost to a music that had been on the wane: it was an incentive to play, or to learn to play. The same thing was happening in the revival in the South; the Northern Irish political struggle was tapped into from afar and its energy productively channelled, (however unaware people were of this)to boost the revival.

'Pure' revivalism

Since the early years of revival there has been a strong feeling abroad that the people who had continued playing 'the music' were in possession of some remnant of a rare and treasured jewel. The lexical toolbox of revival includes lavish expressions of this: 'breathtakingly wonderful', 'a rich heritage', 'cultural treasure' and 'noble tradition' are a few. Culinary similes were, and remain, common: 'cream of tradition', 'essence of Irishness', 'steeped in music', 'steeped in tradition'; these are particularly common in tourist adverts and publications originating outside Ireland. Complementing the wide span of metaphor, the timely efficacy of the revival itself might be described as having prevented all of this artistic noblesse from 'slipping away down the drain-plug'. Such a hugely attractive linguistic bait was typically Victorian, and for Irish music was begun by nineteenth-century collectors such as Edward Bunting. It was still currency, however, in the influential writings and rhetoric of Francis O'Neill in the early 1900s;[2] shades of it are found in Breandán Breathnach's texts, and such verbiage is still inspirational currency in CCÉ documents such as *Treoir* magazine.

It was not an easy task to set about learning the music starting from cold, with an absence of background, as was the case for most beginners, especially those who were out of their teens. People who were attracted enough to the music needed to be inspired to set about learning, and the most inspirational route was (not unreasonably) to trust that it was the living link with the past. Such devotees were often totally defensive about the music – and not without good reason, for there was a deal of absolute hostility to it both from the modern world as well as the old music-education establishment. To Traditional music enthusiasts, for instance, the Beatles and British pop music especially were seen as bad, destructively infatuating for the young, for religious and conservative railing against 'British values' in pop music was fashionable in the 1950s. In this spirit the Catholic Archbishop of Dublin, John Charles McQuaid, 'set up a Vigilance committee which took as much interest in Teddy Boys as it did in writers. "Indecency was the order for the night", a spy reported to McQuaid in 1955 about the Mambo Club, "a mad house" where teenagers went to dance to the new rock and roll. "Without any supervision, anything could happen" the informant wrote'.[3]

Nationalist assumptions

Considering that the revival had its organisational and commercial centre (CCÉ) in Dublin, it is not surprising that there was the implication, if not the conviction, of an inherent *anti-Britishness*, an *Irishness* and, logically (Partition had only happened thirty years before the founding of CCÉ), an *anti-Unionism* in the music. 'Anti-Unionism' for Southern nationalists does not necessarily indicate anti-'Northern Protestantism'. But a level of immature, complacent arrogance – expressed as an incapacity to deal with people of a religion other than Catholic – did persist with the odd Southern musician whose only working model of Protestantism might have been the dated and out-of-place image of wealth and absentee landlords:

> Whenever I was out . . . it never bothered me where anybody went on a Sunday: if they could play music that's all that interested me. I remember one time goin to one of the Pipers' [Na Píobairí Uilleann] dos – it was at Termonfeckin . . . A southern piper and me shared a room together that time, you know, them weekends were great! There was never any hassle, or anythin'. I remember on the Sunday, we were all up on the platform –when you're getting' your pictures taken – my room-mate made a smart-Alec remark about 'Northern Protestants'. Well, I never bothered much about it, but a Dublin friend said to me, 'This boy needs a clout on the ear.' There mustn't have been more than three or four Protestants there, but it was bad taste I thought from a piper who was well known.[4]

As the political situation worsened in Northern Ireland, so too did the status of Traditional music in Protestant areas. Each new crisis brought another sprinkling of Protestant drop-outs from the Fleadh Cheoil travel scene: first internment (1971), then Bloody Sunday (1972), then the hunger strikes (1983). Effectively, this constituted the absenting of more and more Protestant families from that social sustenance without which any music would find survival difficult, and without which young people would be merely playing in a vacuum:

> But then you see the attitude of the musicians changed – after the Hunger Strikes . . . There were people who I was very friendly with. In my lifetime I was never a bigot and that's why I got so disappointed that there were so many bigots. You see before the Hunger Strikes? I would've given my life for them. After that they completely changed, and they wanted nothin' at all to do with me, and that disappointed me terribly. You see I never thought they would ever mix up music and politics. I had no time for that, they just more or less told me in the nicest possible way that they'd prefer that I didnae play with them any more.[5]

County Antrim uilleann piper Wilbert Garvin

While this is demonstrably far from universally applicable, it is nevertheless a profound personal experience. Consider such an awareness in the light of the disappearance of enthusiastic audiences for the music in Protestant communities, the growing perception of it as being more identified with the 'opposition', the pressures on young folk to get involved in their own 'side' in the political crisis, the lure of the drama of politically motivated marching bands; a pretty uninspiring scene for the survival of Traditional music, with it being pushed further into decline in Protestant areas.

Protestantism as a culture, in urban areas, since the 1960s has thus progressively relinquished its participation in Traditional music. The Protestant communities – as opposed to individual Protestant-reared people – because of both the music's perceived political associations and unionist rejection of things Irish, have thereby missed out on those formative years of what is now, arguably, a new music sub-genre However, things are not normally given up in political struggles if they are held dear. One must conclude that the Protestant community has grown away from appreciation of the music, from part of their own heritage.

Today

Traditional music these days in Northern Ireland in very few places[6] is a vital part of any local community (in the sense that a church might be); rather it is participated in by a networking community of musicians and followers who travel widely over all of Ireland and to areas of Irish exile abroad. Traditional musicians, like those in other music fields, operate within a 'community of appreciation', of listeners and off-duty or lapsed instrumentalists. This has its local networks – such as Belfast, East Down, North Antrim, Mullaghbane, Belleek, etc. – which tie into a greater regional one; this in turn blends into a network covering the entire island. Eventually the 'two Irelands' and other centres of Irish music – the biggest being in Britain and the USA – coalesce into a global Irish Traditional music community, in which albums, magazine articles, the internet, gigs and radio/TV programmes are the constantly communicating media. This is no different to what happens in other specialised activities, from pigeon racing to stamp collecting. It is not unique to Irish music either; the same thing happens in other Traditional-style musics, in jazz, baroque, etc., even in post-modern drum-bass or MC rap. A cultural-outsider opinion from an Englishman living and playing in Belfast for many years illustrates an intersection of this global appeal with local ethnocentricity:

> I saw Traditional music in the beginning as the most exciting thing going. Not as having a specific Irishness – 'musical' versus 'affiliated to Irishness' – but it is undoubtedly *Irish* for others. Not me, otherwise I wouldn't be able to do it. I probably disagree with most people on that. I'm used to hearing comments like 'Jesus Christ the way you played that – you must be as Irish as the rest of us', and 'This man here is playin' the fiddle – and he's an Englishman!'[7]

CHAPTER TWENTY-FOUR

Jigging at the crossroads, 2008

Part of the modern face of Traditional music is big-stage performance in which céilí bands (once the providers of music for social dance) and the social dancers themselves (as 'set' dancers) may now be the subjects of sit-down entertainment. This is such a scene from the opening of the Traditional-music-dedicated Glór music centre at Ennis, County Clare in 2001.

Traditional music as played by North of Ireland Protestants in passed-on continuity is, allowing for regional variation, the same as that played by Catholics in both parts of Ireland. It is influenced by Scottish and English musics and is the descendant of the accumulated popular 'folk' music of the island of Ireland prior to the twentieth century, when it was the folk/popular music of all, regardless of religion. The music was eroded first by urbanisation, becoming more exclusively the entertainment of the rural and urban poor prior to the development of modern-day urban living and mass forms of entertainment. It was on the decline in both Protestant and Catholic communities in Northern Ireland prior to the 1950s, but less so in Catholic areas because it was ideologically favoured by nationalism. Traditional music's 1950s 'revival' was contemporaneous with the Civil Rights era and the Troubles in subsequent years. Traditional music after that, benefiting from a climate of nationalist political upheaval, was boosted by the identity demands of submersion in the European Economic Community. It has been tempered by modern tastes, technology, popular music aesthetics and economics to produce a distinctive sub-genre of music.

Most of the Catholics and Protestants (nominally and politically speaking) who now play the music in the North of Ireland only do so since the revival, and not as the result of an immediate, unbroken, handed-down tradition. Protestant musicians today are mostly of the revival era and, like Catholics involved in the music, they may or may not be politically involved. That, like a profession, is considered a different matter, and private. Since the music has come to be, and is still, regarded as a significant attribute of Irish national identity, Catholics do have, and have had, a greater predisposition towards liking and supporting it, while most Protestants regard it as 'Catholic'. For loyalists/unionists, music has been an important descriptive emblem and spatial marker historically. This contributes to Protestant suspicion that Irish Traditional music is politically emblematic of nationalism, an appellation of Catholicism/Irishness. Therefore, among Protestants, Irish Traditional music doesn't exist confidently as part of the culture. Indeed, Irish Traditional music played by Protestants is seen by loyalists as a dangerous agent of a rival constituency; it is typically rejected by them, most strongly in urban areas, this done in pursuit of clarification of political/ethnic boundaries.

What is to be done?

As a human self-location point in the massiveness of the melodic world, Scottish composer Judith Weir holds strongly that 'everyone should have their Folk music'.[1] In Ulster the matter is part political, part absence of information. Had Traditional music not been set aside by the Protestant communities that contributed to its production, it might still be valued and taught within them. The fact that it could so easily be forgotten is itself partly the result of ignorance as to – and carelessness about – how it was created. Had the music been taught seriously in schools (to all children, not just as a religion-conditioned option), this kind of thing would not have happened. But then Traditional music was not formally supported anywhere on the island until relatively late in the age of technology. There is no doubt that people's need for music performance *can* be satisfied by whatever form of music is available, whether it be dance music or agitational or classical-music-based bands. But it is obvious too that this will not always be the case. It is likely that if the participants in these were to broaden their repertoire to include acknowledged indigenous music (as the pipe bands have done), then a new awareness and popularity for Traditional music would be seeded. Such a vista is also the most likely outcome of the present-day Ulster-Scots music education initiatives. There is no reason why Traditional music should not be played exclusively by Protestants in a local, Protestant bar or theatre, as much as by Catholics in a Catholic one. If Italians, French, Germans, Dutch, Swedes, Finns, Jewish-Americans, Scandinavian-Americans, Norwegians, Danes, Bretons, Scots, English and Japanese can do it, so too – if they wish to – can Northern Irish Protestants. And with considerably more connectedness.

Notes and references

Preface

1 See Chapter 14 for fuller definitions.
2 Most of the bands are Protestant – possibly a thousand or more according to Hastings' *With Fife and Drum*, making band culture very much part of Protestant life.
3 Lambeg drumming is adequately dealt with elsewhere by Prosser 'The Lambeg Drum' PhD, QUB (1977), Hastings, *With Fife and Drum* and Schiller (2001), *The Lambeg and the Bodhrán*.
4 This has been done in various media by, among others, Georges Zimmerman, *Songs of Irish Rebellion – Political Street Ballads and Rebel songs 1780–1900* and Hugh Shields, *Narrative Singing in Ireland*. May McCann has analysed republican song practices (PhD, QUB, 1985), as has Katy Radford (PhD, QUB, 2002) those of loyalists.
5 Orange and republican songs use both old airs (which may also be borrowed from non-political songs) and more modern popular-music airs.
6 For example, Zimmerman, *Songs of Irish Rebellion* (1967, 2003) and Mulcahy and Fitzgibbon (eds), *The Voice of the People* (1982).

1. Sound, assumption and symbolism

1 The large bass drum developed out of largely Orange Order music process in the later 1800s. Waning in popularity as the twentieth century progressed, the drum has become iconic of Unionism – partly due to the visual appeal it lends to TV journalism – this particularly so since the onset of 'the troubles' in the 1960s. The 'Lambeg' is named after a village of the same name in County Down which is now a suburb of Belfast (see Hastings, *With Fife and Drum*).
2 '. . . it seems likely that the general characteristics of a language, its stress patterns, its patterns of intonation, and of course the structure of its poetry, are reflected in the music of its people' (Nettl, *Folk and Traditional Music of the Western Continents*, p. 7). The Ulster-Scots Agency, for instance, sees it as important to set about formalising an appropriate music for the linguistic territory it applies itself to.
3 See for instance Rosenberg, *Transforming Tradition*.
4 The identities of contributors are occasionally omitted in deference to expressed wishes.
5 'There will be no attacks made simply because of folk music – there is no threat from us'– Red Hand Commando statement quoted in *Down Spectator*, 2 September 1993, p. 1.
6 ibid.

2. 'Folk' music and 'traditional' music

1. The logo and trademark of the Archive derives from the bell of a bronze horn of the Iron Age, the Loughnashade Horn, which is one of the oldest surviving Irish music instruments. Decorated in curvilinear Celtic style, it was discovered with three similar instruments in a lake in County Armagh where it is believed to have been deposited as a religious offering sometime about the beginning of the Christian era (see Barry Raftery, 'The Loughnashade Horns', *Emania*, no. 2, 1987). The horn is in the National Museum of Ireland, and the logo is used with permission of the museum.
2. John Moulden.
3. '... the work of Bishop Percy in the middle of the eighteenth century ... first aroused a largely town-living world, that was beginning to lose touch with its own countryside, to the fact that something valuable had, in the migration, been left behind ... The expressions "Folk Music", "Folk Song" and "Folk Dance" ... are extensions of the term "Folk Lore" which was coined in 1846 by W. J. Thomas ... to cover the idea of the traditions, customs, and superstitions of the uncultured classes ... It is self-evident that the germ of all music lies in folk music ... folk music represents the culture of the countryside and art music the culture of the city ... no complete understanding of life is possible to a man who knows it only in its city complexities' (Scholes, *Oxford Companion to Music*, pp. 365–8).
4. English collector W. Christie used the title *Traditional Ballad Airs* for a collection in England in 1876. Frank Kidson also published *Traditional Tunes* in 1891. In 1910, American-Irish collector Francis O'Neill used the term 'folk' music, but in 1913 began to use 'traditional' without the need for explanation. National-centred books and pamphlets in the 1930s – the era that produced European fascist movements and their counterpart in Ireland, the Blueshirts – refer also to 'Traditional' music (but without any descriptive indication of what it is).
5. Initiated in 1987 under director Nicholas Carolan, the Irish Traditional Music Archive has amassed a large multimedia resource library of books, cylinders, tapes, records, discs, etc., of and relating to all forms and shades of Traditional music in all of the island of Ireland and its exile communities, past and present. www.itma.ie.
6. Carolan, 1991, 4.
7. 'Folk music is a heritage which is passed on from one age to the next – hence the term "Traditional", which is usually applied to it in Ireland. Irish Folk music includes not only the older songs and melodies of the Gael ... but also the Anglo-Irish and English ballads of the countryside and the extraordinarily rich vein of dance music' (Breathnach, *Folk Music and Dances of Ireland*, p. viii).
8. Carolan, 2–4. *What is Traditional Music?*
9. ibid.
10. ibid.
11. ibid.
12. 'The instrumentarium of the folk musician expands, admitting new instruments while rendering others obsolete. There are also deeper transformations of the instrumentarium, including the mass production and reproduction of instruments that were previously hand-crafted and personalised' (Bohlman, *The Study of Folk Music in the Modern World*, pp. 124–7). See also Chapter 11.
13. Carolan, *What is Traditional Music?*
14. ibid.

15 ibid.
16 Nettl, *Folk and Traditional Music*, p. 2.
17 For instance, Cole's collection (USA, 1890) and O'Neill's (USA, 1903, 1907). See Breathnach, *Folk Music and Dances of Ireland*, pp. 60–1).
18 Seán O'Boyle, *Ulster Folklife*, Vol. 5, 1959, quoted in Vallely, *Companion to Irish Traditional Music* (1999), p. 363 (hereafter *CITM*).
19 John Moulden, 'Songs of the People' in Vallely, *CITM*, p. 363.
20 Mary Holland, *The Guardian*, 7 October 1990; report on the 'Whose Music?' conference at Enniskillen.
21 Ó Súilleabháin (review of Cowdery), in *Ethnomusicality*, 37 (1990), p. 111

3. Dance music and song

1 John Moulden.
2 'Crack' means fun, 'news' or 'gossiping' engaged in with lively wit and conversation. It often appears in the fashionable spelling 'c-r-a-i-c', a new addition to the Irish language since the time of the De Bhaldraithe dictionary (1977). As *craic*, it has come to be used inaccurately (unitalicised), particularly by publicans, southern newspapers and in tourism paraphernalia in otherwise English-language sentences, the assumption in this being that the original word is Gaelic in origin. In fact it is not Gaelic, but is decidedly (in the Irish context) part of English and has been used widely in Ulster, Scotland and all of England in continuity for long before it emerged in today's common parlance in the southern part of Ireland. See also Vallely, *CITM*, p. 91.
3 John Kennedy.
4 See Morton, *Folksongs Sung in Ulster* (1970), p. 15.
5 John Kennedy.
6 John Kennedy.
7 Leslie Bingham, flute player (McNamee, *Traditional Music – Whose Music?*, p. 44).
8 'Music functions as expressive, and instrumental political behaviour' (Pratt, 1992, p. 4).
9 David Bushe, *Ulster Society*, quoted in McNamee, op. cit., p. 16.
10 County Antrim, fiddler, piper.
11 John Kennedy.
12 Andy Dickson.
13 Zimmerman, *Songs of Irish Rebellion – Political Street Ballads and Rebel Songs 1780–1900*, has detailed comment on and texts of 100 nationalist, republican and Orange songs.
14 Shields, *Narrative Singing in Ireland*, pp. 113–33.
15 Abbreviated as CCÉ, and often referred to as just 'Comhaltas', this was the major revival Traditional music organisation.

4. Loyalty, identity and religion in Northern Ireland

1 Based on poll-tax returns c.1659, the Scots/English bloc of the old Ulster province's adult population was approximately 37 per cent (Robinson, *The Plantation of Ulster*, p. 105).
2 'In just over fifty years after the Plantation had begun the freehold ownership of land by Catholics in Ulster had been reduced to an insignificant level' (ibid., p. 192).
3 'Almost without exception the reserved quarters were the poorest and most isolated sections. Indeed many of the townlands which were the "most fit parts to be

let to the natives" were precisely the same townlands as had already been leased to Irish tenants' (ibid., p. 102).
4 Gary Hastings.
5 Similar Catholic/nationalist bodies that do not directly engage with music are not covered here for the same reasons.
6 Long, 'A Celebration: 1690–1990 – The Early Years', in *The Orange Institution*, p. 6.
7 On 17 March, 2001 while on a visit to the snow-layered environs of St Johns, Newfoundland, a Catholic woman could tell me 'This mornin' a Orangeman brought me a rabbit.'
8 Bastille day, the French celebration of the declaration of the 1787 Republic, was celebrated in Belfast in 1791 mostly by Protestants, with green cockades and green ribbons, carrying a banner with the caption '4th Year of Liberty'; a Belfast broadside (song-sheet) of the period commemorates this (1993), Len Graham, singer, Co. Antrim, personal communication).
9 This has parallels in other cultures and corresponds to, for instance, the *Indigenista* period (1910–1940) of Peruvian history (Turino, 1988, p. 131). Similarly the *tango* dance form was adopted as a national unity emblem in Argentina from 1913–1930 and went on to become an all-class-alliance emblem in the Peron years (1945–1955) (Manuel, *Popular Music of the Non-Western World*, p. 63).
10 Doherty and Hickey, *A Chronology of Irish History since 1500*, pp. 143, 190.
11 Partition was initiated following the War of Independence (1919–1921); the separate parliament for the new Irish state was located in Dublin and that for the new, distinct Northern Ireland state was located near Belfast at Stormont, opened in October 1924 (ibid., pp. 190, 208).
12 This is expressed in the regional organisation structures, for instance, of both Gaelic football (the Gaelic Athletic Association [GAA]), and Traditional music itself (Comhaltas Ceoltóirí Éireann [CCÉ]). All is presently undermined by post-1991 changing philosophies in tourism marketing, academic life, economic planning and sport.
13 See History and Ethnicity (1989) – intro. by Malcolm Chapman, Maryon McDonald and Elizabeth Tonkin, pp. 11–17.
14 John Taylor's 'Jigging at the cross-roads' remarks, as reported in *The Irish Times*, 7 December 1993, and also on RTÉ, *Today at Five*, 8 December 1993 (see also Chapter 7).
15 DUP leader the Rev. Ian Paisley used the (trivialising) term 'Bogmen!' in dismissal of the acknowledgement of the rights of Irishness in the course of the 'Ireland Joint Declaration' debate in Westminster, 15 December 1993. Record of this was not noted in Hansard, but the incident was broadcast on TV evening news bulletins.
16 Described by poet Michael Longley, he likened the trepidatory entry of one such tour of *You and Yours* musicians into a basement UDA club in Belfast as: 'Like Egyptologists descending into a tomb' (McNamee, *Traditional Music – Whose Music?* pp. 102–7).
17 David Bushe, Ulster Society (McNamee, p. 16). The Ulster Society was set up in 1985 (the period of the signing of the Anglo-Irish Agreement, which involved the government of Ireland in Northern Ireland affairs; the accord was hotly disputed by most unionists and all loyalists). The Ulster Society's aims were to promote 'Ulster-British culture and heritage in all its rich and varied forms', as distinctive. Its chairman at that point was David Trimble, then a unionist MP at Westminster (Hanvey, 1987, pp. 1, 102).
18 See McWhiney, *Cracker Culture* (1988), for instance.

19 See Vallely, in Tonge et al., 2008, and Dowling, 2007.
20 Such as Willie Drennan and the 'Ulster-Scots Fowk Orchestra' (c.2001).
21 John Purser (on music history), or T. M. Flett (on dance).

5. THE MYTH OF 'THE WEST'

1. An abusive term of urban supremacy applied occasionally by dwellers of larger towns to those from smaller. It may relate to the assumed remoteness, social inferiority and backwardness of the town of Kiltimagh in the west of Ireland in County Mayo, but may also be derived from *coillte* (Gaelic, 'woods'), i.e. 'backwoodsy' or 'backward'.
2. *Deliverance*, 1972, directed by John Boorman, based on the novel of the same name by James Dickey.
3. *Zorba the Greek*, 1964, a film by Michael Cacoyannis.
4. Morton, *Folksongs Sung in Ulster*, Foreword.
5. George Patton.
6. Michael Healy, Catholic-background Alliance Party policy committee member (1991).
7. Gary Hastings.
8. A ballad group, seminal in the Revival period, they achieved huge popularity, first in the USA, then all over Ireland during the 1960s. Despite the fact that they are not what Traditional musicians would aspire to musically, nevertheless they (and the similar Dubliners) are accorded fond remembrance on account of their having been the catalyst which got many, many revival musicians-to-be 'hooked' in the sixties and seventies. This is the case in both the north and south of Ireland, in Britain and the USA. Also, because the Clancys are perceived as being 'Irish traditional' by both uninvolved Protestants and Catholics, their popularity can be taken to be an indicator of the public acceptance of Traditional music.
9. Old-English usage, meaning 'remember'.
10. Gary Hastings.
11. Gusty Spence.
12. A major competition forum for traditional step dance.
13. Seventy-year-old woman born and living on the Shankhill Road, Belfast (1992).
14. Gusty Spence.
15. Gusty Spence.
16. Reference in the song to the speaking of the Irish (Gaelic) language in County Galway.
17. 'One or two' is a cosy expression for 'drinks' – bottles of Red Hand Guinness, or whiskies perhaps.
18. Gusty Spence.
19. A popular singer from County Donegal, whose heyday was the 1950s–60s. Her repertoire was sentimental ballads about Ireland, often done in 3/4 time, most of them modern compositions. This was the last fling of popular Irish song, for it was suddenly eclipsed by the rock style and cover-pop instrumentation and lyrics of the showband era.
20. A form of Traditional-music dance band developed after 1919 on the lines of more mainstream popular-music orchestras. It became hugely popular and waned only in the 1950s, a victim of the internationalisation of popular music and dance taste.
21. Moulden, 1999, p. 8.
22. For example, see Len Graham, in Vallely, Piggott and Nutan, *The Blooming Meadows*, p. 79.
23. A popular colloquialism meaning 'Comhaltas Ceoltóirí Éirean or "CCÉ"'.

24 Wilbert Garvin.
25 An outstanding and stylistically influential flute player from the heartland of Traditional-music flute playing, the Gurteen area of County Sligo.
26 Fiddler; 'other side of the house' indicates a person of the opposite religion to the narrator.
27 Wilbert Garvin.
28 County Antrim, fiddler, piper.
29 Alec Crawford.
30 Doris Crawford.

6. THE 'SOUND' OF MUSIC

1 Tony McAuley, in McNamee, *Traditional Music – Whose Music?*, p. 59. 'Taig' [tay-g] is a derisory colloquial term used by some Protestants to denote Catholics, derived from the Irish name 'Tadhg' (= Tim), which is pronounced 'Tye-g'.
2 Traditional singing organiser, Joe Mulhearn, recounting an experience with John Kennedy, a flute player and traditional singer from a Protestant community.
3 The Ulster Workers' Council was a loyalist extra-parliamentary body which organised opposition to the 'Sunningdale' Northern Ireland Assembly (an early initiative in political settlement). Its activity peaked in a strike of Protestant workers in May 1974, which ultimately brought that Assembly down.
4 Tony McAuley.
5 Andy Crockhart, television producer.
6 Tony McAuley.
7 Gary Hastings.
8 In the men's senior ballad competition at the 1980 All-Ireland Fleadh Cheoil held at Buncrana (County Donegal), the County Mayo adjudicator criticised the Ulster style of singing, claiming that it 'should be kept to the back rooms of pubs where it belongs'. This, and his opinion that Ulster singers were unlikely to be able to sing Munster songs, caused an uproar and walkouts from, among others, Fermanagh singer Paddy Tunney. The incident, and its subsequent immortalisation in a satirical ballad, identifies the existence and personality of regional styles, and also marks the confidence and esteem attached to them. A classic verse from the satire goes:
   He said the Ulster Style was wrong, and my choice of song was shockin'
   And my ornamentation nil – boys, I was goin' to clock him,
   My song-had-been sung by the Fenian Men, the bard John Reilly later,
   'You got that from Christy Moore,' says this Free State adjudicator (Mulhearn, 1981; see Vallely, 2008).
9 John Moulden, referring to the above incident, which for many symbolises the notion of the 'standardisation' of taste, a hazard inimical to competition adjudication.
10 Geordie McAdam, fiddle and flute player.
11 Meaning 'insisted on learning'.
12 Geordie McAdam.
13 Brian Moore, 1990, a response to the burning out of Protestant houses in a mixed but Catholic-dominated area of Belfast.
14 Geordie McAdam.
15 Colm Sands, singer and songwriter, speaking of a rural, County Down, session.
16 Geordie McAdam.
17 Geordie McAdam.
18 The uilleann pipes in Ireland have a long association with 'big-house', 'gentleman' players, several of whom were significant composers, and whose contribution to the body of tunes and to design of the instrument is most likely grossly underestimated. As documented by O'Neill (1913) such players were largely Protestant.

19 Wilbert Garvin.
20 Written by a Scottish songwriter now resident in Australia, Eric Bogle, this song is part of a trilogy of works which denounce – from the point of view of the squaddie – the pointlessness of slaughter in World War I. It is a modern song in the 'folk' genre but, sung by the Fureys ballad group and in the Irish charts for several months, it took on the characteristics of a 'rebel' song. Because of the importance attached by Protestants to the WWI roll of honour, and indeed because of the importance in Protestant tradition of WWI songs, and songs of all imperial wars, it was not difficult to interpret the songwriter's intentions – accurately – as, in fact, pacifist and therefore, objectively, anti-imperialist, anti-Protestant or even subversive. But the fact that Bogle's 'subversion' was on the side of the squaddie victims – who in many cases were Catholic – also gave the song universal appeal and so it was familiar to practically everybody, Catholic and Protestant. So cloying indeed was its popularity that east Belfast lyricist, Crawford Howard, wrote a popular satirical parody on the ballad in the 1980s (see Vallely, 2008, p. 7).
21 Singer.
22 John Moulden.
23 Singer.
24 EMU – 'Education for Mutual Understanding' – through which a broader music curriculum, which could include indigenous music, was made available in Northern Ireland schools.
25 George Patton.
26 George Patton.

7. GAA, CULTURE AND THE VICTORIAN MODEL

1 Max Weber, quoted in Geertz, *The Interpretation of Cultures*, p. 5.
2 See *Crosbhealach an Cheoil – The Crossroads Conference* (1996), for fuller exploration of this term in relation to Traditional music.
3 For instance in Ernie O'Malley's *On Another Man's Wound*: 'The tradition of nationality, which meant not only the urge of the people to possess the soil and its products, but the free development of spiritual, cultural and imaginative qualities of the race, had been maintained not by the intellectuals but by the people who were themselves the guardians of the remnants of culture' (Introduction).
4 This was interpreted in satire by Sinn Féin supporters as: 'Paisley also had a unique analysis of the paramilitary situation: "O Father, we can see the great pan-nationalist conspiracy, with the Pope at its head, sending his secret messages to the IRA"' (O'Toole, 1995).
5 The very real political loyalty and significance of the GAA was emphasised by the symbolic entry of rugby to its prime stadium, Croke Park, in 2007, and in the reaction to the defeat of the British national rugby side there. British television reportage leading up to those events acknowledged that footballers had been slain by British soldiers on the pitch in 1913 during a match between Dublin and Tipperary, and that the main stand – the Hogan stand – was named after the Tipperary captain who was one of the victims on that day. It is hardly surprising that in an interview in the 1967 film, *The Rocky Road to Dublin*, the then secretary of the GAA could state that the organisation 'provided the fighting men for Irish republicanism'.
6 Mandle, *The Gaelic Athletic Association and Irish Nationalist Politics 1884–1924*, p. 13.
7 ibid., p. 14.
8 Puirséal, *The GAA in its Time*, p. 26.
9 *Freeman's Journal*, 1 January 1883, quoted in Mandle, 1987, p. 3.
10 Mandle, op. cit., p. 27.
11 E. Vallely, 'Jackets on the Grass Verge', in *Causeway*, vol. 1, no. 1 (1993), p. 39.

12 Puirséal, op. cit., p. 39.
13 Sheehy, *The Rediscovery of Ireland's Past – the Celtic Revival: 1830–1930*, p. 7.
14 ibid., p. 189.
15 Published as *Origin of Species by Means of Natural Selection* (1859), and *The Descent of Man* (1871).
16 Sheehy, op. cit. p. 7.
17 A caricature created in Britain to ridicule the perceived inferiority of the Irish, but which became adapted as friendly by the Irish in America when utilised by and among themselves. Such an image is used widely in St Patrick's Day, Irish bar and Irish festival iconology, and by international soccer supporters today.
18 Stumpf (1908), quoted in Simon, *Das Berliner Phonogramm-Archiv. 1900–2000*, pp. 65–6.
19 From Herbert Moore-Pim, *Unconquerable Ulster*, pp. 92–5.
20 E. Crooke, *Politics, Archaeology and the Creation of a National Museum in Ireland*, p. 80.
21 ibid., p. 81
22 ibid., p. 103 (quoting from *Saunders Newsletter*, 4 December 1840).
23 ibid., p. 128.
24 ibid., p. 141.
25 ibid.
26 GAA, 2003, p. 1.
27 Such is epitomised in the following County Kerry GAA website information: SCÓR – 'A fundamental part of the GAA' – by Ann Mangan, East Kerry Board Scór Officer. The GAA of course is much more than a sporting organisation. It promotes our games, but it also embraces the cultural aspect of Irish life. Since the birth of Scór in 1969, our clubs have become involved in promoting our culture in an enjoyable manner through the medium of Scór. The organization has been uniquely successful in instilling into every boy and girl a sense of place and a deep and lasting pride in that special place, their club. Scór affords all GAA clubs the opportunity to give public expression to their affection for their own area and to promote the core values of the organisation to which they belong. It provides a platform to show their talents, to derive enjoyment from doing so and at the same time, providing delightful entertainment to thousands throughout the country. The element of competition, the opportunity to represent and bring honour to your club, county and province, elevates the whole experience to a different realm. The club and county colours so proudly displayed, the electric atmosphere and the welcoming cheers are obvious signs that Scór is a fundamental part of that pride that we all have in our roots and affinity we have to our own club.

As we enjoy the entertainment and excitement generated at Scór competitions, it causes one to reflect on what is being missed by clubs who fail to make a serious effort to become involved in Scór. What a disservice they are doing to their own members! (See http://www.setdancingnews.net/news/ireland.lp.)
28 Source: http://www.risingsonsofdown.co.uk LOL website, 2004. Additionally, in Scotland the LOL has a membership of 20,000 distributed among 300 lodges. England has forty-four lodges. The GAA also organises games, teams and social life in areas of exile abroad, including Scotland and England as well as, substantially, in the major cities of the USA.
29 Source: David Kerr, summary of Ulster Bands Association conference 2002, on http://www.the-twelfth.org.uk/Ulsterbandsassn2002. George Patton, former Orange Order director, thought in 1992 that 'roughly there must be 1,000 marching bands, from silver down. We have 1,500 lodges and we can't get a band for each

lodge. The number of bands has grown since the seventies with the growth of the Blood and Thunder bands . . .'(interview). Hastings (2003, p. 76), however, asserts that 'there are more performers connected with the marching bands in Ulster than with any other music in the whole of Ireland, including pop, country and western, classical, and so on.' However, he gives no statistics to back up this extraordinary claim on behalf of perhaps only 20 per cent the island's population. In 2005, one website claimed that there are 900 Orange Lodges, each with an average membership of seven. The most informative loyal band website in 2006 (that of The Pride of Ballinran Flute Band) lists some 160 bands of all kinds, including Scottish bands. The Ulster Bands Association itself can make no estimate. The Select Committee on Northern Ireland Affairs' Second Report (The Public Processions (Northern Ireland) Act 1998 and the Parades Commission) states that 'There are several hundred bands in Northern Ireland which are involved in parades. While some of them are attached to individual lodges, many are not. There are a number of different types of band associations in Northern Ireland, including the Ulster Bands Association, the loyalist Band Association, the Northern Ireland Pipe Band Association and the Flute Band League of Northern Ireland' (North, *Independent Review of Parades and Marches*, p. 28). Considering that there are some 160 bagpipe bands (including Catholic bands) in Northern Ireland, ninety of them affiliated to the main competition network (Garvin, 2002, personal communication), the total number of bands today may perhaps be closer to 1,200.

30 Until a decision taken as recently as November, 2001, the GAA did not permit membership of its clubs to members of the British army or Northern Ireland police forces, for political reasons. Few, however, might have taken part anyway, because of both the internal religious balance of the older police force, the RUC, and the prevailing political situation. The change in policy is symbolically marked by teams from the PSNI (the current Northern Irish police force) and the Garda Síochána (Irish police force south of the border) playing each other annually.

31 'The population of Ulster then [1659 survey] was returned as 103,923, of whom 63,272 were Irish and 40,651 were listed as 'English and Scotch'. In every county the Irish outnumbered the others, though in Tyrone and Antrim the differences were not so great. Further, the survey shows that English (and Scots was then listed as English for the purposes of the survey) was the majority language in the following areas only: some towns, e.g. Derry, Carrickfergus and Coleraine; East Donegal; the barony of Coleraine and the area between Lisburn and Larne. Irish was the majority language everywhere else in Ulster' (Ó Snodaigh, 1973, p. 2).

'Rev John Richardson, Church of Ireland rector of Belturbet, County Cavan, was a native Irish speaker. Visiting Glenarm in County Antrim in 1711 he had this to say: "I met many of the inhabitants, especially of the Baronies of Glenarm and Dunluce . . . who could not speak the English tongue, and asked them in Irish what religion they professed. They answered they were Presbyterians. Upon which I asked them further how they could understand the minister preaching. To that they answered "He always preaches in Irish". In 1833 the synod of Ulster of the Presbyterian church passed an overture requiring a knowledge of Irish from some of their students, and two years later some Irish was made imperative upon candidates for Holy Orders. In 1841 the General Assembly of the Presbyterian Church in Ireland issued for their teachers an instruction to foster the Irish language which was referred to as "our sweet and memorable mother tongue".' Source: Len Graham, singer and song collector, Portaferry, County Down, 30 January 1993; Ó Duibhín, 1991.

32 *Gaeltachtaí* is plural of *Gaeltacht*, indicating an area where the dominant language spoken is Irish. The *gaeltachtaí* are located largely in the extremities of maritime counties – NW Donegal, Mayo, Galway, Kerry, Cork and Waterford. A small *Gaeltacht*, comprised of people transplanted from other areas, thrives in the Rath Carn area of County Meath. A modern-day Irish-speaking street was set up in Belfast in the mid-1960s also. Irish-language colleges are located in most of these areas, where children and adults take intense, holiday-time immersion courses in the Irish language. Such colleges were major promoters of céilí dancing in the last half of the twentieth century.

33 The Scottish island of Lewis is Gaelic speaking. It is also largely Free Presbyterian. To the south, the island of North Uist is also Protestant and Gaelic speaking. South Uist, and Benbecula, are Catholic and also Gaelic speaking. The western portion of Skye is also Gaelic speaking.

34 O'Donovan, *The O'Growney Memorial Lecture*. Ironically, as Prof. John A. Murphy pointed out at the conclusion to the 2006 Merriman School at Lisdoonvarna, County Clare, the Gaelic League organised itself through the medium of the English language.

35 These figures were supplied by Róise Ní Bhaoill of the Ultach Trust, Belfast. They are deduced from the Northern Ireland Census 2001, pp. 85–102.

36 Cooper, 'Lámh Dearg: Celtic Minstrels and Orange Songsters', in *Celtic Cultural Studies*, p. 4.

37 Reid, 'Patterns of Memory Fragmented: the Townland in Northern Ireland', paper presented at Irish Conference of Historians, UU Magee, May 2003.

38 The major station – Telefís Éireann – was launched in 1961, and was combined with radio in 1966 as Raidió Telefís Éireann (RTÉ). A second channel, RTÉ 2, was later added, with Telefís na Gaeilge (TnaG, now TG4, strong on Traditional music) following as an all-Irish station in 1997. A further commercial channel, TV3, began broadcasting in 2001.

8. Fetishising the Crossroads

1 Many N.I. citizens hold Irish passports. Some of these are Protestant, for most of whom this is an ideological decision; for others it is because the Irish passport was considerably cheaper than the British one. Under the original Irish constitution, those born in the thirty-two counties of the island of Ireland before the year 1921, and their children, are entitled to an Irish passport.

2 During the 1993 season Independent Television ran a series of advertisements for the Northern Ireland Tourist Board featuring a large, lively pub session of jolly people drinking. The slogan was 'The Northern Ireland you'll never know – unless you go'. It was selling a familiar image of Ireland, for tourists from England will presumably come to either part of Ireland to see round towers, ruined churches and scenery and to listen to the local music more quickly than to see their own (Union) flags waved; the NI Tourist Board consequently engaged itself with selling 'Ireland'. This bi-lugged spade was finally credited as the versatile implement it is by both tourist boards coming together formally to globally market 'Ireland' as 'the island of memories' in 2002.

3 Reported in *The Irish Times*, 7 December 1993.

4 He was interviewed by Pat Kenny, a host on the popular RTÉ Radio One (Irish national radio) show, *Today at Five*, RTÉ , 8 December 1993.

5 The term 'Northern Ireland' did not come into use for some three centuries after the Plantation; Scottish settlers then moved to Ireland.

6 John Taylor, op. cit., *Today at Five,* RTÉ, 8 December 1993.
7 Interview with David Hanley, RTÉ *Morning Ireland,* 9 December 1993.
8 Charles Kingsley (1819–1875), an evolutionist English clergyman, while on a visit to post-famine Ireland in 1860 wrote in a letter to his wife concerning famine survivors: 'I am haunted by the human chimpanzees I saw along that hundred miles of horrible country . . . to see white chimpanzees is dreadful; if they were black, one would not feel it so much, but their skins, except where tanned by exposure, are as white as ours' (Curtis, *Anglo-Saxons and Celts,* p. 84).
9 President of the Irish Republic from 1959 until 1973. His recorded St Patrick's Day speech of 1943 addressed his ruralist, folk vision of the way forward. He spoke of 'the contests of athletic youths and the laughter of comely maidens'. This was redisposed – probably by satirist Flann O'Brien – as 'comely maidens dancing at the crossroads' and in that form is most often utilised to retrospectively ridicule De Valera. It probably does get the sentiment right though, and the words are now a modern myth – real enough not only for writer John Waters to parody in the title of his 1991 book *Jiving at the Crossroads,* but also for a Westminster MP to recruit as a hallmark of Protestant differentiation, and a Swedish dance scholar Helena Wulff to use (accurately qualified) as her analysis of Irish dance. 'Dancing at the Crossroads' (2007).
10 BBC has often used Irish Traditional music imagery (addressed, presumably, to its bulk UK audience) to illustrate the difference between North and South in Ireland. For instance, there is the *Timewatch* TV series for BBC 1, a programme on 'how it all began'. Entitled *The Sparks that Lit the Bonfire* (21 January 1993) this first documented Civil Rights marches and the peak of the riots in 1970. Then it cut to Dublin with the remark, *'Meanwhile down in Dublin . . .',* showing (contemporary 1990s style) visuals of an accordion and flute being played for set dancers. In the 1960s, in actual fact, traditional music was a long way from its modern-day iconicity and popularity, and there was little or no music and song, or set dancing, to be found in Dublin pubs. Indeed in many the 'No Singing Allowed' notices indicated quite the opposite.
11 Baskervill's 1929 title, *The Elizabethan Jigg,* evidences the dance-form as a feature of sixteenth-century English music life.

9. Religion, Nationality, Difference and Inequality

1 Angrosino, *The Essentials of Anthropology,* p. 75.
2 Implying all the emotive and dogmatic suggestive power of the term – i.e. *as of right.* 1966 is chosen, as it is the beginning of the Civil Rights movement, which challenged such supremacy.
3 Up until the year 2000, Catholics generally boycotted the security forces as an employment option. The police – RUC – were predominantly Protestant; the locally recruited militia, the Royal Irish Rangers (formerly known as the Ulster Defence Regiment), were almost totally Protestant too. As of 2000, both bodies became the subject of considerable restructuring and religion balancing, with the police force being renamed PSNI (Police Service of Northern Ireland).
4 Today there is an alarming tendency for young Protestants to take up further education options in England or Scotland, and to remain there.
5 The war against EOKA. This involved 40,000 British troops, 99 of whom were killed. See also http://www.britains-smallwars.com/cyprus/war. html, andhttp://users.skynet.be/terrorism/html/cyprus_eoka.htm.
6 Gusty Spence.

7 The dictum 'The strongest are not those who can inflict the most, but those who can endure the most'.
8 Lavish homes and expensive cars are a universal status symbol, particularly so in Northern Ireland, where for an otherwise apolitical nominal Catholic, driving a BMW may be intended as – and/or perceived as – a kind of political triumphalism. For the less wealthy Catholic, so too was driving non-British-made – particularly Japanese – cars in the 1970s, when the religion of the participants at a gathering could be gauged by the nationality of the makes of vehicles parked outside: Vauxhall and BMC (= British industry): Protestant; Toyota, Datsun, Renault (= foreign import, undermining British industry): Catholic. Among farmers, Ford tractors (blue) were sometimes seen as at least American-inspired, against thoroughly British creations like Massey-Ferguson (red) and David Brown (white).
9 Opsahl, *Report of the Opsahl Commission*, p. 107.
10 Quoted in Larsen, Kilbroney, p. 152.
11 For instance, the Catholic Christian Brothers' (boys') Grammar School in Armagh had a small percentage of Protestant students through the 1960s (15 per cent in this writer's year). This may have been a political statement by parents. It appears to have been partly to do with economics too, and was also connected with the school's track record of good examination results being achieved by children from poorer backgrounds.
12 Opsahl, *Report*, p. 107.
13 Aughey, 'Ethnic Mending', in Rawls and Dworkin (eds), *Conflict and Community*, supplement to *Fortnight*, November 1992, p. 9; Morgan, 'Milesians, Ulstermen . . .,' in *Linenhall Review*, vol. 18, no. 4 (1992), p. 15.
14 Gillespie, Lovett and Garner, *Youth Work and Working-Class Youth Culture – Rules and Resistance in West Belfast*, p. 194.
15 Unidentified Asian floor speaker at the ESRI conference, University of Ulster, Belfast, June 2002.
16 Opsahl, *Report*, p. 95.
17 O'Doherty, Michael, 'Bitter' in this context means 'bigoted'.
18 Lee, *Ireland 1912–1985*.
19 This was modelled on the Civil Rights campaign of African Americans in the USA.
20 The figures for Table 1 are primarily from Walker, 1996, pp. 115–27. Here Walker uses figures from Rose, 1971, pp. 208–17; survey by Edward Moxon Browne; and Report of a social attitude survey in *The Irish Times*, 19 May 1993.
21 'In 1776 Benjamin Franklin reckoned that the Scotch-Irish and their descendants formed one-third of Pennsylvania's 350,000 inhabitants. By that year perhaps one quarter of a million Ulster people had emigrated to the American colonies. The peak of the emigration was reached in the first half of 1773' (Bardon, *A History of Ulster*, p. 210).
22 Buckley, 1991, p. 184.
23 Barth (ed.), *Ethnic Groups and Boundaries – The Social Organisation of Cultural Differences*.
24 Buckley, op. cit., p. 185.
25 Gusty Spence.
26 George Patton.
27 John Kennedy.
28 John Moulden.
29 Alec Crawford.
30 Wilbert Garvin.

31 Geordie McAdam.
32 See note 20 above.
33 Walker, *Dancing to History's Tune: History, Myth and Politics in Ireland*, pp. 115–27.
34 Triangular-shaped portions of bread traditionally cooked on a griddle iron or frying pan on top of an open fire or kitchen stove. The shape is peculiar to Ulster, among Protestants and Catholics alike, and is not found in other parts of Ireland. A modern, fast-food adaptation is the 'filled soda'– rather like a filled pitta bread. In the rest of Ireland a cake of soda bread might be baked in an oven (in earlier times a 'pot' oven – a closed iron vessel placed directly in the open fire).
35 Philip Robinson.
36 An old and well-known republican, a renowned poteen maker.
37 County Antrim, fiddler, piper.
38 It isn't rightly known how many people outside of a small number of experts actually read these, certainly not the broad public at whom job advertising is aimed. Outside of linguistic posts, and unlike job advertising in the Irish language in the south of Ireland – which is typically for positions in which full comprehension of the language is a working necessity – the speaking of 'Ulster-Scots' or 'Ullans' is not a requirement for positions advertised in that language: this was tested by an application made by the writer for the prime one of these posts – that of Director of the Ulster-Scots Agency – in 1992. He was told, additionally, by the job agency (Price Waterhouse Cooper) that the application form could not be supplied in, nor could it be completed in, Ulster-Scots. The position ultimately went to one of the original interviewees for this book, George Patton. Balancing the religion equation in NI, however, demands that public service jobs appear in English, Irish and Ulster-Scots, an intriguing situation since the majority of NI Catholics cannot read Irish-language adverts (but they do take a curmudgeonly political satisfaction from seeing them in print).

10. The radical impetus of 'folk'

1 Pratt, *Rhythm and Resistance: Explorations in the Political Uses of Popular Music*, p. 100.
2 Peterson, *Creating Country Music – Fabricating Authenticity*, p. 48.
3 Pratt, op. cit., p. 105.
4 Lawrence Goldwyn, 1926, quoted in Pratt, op. cit., p. 352.
5 Pratt, op. cit., p. 106.
6 Revolutionary tourist (RT) is a faintly sceptical term devised by ex-Edinburgh restaurateur Margaret Gaj ('guy') in order to classify the many well-intentioned English and European idealists and revolutionaries who visited Ireland from 1968 onwards to view at first hand, if not participate in, 'in-the-field' revolutionary struggle. Inevitably they passed through her premises in Baggot Street, Dublin, not just for the wholesome quality of the Polish-style food, European ambience and reasonable prices, but also for the intellectual ethos, and her overseeing of all with socialist consciousness. A major part of her clientele, particularly in the evenings, included the active leftists, socialists, republicans and communists of the day, many of whom subsequently established leading careers in the Irish Labour Party, media and government. Her uncompromising political thought made 'Gaj's' a stimulating salon of ideas and beacon of change; her generosity and consideration, as well as her sharp focus and intolerance of half measures, remain legendary. She played a background, but key, inspirational role in many campaigns, particularly those for unfashionable and unrepresented sections of society, and her major achievement was in initiating the Prisoners' Rights Organisation. A measure of the regard in

which she was held publicly, and indeed of the complementarity of music and political identity, is the fact that Thomas McCann (later a militant organiser among Travelling people) and the younger Keenan brothers instinctively chose, and were welcomed, to busk with whistles and pipes at the entrance to the restaurant.
7. Pratt, op. cit., p. 108.
8. Thomas More's *Utopia* (1516, 1901) presents an ideal society without private property and where religious toleration is the norm; William Morris' *News From Nowhere* (1890; 1918; 1972) explores a socialist future with common ownership and democratic control of production, looking back from nineteenth-century air and water pollution to a golden age of tranquillity and leisurely, healthy recreation time in a world respectful of seasonal impulse.
9. Pratt, p. 108.
10. ibid., p. 109.
11. Bender, *Community and Social Change in America*, p. 6.
12. Pratt, op. cit., p. 109.
13. Peterson, op. cit., p. 198.
14. Pratt, op. cit., p. 117.
15. ibid.
16. Cooney, 1999, p. 294.
17. Pratt, op. cit., pp. 110–24.
18. Carson, *Pocket Guide to Irish Traditional Music*, p. 53.

11. Traditional Music in a Modern World

1. Cathal Goan, quoted in McNamee (ed.), *Traditional Music – Whose Music?*, p. 95. Organised by Cooperation North, *Traditional Music – Whose music?* was held at the Killyhevlin Hotel, Enniskillen, on 6–7 October 1990. As part of a series of investigations of North–South cultural attitudes, the event highlighted the differences in perception of what 'Traditional' music meant, taking as the basic premise that all that was traditionally done in music is 'Traditional' music. The intention was to air the opinions of those involved in (perceived) Catholic and Protestant musics, viewed respectively by the organisers as 'Traditional' and 'Political'. The fundamental supposition that these were equivalent, active, politically experienced opposites was not convincingly demonstrated either by panel speakers or the majority of those who attended and spoke. All the Traditional musicians who contributed – Protestant and Catholic – claimed they saw Traditional music in fact as *non-political*. The conference proceedings were published as *Traditional Music – Whose Music?*
2. JAlan Jabbour, et.al., in Rosenberg, 1993, pp. xii, 198, etc., examines in fine focus the notion of 'revival', and acknowledges clearly that these kinds of music had not diminished enough to justify such an extreme measure as revival. The term persists, however, as an (arguably) useful line in the sand which ultimately marks off the 'folk' from the 'classical' and modern 'popular'.
3. Many bars host sessions there, and a number of well-known performers are based in the town; they are attracted by the county's very real association with Traditional music. The town also has a dedicated Traditional music educational and performance centre – Cois na hAbhann – run by CCÉ, and in 2001 Glór (lit. 'voice') opened as a purpose-built, commercial Traditional music facility.
4. Vallely, *CITM*, p. xv.
5. The late Frank Harte held that these notices were a reaction by bar staff and/or conversationalists to the over-zealous enthusiasm for tonal self-expression among

chorus-lovers, which was created by an earlier (1950s to early 1960s) fashion of 'singing lounges'.
6 Today, in fact, some forty different kinds of instrument are found in Irish Traditional music: banjo, button accordion, piano accordion, bagpipes, bodhrán, bones, Greek bouzouki, Irish bouzouki, cello, cittern, concertina, didgeridoo, djembe, double bass, drum kit, dulcimer, flute, fiddle, guitar, guitar-bouzouki, harmonica, harp, harpsichord, horns, Jew's harp, keyboard, low whistle, mandocello, mandolin, melodeon, piano, saxophone, snare drum, spoons, synthesiser, tables, tin whistle, uilleann pipes, washboard and woodblock. Among all of these, however, the core melody instruments are tin whistle, fiddle, flute, button accordion, melodeon, concertina, uilleann pipes, banjo and harp. Since rhythm and harmony have now become a key feature in addition to any or all of the melody instruments, piano, keyboards, guitars, bouzoukis and bodhráns are all standard items that colour the music today.
7 Much has been written on the session, and the web has much information. Commentaries include many postgraduate dissertations (e.g. Hamilton, 1983; Lundh, 1991, 1994) and journal articles; also Hast and Scott's 2005 narrative addresses a particular session format in County Clare.
8 Frank Harte, personal communication, 1992.
9 Isao Moriyasu, 2000, interview.
10 This application is typically referred to as 'ambient' or 'wallpaper' music, and as 'carpet' music by former RTÉ television producer Tony MacMahon, on account of his perceived trampling of the artistic finesse of the music in such situations.
11 'Ethnic' is used in this context to describe distinctive national, geographical location, language and cultural differences.
12 Alec Crawford.
13 Vaguely equivalent to 'music festival' but with much more roving and casual participation. These events – about forty-five each year – are just as much about social intercourse and good fun as they are about music.
14 See later in this chapter; also Henry, 'The case for Ireland's Comhaltas Ceoltóirí Éireann', in *Ethnomusicology*, vol. 33, no. 1, 1989, and Vallely, *CITM*.
15 The Royal Irish Academy of Music, Dublin, a music-dedicated institution, formerly specialising only in 'classical' music. Its connection with these grades was abandoned due to irreconcilable tensions after a couple of years, however, and they are now administered directly by CCÉ itself.
16 Most prominent among these is Na Píobairí Uilleann (NPU), an organisation dedicated to the art of uilleann piping, a body with members all over Ireland and abroad. Cairde na Cruite and the Harp Foundation are the harp organisations. Smaller organisations are Armagh Pipers' Club, the Counties Antrim and Derry Fiddlers' Association, and committees which run local summer schools. The biggest of the latter is Scoil Samhraidh Willie Clancy, held at Miltown Malbay, County Clare, in July of each year, which teaches more than a thousand students
17 All television stations on the island have had such dedicated programmes during the revival years. In the 1960s–1980s UTV had *From Glen to Glen*, BBC had *As I Roved Out* and *The Corner House*, and RTÉ had *Bring down the Lamp, Aisling Geal* and *The Pure Drop*. Currently only TG4 has regular programmes, such as *Geantraí*, with RTÉ offering periodic series and re-runs, as well as a high viewership archive show, *Come West Along the Road*. Other stations have occasional features – with BBC having several shows, some featuring also the Irish language.
18 E. Vallely, 'Education', in Vallely (ed.), *CITM*, p. 114.

19 Royal Irish Rangers, a local regiment of the British army, originally set up as the Ulster Defence Regiment, which in ethos was intended as merely 'loyal' to the crown, but in the political reality of a divided society became an almost exclusively Protestant armed force.

12. PERFORMANCE STYLE AND POLITICAL IDENTIFICATION

1 Leslie Bingham.
2 Stokes, *Ethnicity, Identity and Music*, p. 1.
3 Known colloquially as 'thumb piano', and described as the 'national' instrument of Zimbabwe, this plucked instrument has tuned metal or wood lamellae of different lengths fixed in a frame, usually with a spherical gourd resonator (Berliner, 1978, Introduction).
4 Berliner, 1978, p. 53.
5 Con Cassidy, Donegal fiddler, quoted by Gary Hastings in Vallely, 1998, p. 86.
6 Bishop Thomas Percy (1729–1811), once the Established Church bishop of Dromore, County Down, who while in ministry in England rescued part of a manuscript of old ballads from his housemaid's morning incendiary ritual, and subsequently published this in 1765 as *Reliques of Ancient English Poetry*. The work acted as inspiration to a German romantic literary movement, which in turn influenced that of Britain (Wordsworth, Coleridge, Scott). So was begotten a similar approach in music, this influencing the compositions of such as Weber, Schumann and Wagner (Scholes, *Oxford Companion to Music*, p. 74).
7 Pratt, *Rhythm and Resistance*, p. vii.
8 Simon Mashoko, in Berliner, 1978, p. 185.
9 O'Neill, *Irish Minstrels and Musicians*.
10 Henebry, *A Handbook of Irish Music*.
11 Tansey, 'Irish Traditional Music – the Melody of Ireland's Soul, its Evolution from the Environment, Land and People', in F. Vallely, Doherty, Hamilton and E. Vallely (eds), *Crosbhealach an Cheoil*, p. 47.
12 Pratt, op. cit., pp. 11–12.
13 Waterman, *Juju – A Social History and Ethnography*, p. 89.
14 Stokes, *Ethnicity, Identity and Music*, p. 14.
15 Bailey, 'Recent Changes in the Dutar of the Heart', in *Asian Music*, vol. 8, no. 1 (1976), p. 55
16 Latterly known as 'Co-operation Ireland'.
17 See chapter 10, and McNamee, *Traditional Music – Whose Music?*
18 Cohen, 1988, p. 6.
19 Charlie Menzies, Sutherland fiddler (1990).
20 Leslie Bingham.

13. DREAMS AND REALITIES – FOLK MEMORY AND GAELIC IDENITY

1 Fiddler.
2 This view is articulated most clearly by Martin Hayes in Vallely, *CITM*, p. 91.
3 Each of these aspects was of course fulfilled among earlier generations of musicians, particularly in the early twentieth century on 78 RPM albums by recording artists such as Michael Coleman and James Morrison, who found their primary audiences among Irish people in the USA.
4 See Vallely, 2002–7, for a fuller development of this theme of Traditional music as a 'classical' music.
5 Mandle, *The Gaelic Athletic Association and Irish Nationalist Politics 1884–1924*, p. 221.

6 Sheehy, *The Rediscovery of Ireland's Past – The Celtic Revival*: 1830–1930, p. 190.
7 O'Neill, *Irish Folk Music: A Fascinating Hobby*, p. 8.
8 Ó Murchú, *An Ród Seo Romhainn – A Future for Irish Traditional Music*, pp. 1–2; these words have been repeated in various other articles by this writer.
9 From the *Irish Independent*, 2 August 1933, quoted in 'Some Aspects of the present Condition of Catholic Secondary Education in Ireland', cited in Cooney, 1999, p. 24.
10 *Treoir*, No. 4, 1983, p. 1.
11 Fiddler.
12 Gary Hastings; see also Vallely, 1998, p. 83.
13 John Moulden.
14 *Treoir,* Sept–Oct 1971, p. 3.

14. THE WAY IT WAS?

1 Title of a film written by Dave Duggan, directed by Tim Loane and produced by Pearse Moore, from Raw Nerve Productions, Derry, financed by the Northern Ireland Film Council and BBC Television Drama, Northern Ireland, in 1996. The film dealt with the innocent eagerness of a young Protestant girl to learn *Riverdance* style Irish dancing, and all the contradictions and major political issues which that threw up.
2 'Set' dance is the colloquial term used to indicate the nineteenth-century popular social dance forms quadrille and lancers. Since these dances involve a collection of independent, but related, groupings of movements separated by pauses in the music, they came to be known as 'sets of quadrilles' (etc.), this abbreviated in modern time to 'sets'. In their original French form they were done to different music, and involved a more genteel style of stepping, but within Ireland they were adapted to fit local polkas, reels and jigs, and an indigenous *style* of dancing was applied to articulating and decorating rhythms with the feet.
3 Gary Hastings.
4 Tony McAuley.
5 Alec Crawford.
6 County Antrim, fiddler, piper.
7 Well-known County Antrim fiddler.
8 John Kennedy.
9 Michael Beattie, BBC TV.
10 Meaning 'function' or 'event'.
11 County Antrim, fiddler, piper.
12 Fiddler.
13 Leslie Bingham.

15. THE BRIDGE OF GLASS – SCOTLAND AND IRELAND

1 The Scottish island of Islay.
2 Campbell quoting *Chronicom Scotorum*, in *Popular Tales of the West Highlands*, vol. 1, pp. 394–409.
3 *An Leabhar Mór* – The Great Book of Gaelic. This assembly of visual and literary works in a book format was undertaken as 'an international celebration of contemporary Celtic culture . . . a major contemporary artwork', seen 'as 21st century "Book of Kells", that brings together the work of more than 200 visual artists, poets and calligraphers from Scotland and Ireland'. It generated an international touring exhibition of 100 artworks, a book publication, a website, a TV documentary, a series of BBC radio programmes, a music CD, a schools pack and an events programme. Ref. http://www.leabharmor.net/.

4   Margaret Bennett, in Vallely (ed.), *CITM*, pp. 331–2.
5   ibid., p. 332.
6   Breathnach, in *Folk Music and Dances of Ireland*, lists a number of the most popular of these, including 'Bonnie Kate', 'Lord Gordon' and 'The Perthshire Hunt' (known in Ireland as 'The Boyne Hunt').
7   Bennett, op. cit., p. 332.
8   Arising from the Gaelic colonisation of Scotland from Antrim in late AD 500 (Bardon, *A History of Ulster*, p. 17) and, for example, McDonnell's ownership of the Antrim Glens (Robinson, *The Plantation of Ulster*, p. 45).
9   Yeats, 1999, pp. 170–3.
10 Maxwell, 1973, p. 228.
11 Ó Snodaigh, *Hidden Ulster*, p. 2.
12 The Italians make their galliardes . . . plaine, and frame ditties to them, which in their mascaradoes they sing and daunce, and manie times without instruments at all, but in steed of instrumentes they haue Curtisans disguised in mens apparell, who sing and daunce to their owne songes'; from Morley's *Plaine and Easie Introduction to Practicall Musicke* (1597), quoted in Baskervill, *The Elizabethan Jigg*, p. 37.
13 Vallely (ed.), *CITM*, pp. 14–18.
14 Johnson, *Music and Society in Lowland Scotland in the Eighteenth Century*, p. 6.
15 The Reformation took hold in Scotland in 1560. It was marginally in favour of folk tunes, if used as vehicles for spiritual lyrics; in the later seventeenth century, Lowland Scotland was a centre of episcopacy (ibid., p. 164).
16 ibid., p. 15.

16. 'Crossing over' of tunes and songs

1   P. J. Flood, personal contact, 1993.
2   Gary Hastings.
3   The full text of this article appears on the web (http://www.celtic-cultural-studies.com/papers/01/cooper-01.html).
4   See Chapter 11 for reference to this event. It was held in Enniskillen, hosted by Co-operation North with assistance from the Arts Council of Northern Ireland (and not, as Cooper inadvertently states, QUB – his source is the proceedings of the event). See note 1 to chapter 11 above.
5   For analysis of this see Éamonn Ó Bróithe's summary of Irish song distinctiveness, involving interplay of internal rhyme and verse structure (Ó Bróithe, 1999, pp. 352, 353)
6   O'Boyle, *The Irish Song Tradition*, p. 7.
7   Cooper, op. cit., p. 5.
8   *The Petrie Collection of the Ancient Music of Ireland* (1855), p. 2.
9   Cooper, op. cit., p. 5.
10 ibid., p. 7.
11 ibid., p. 8.
12 ibid.
13 ibid., p. 11.
14 ibid.
15 ibid., p. 18.
16 These examples were for some years located on BBC Northern Ireland's website. With the revamping of that in 2007 the material is now either removed or shifted to obscurity. However, the same material is covered by Mullen (along with Gary Hastings) in their 2007 presentation to the Library of Congress in the USA. This

can be consulted via several web routes, most conveniently at http://www.loc.gov. Search for 'Hastings' in the 'webcast' menu. The material was Brian Mullen's subject for the 1993 symposium 'Swinging Shoulders – Dancing Feet', hosted at University of Ulster.
17 Brian Mullen, *Swinging Shoulders – Dancing Feet* (forthcoming).
18 BBC music, www.bbc.co.uk (2006), see note 16 above; *Swinging Shoulders – Dancing Feet* (forthcoming).
19 Mullen, BBC website, www.bbc.co.uk (2006); see note 16 above. He attributes the research information on 'Irish Molly' to County Down singer Tommy Sands.
20 The full texts of the writers quoted here bear closer inspection for a more fulfilling appreciation than this brief resumé can afford. See the bibliography for websites and other published references.
21 See also Hastings, *With Fife and Drum*, for fuller development of this information in relation to Protestant political and recreational music.

17. A MUSIC- AND SONG-TRANSMISSION CORNUCOPIA

1 Blaney, *Presbyterians and the Irish Language*, p. 9. See also Cooper, 'Lámh Dearg: Celtic Minstrels and Orange Songsters', p. 4, for further references on the Irish language and Protestantism.
2 The 1763 Neil Stewart collection is hand-scribed. One copy is presently housed in the King George V Library at Edinburgh. The music it contains suggests a style of playing that is close to present-day Irish and Cape Breton practice. This book also contains some tunes that have been played in Ireland for at least a hundred years in the Traditional dance-music repertoire, and also for at least the same length of time in the repertoire of Orange bands. See example of 'The Duke of Atholl's Rant'.
3 This is a key ingredient, passed on exclusively by an oral tradition.
4 The ancestors of a large proportion of the present-day Cape Breton population went there as a result of the Highland Clearances in the eighteenth century. They brought their Highland pipes and fiddle music with them, where it retained its individual character and coexisted and blended with Irish music, remaining unaffected by mainstream Scottish folk music until the post-World War II period of the twentieth century (Paul Cranford, interview). Cape Breton has a strong Scottish orientation. Its population is approximately 60 per cent Scottish, 30 per cent Irish by origin (MacPhee, personal communication, 1992); Gaelic was still being spoken by many of the older generation at the time or this study in 1992, and the tartan was important to identity.
5 As evidenced by O'Neill's collection of music in those years. While this body of music did undoubtedly influence subsequent repertoire in Ireland by a process of reintroduction to the oral tradition via music-literate players, its expense and relative unavailability, taken with the general absence of literacy among traditional musicians, must have left ample space also for local repertoire to survive through usage and preference. That it is unlikely that bands would jettison well-liked, community-selected, older tunes for the newer is borne out by the McCusker Brothers' Céilí Band from County Armagh, which in the late 1940s was able to sport locally favoured pieces as its trademark.
6 Breathnach, *Folk Music and Dances of Ireland*, p. 88.
7 Munnelly and Shields, 'Scots Ballad Influences in Ireland', in *Lore and Language*, vol. 3, no. 4/5 (1981), p. 90; Hamish Henderson, School of Scottish Studies (interview, 1992).
8 Liam O'Connor ran an Irish-language college in Cushendall, County Antrim, in

the early 1960s. While attending there at that time this writer met native speakers of the language who were still living in the vicinity of the town.
9 Gary Hastings.
10 Smyth, *Rome our Enemy*, p. 14.
11 ibid., p. 13.
12 David Johnson, *Music and Society in Lowland Scotland in the Eighteenth Century*, assumes tthat Highland and Lowland musics 'differed considerably' (4). But he states this in reference only to the extreme precision of his study. In the Lowlands he goes on to identify (120) English country dance (also popular in Ireland) by the late 1600s and notes the widespread popularity of dancing in general. If 'country' dancing began elsewhere, but gradually moved to Scotland where it eventually became localised, and was being done then to Scottish reels and jigs, it seems logical that any earlier forms of dance must have used the same 'Scottish' style of dance music, the close relative of that which was popular during the same period in Ireland.
13 Moore Pim, *Unconquerable Ulster*, p. 3.
14 Gusty Spence.
15 Moore Pim, op. cit., p. 46.
16 Hyde, *A Literary History of Ireland*, pp. 34, 106.
17 See Charlotte Milligan Fox, *Annals of the Irish Harpers* and Dónal O'Sullivan, *Carolan – The Life and Times of an Irish Harper*.
18 Munnelly, 1979, p. 90.
19 Gusty Spence.
20 Fraser, *The Airs and Melodies Peculiar to the Highlands of Scotland and the Isles*, p. viii. His use of the word 'electrify' is interesting.
21 Shields, 1979, p. 82.
22 Shields, op. cit.
23 ibid.
24 Alec Crawford.
25 Paul Cranford (1993) and Liz Doherty (1994) (personal communication).
26 County Antrim, fiddler, piper.
27 This very issue, however, is precisely what has been taken up by the Ulster-Scots in the early twenty-first century, with a heavily funded visual promotion of identity as vividly Scottish. Dowling (2007) deals with this in academic detail, and *The Ulster Scot* news-sheet is an excellent demonstration of how it is represented.
28 Gary Hastings.

18. Migration, movements and music

1 Robinson, *The Plantation of Ulster*, p. 173.
2 Johnson, *Music and Society in Lowland Scotland in the Eighteenth Century*.
3 ibid.
4 Swedish singer Jenny Lind (1820–1887), for instance, was a huge earner, with a publicity machine operating through the press even in America. In her time she was commemorated in images on cards and mugs and, notably, had music named in her honour. Of this the 'Jenny Lind' polka is still played in Ireland, and 'The Jenny Ling' (so-called) set-dance is still performed in County Fermanagh.
5 Robinson, op. cit., pp. 106–7.
6 ibid., p. 111.
7 Ireland also had direct contact with continental Europe, which provided an additional source in the same period.

8 Johnson, op. cit., p. 111.
9 MacNeill and Richardson, 1970.
10 Philip Robinson.
11 'Fife' is the term for the original (Swiss) short military flute with a cylindrical bore. The name is a corruption of the German term *pfeife* (pipe). (See Vallely, from *Fifth Column to Pillar of Society*, p. 11.)
12 'Flute' in this context indicates a short, band-style flute with tapered bore, technically more advanced than the original 'fife'.
13 Gary Hastings.
14 Johnson, op. cit., pp. 11–129; Carolan, *Irish Traditional Music*, p. xii.
15 See for instance Mac Aoidh, 1999, p. 126.

19. THE FLUIDITY OF CHANGE

1 Marie McCarthy, 1999, p. xii.
2 John Kennedy. The Wright collection is now housed in the Ulster Folk Museum at Cultra, Hollywood, on the outskirts of Belfast.
3 'Radio-gramophone', a two-in-one radio and electrical record player which became fashionable in the 1950s. It could play the older 78 rpm discs, and modern 45 rpm 'singles' and EPs (extended play), as well as the LP (long play) vinyl albums.
4 Gusty Spence.
5 Gary Hastings.

20. NEW NATIONS, NEW TIMES, NEW CULTURES

1 See Moloney, 1999, pp. 46, 47, and also Moloney, 2000.
2 Gary Hastings.
3 The major collectors and commentators include Joseph Cooper Walker (published 1786 and 1818), Edward Bunting (1773–1843), Charlotte Brooke (c. 1740–1793), Henry Hudson (1798–1889), James Goodman (1828–1896), George Petrie (1790–1866), John Edward Pigot (d. 1853), P.M. Levey, William Allingham, Patrick Weston Joyce (1875–1909), Francis O'Neill (1848–1936) and Sam Henry (1878–1952).
4 See Vallely, 2005, chapter 14, for some development of this; also Cooper, 1999, and Mulcahy and Fitzgibbon ,1982 (as indicated previously). Significant scepticism has been expressed concerning nationalist sentiment in the balladry of Catholic Ireland also, however. Take for example the searing opinions of poet Eavan Boland in her analysis of the 'great' political songs of Irish nationalism: '. . . the songs and the ballads . . . a sequence of improvised images . . . wonderful and terrible and memorable as they are, propose for a nation an impossible task – to be at once an archive of defeat and a diagram of victory' (Boland, *National Identity and Poetry*, p. 8); 'These songs are effect, not cause. They were only the curators of the dream, not the inventors' (ibid., p. 9).
5 In County Clare, late well-known fiddler and composer Martin (Junior) Crehan had, among the tunes he made, a jig called 'The Mist Covered Mountain'. The fact that this is close to a tune played by Shand (with the same title) does not imply plagiarism. But it is highly interesting that the tune – and presumably Shand's style – was so familiar as to have become part of the subconscious, and could re-emerge in an Irish context (and in a different, Clare, style), unsuspectingly, as a 'new' tune. The piece was not original to Shand anyway, but is the renamed, retimed, Jacobite 'Caoineadh na Mordhbhna', from the Gaelic-associated Morar Peninsula on Scotland's western coast.
6 This commentary was broadcast on Radio Éireann in 1957, and Boyle subsequently

played some 'jazz' himself anyway. The same notions as espoused by Boyle were already common also in Britain and in the USA, where the ideology had originated, expressed in such as: '. . . in its sinister aspects, jazz is doing a vast amount of harm to young minds and bodies not yet developed to resist evil temptations' (1925 comment in *Étude* magazine, quoted in Merriam, *Anthropology of Music*, p. 242); 'Jazz was borrowed from Central Africa by a gang of wealthy international bolshevists from America, their aim being to strike at Christian civilisation throughout the world' (Mgr. Conefrey, 1934, quoted in Merriam, op.cit., p. 243). The term was claimed back anyway by jazz player Duke Ellington and later hip hop stylists.

7 At this same time in the Republic, Partition and independence had radically cut the Gaelic League's membership, since people assumed that having achieved independence all was well, and the language – and presumably the music too – didn't have to be fought for any more. The logic of this is that they were seen as having been vehicles of nationalist mobilisation. This clarifies how the music waned there too, in the absence of the political antipathies that continued in the North (Breandán S. Mac Aodha, 'Was This a Social Revolution?' in Ó Tuama, *The Gaelic League Idea*, pp. 20–30).
8 County Antrim, fiddler, piper. 'Druth' is a Scots borrow-word meaning 'dryness' or 'drought'. It is used in Ulster counties in the context of drinking alcohol and alcoholism. Thus 'I have a druth on me' means 'I'm needing a drink' (or, outside of alcohol, 'I'm thirsty'), and 'he was a real druth' means 'he was a drunkard' or 'he was fond of a drink', or 'he drank too much'.
9 Alec Crawford.
10 For instance, the *Government of Ireland – Houses of the Oireachtas Joint Committee on Heritage and the Irish Language Report on Traditional Irish Music* (1999), prepared by Senator Labhrás Ó Murchú, produced considerable controversy and was eventually withdrawn.
11 Bohlman, *The Study of Folk Music in the Modern World*, p. 130.
12 John Moulden.
13 Leslie Bingham.
14 B. Lloyd, quoted in Boyes, *The Imagined Village – Culture, Ideology and the English Folk Revival*, p. 211.
15 ibid., p. 220.

21. THE CREATION OF MODERN STYLE

1 Baumann, 1987, p. 26.
2 This concept of differing 'music pathways' crossing a society's lateral (locale) and vertical (class) profiles was put forward by Ruth Finnegan in her book *The Hidden Musicians* 1989.
3 An attempt at a neutral title for a cross-community folk and Traditional music festival begun in the early 1990s at Ballycastle, County Antrim. Despite the noble intention it rapidly became known, pragmatically, as a 'fleadh'.
4 Meaning 'not received from an older generation in a context of use value'; 'having little deep emotional or rooted social meaning'.
5 Not only did official unionist MP John Taylor reject it, but so too do urban working-class Protestants (see Chapter 7 for his 'jig at the crossroads' remarks).
6 Carson, *Pocket Guide to Irish Traditional Music*, p. 56.
7 Uilleann piper, collector, broadcaster and hands-on authority. Séamus Ennis (1919–1982) was a musician of great talent and charisma. Browne (1999), Uí Ógáin (1999, 2007) and Mitchell (2007) have documented his life, work and music collection.

8 Also an uilleann piper, Breathnach (1912–1985) was the major ideologue of the revival period (see Moylan, 1999, pp. 39–40).
9 Kaemmer, 1980, p. 61.
10 ibid., p. 70.
11 In 1999 there were more than 1,500 session venues running weekly in Ireland and abroad (Vallely, *CITM*, p. xv).
12 Blacking, 1980, p. 40.

22. TONAL BOUNDARY-MARKING
1 Morris, *Signs, Language and Behaviour*, p. 25.
2 Patton, op. cit.
3 Michael O'Doherty, SDLP (Social, Democratic and Labour Party – nationalist), local-government politician.
4 Kluckhohn, 1962, p. 35.
5 Max Weber, quoted in Geertz, *The Interpretation of Cultures*, p. 5.
6 ibid., p. 5.
7 'Haet', a word popular in older Northern Irish parlance, indicating that the Catholics present (on this occasion) 'couldn't care less' or 'weren't bothered by' the presence of a Protestant; i.e. there was nothing to be worried about.
8 Gary Hastings.
9 Heslinga, *The Irish Border as a Cultural Divide*, p. 134; this refers to Barth's earlier study.
10 Barth, *Ethnic Groups and Boundaries*, p. 15.
11 ibid.
12 ibid., p. 204.
13 Bell, 1990, p. 167.
14 Jarman, 'Troubled Images', in *Critique of Anthropology*, vol. 12, no. 2 (1992), pp. 148–9.
15 ibid.
16 Morgan, 'Milesians, Ulstermen . . .', in *Linenhall Review*, vol. 18, no. 4 (1992).
17 Interview with student, 1991. That (mature) student's father (then deceased) ironically was a Catholic musician who had been familiar with performance in the company of Protestants.
18 Gary Hastings.
19 Middleton, *Studying Popular Music*, p. 132.
20 Blacking, 'The Structure of Folk Models', in *Political and Musical Freedom*, p. 37.

23. WITHERING AND BLOOMING IN THE SEVENTIES
1 Nettl, *Folk and Traditional Music of the Western Continents*, p. 6.
2 Notably in his 1913 work, *Irish Minstrels and Musicians*.
3 Cooney, 1999, p. 308, quoted from *John Charles McQuaid: What the Papers Say*, Producer Peter Kelly, Esras films, presented by John Bowman.
4 County Antrim, fiddler, piper.
5 ibid.
6 There are exceptions, for instance around Derrygonnelly in County Fermanagh, or music in the recreational life of the odd Orange hall in County Down where The Lancers set was still danced up to the present.
7 Andy Dickson.

24. JIGGING AT THE CROSSROADS, 2008
1 Judith Weir, speaking on *Start the Week with Andrew Marr*, BBC Radio 4, 14 January 2008.

Bibliography

Angrosino, Michael V. *The Essentials of Anthropology* (New Jersey: REA, 1990).
Aughey, Arthur. 'Ethnic Mending', in John Rawls and Ronald Dworkin (eds), *Conflict and Community*, supplement to *Fortnight* magazine, November 1992, p. 9.
Bailey, John. 'Recent Changes in the Dutar of Heart', in *Asian Music*, vol. 8, no. 1 (1976), pp. 29–83.
—. *Music in Afghanistan, Professional Musicians in the City of Heart* (Cambridge: Cambridge University Press, 1988).
Bardon, Jonathan. *A History of Ulster* (Belfast: The Blackstaff Press, 1992).
Barth, Frederick (ed.). *Ethnic Groups and Boundaries – The Social Organisation of Cultural Differences* (Boston: Little Brown & Company, 1969).
Baskervill, Charles Read. *The Elizabethan Jigg* (Chicago: University of Chicago Press, 1929).
Baumann, G. *National Integration and Local Integrity: The Miri of the Nuba Mountains in the Sudan* (Oxford: Clarendon Press, 1987).
Bell, Desmond. *Acts of Union: Youth Culture and Sectarianism in Northern Ireland* (London: Macmillan, 1990).
Bender, Thomas. *Community and Social Change in America* (New Brunswick, NJ: Rutgers University Press, 1978).
Bennett, M. 'Scotland', in Vallely, F (ed.). *Companion to Irish Traditional Music (CITM)* (Cork: Cork University Press, 1999), pp. 331–3.
Bergin, Osborn. *Irish Bardic Poetry* (Dublin: The Dublin Institute for Advanced Studies, 1970).
Berliner, P. *The Soul of Mbira: Music and Traditions of the Shona People of Zimbabwe* (Chicago: University of Chicago Press, 1978; 1981).
Blacking, John. 'The Structure of Folk Models', in *Political and Musical Freedom in the Music of some Black, South African Churches* (London: Academic Press, 1980), pp. 35–62.
Blaney, R. *Presbyterians and the Irish Language* (Belfast: Ulster History Foundation, 1996).
Bohlman, Philip V. *The Study of Folk Music in the Modern World* (Bloomington: Indiana University Press, 1988).
Boland, Eavan. *National Identity and Poetry*, LIP pamphlet (Dublin: Attic Press, 1990).

Boyes, Georgina. *The Imagined Village – Culture, Ideology and the English Folk Revival* (Manchester: Manchester University Press, 1993).
Boyle, Harry and Sara Evans. *Free Spaces* (New York: Harper & Row, 1986).
Breathnach, Breandán. *Folk Music and Dances of Ireland* (Cork: Mercier, 1971).
Browne, Peter, 'Ennis, Séamus (Séamus Mac Aonghusa)', in F. Vallely (ed.), *The Companion to Irish Traditional Music* (Cork: Cork University Press, 1999), p. 118.
Buckley, Anthony. 'We're Trying to Find Our Identity: Uses of History among Ulster Protestants', in Elizabeth Tonkin, Maryon McDonald and Malcolm Chapman (eds), *History and Ethnicity* (London: Routledge, 1989), pp. 183–97.
Bunting, Edward. *The Ancient Music of Ireland* (Dublin: Walton's, 1969) [Reprinted from 1796, 1809, 1840].
Buttimer, Anne. 'Social Space in Interdisciplinary Perspective', in John Cabree (ed.), *Surviving the City* (New York: Ballantine Books, 1973).
Camden, William. *Britannia: or a Chorographical Description of Great Britain and Ireland Together with Adjacent Lands* (London: Edmund Gibson, 1588); English translation (London: Philemon Holland, 1610).
Campbell, J.F (ed.). *Popular Tales of the West Highlands,* Vol. 1 (Dublin, London, Glasgow, Cambridge: 1860 [digitised on Google, 2007]).
Carlin, Richard. *English and American Folk Music, Facts on File* (New York: 1987).
Carolan, N. *Irish Traditional Music* (Dublin: ITMA, 1986).
—. *What is Irish Traditional Music* (Dublin: ITMA, 1987).
Carson, Ciarán. *Pocket Guide to Irish Traditional Music* (Belfast: Appletree Press, 1986).
Chapman, M., McDonald, M. and Tonkin, E., 'Introduction – History and Social Anthropology', in Elizabeth Tonkin, Maryon McDonald and Malcolm Chapman (eds), *History and Ethnicity* (London: Routledge, 1989), pp. 1–21.
Cohen, S. *Against Criminology* (New Brunswick, NJ: Transaction Books, 1988).
Conran, Michael. *The National Music of Ireland* (Dublin: Duffy, 1846).
Cooney, John. *John Charles McQuaid, Ruler of Catholic Ireland* (Dublin: The O'Brien Press, 1999).
Cooke, Peter. *The Fiddle Tradition of the Shetland Isles* (Cambridge: Cambridge University Press, 1986).
Cooper, David. 'Lámh Dearg: Celtic Minstrels and Orange Songsters', in *Celtic Cultural Studies*, 1999 (http://www.celtic-cultural-studies.com/papers/01/cooper-01.html).
Cowdery, James R. *The Melodic Tradition of Ireland* (Ohio: Kent State University Press, 1990).
Crooke, Elizabeth. *Politics, Archaeology and the Creation of a National Museum in Ireland: An Expression of National Life* (Dublin: Irish Academic Press, 2002).
Curtis, Edmund. *A History of Ireland* (London: Methuen, 1945).
Curtis, L.P. Jr. *Anglo-Saxons and Celts* (Connecticut: University of Bridgeport, 1968).
De Bhaldraithe, Tomás. *Foclóir Gaeilge-Béarla* (Dublin: Foilseacháin Rialtais, 1977).

Denisoff, R. Serge. *Sing a Song of Social Significance* (Bowling Green, Ohio: Popular Press, 1983).
Dinneen, Pádraig. *Irish–English Dictionary* (Dublin: Irish Texts Society, 1927).
Doherty, J.E., and D.J. Hickey, *A Chronology of Irish History since 1500* (Dublin: Gill & Macmillan, 1989).
Dowling, Martin W. 'Confusing Culture and Politics: Ulster Scots Culture and Music', in *New Hibernia Review*, vol. 11, no. 3, Autumn 2007, pp. 51–80.
Feldman, Allen, and Eamonn O'Doherty. *The Northern Fiddler* (Belfast: The Blackstaff Press, 1979).
Finnegan, Ruth. *The Hidden Musicians* (Cambridge: Cambridge University Press, 1989).
Flett, T.M. (ed.), *Traditional Dancing in Scotland* (London: Routledge, 1985).
Fraser, Simon. *The Airs and Melodies Peculiar to the Highlands of Scotland and the Isles* (Edinburgh: Highland Society of Scotland, 1816, 1874; St. Paul's Island, Nova Scotia: Cranford Publications, 1982).
Frith, Simon. *Sound Effects* (New York: Pantheon, 1981).
GAA. *Annual Report 2004*: Part 4 – Information & Statistics (Dublin: GAA, 2004).
Garvin, Wilbert. 'Pipe Bands and their Organisations', in Brian Lalor (ed.), *The Encyclopaedia of Ireland* (Dublin: Gill & Macmillan, 2003), p. 874.
Geertz, Clifford. *The Interpretation of Cultures* (New York: Basic Books, 1973).
Genovese, Eugene. *Roll, Jordan, Roll: The World the Slaves Made* (New York: Random House, 1972).
Gillespie, N., T. Lovett, and W. Garner. *Youth Work and Working Class Youth Culture – Rules and Resistance in West Belfast* (Buckingham, Philadelphia: Open University Press, 1992).
Goldwyn, Lawrence. *Democratic Promise: The Populist Movement in America* (New York: Oxford University Press, 1926).
Guralnik, Peter. *Feel Like Goin' Home* (New York: E.P. Dutton, 1971).
Hamilton, Colin. *The Session – A Socio-Musical Phenomenon in Irish Traditional Music* (Belfast: Queen's University, 1983) [MA Dissertation].
Hamm, Charles. *Yesterdays – Popular Song in America* (New York: W.W. Norton, 1983).
Handler, R. *Nationalism and the Politics of Culture in Quebec* (Madison: University of Wisconsin Press, 1988).
Hanvey, Bobby (ed.), *The Orange Lark* (Lurgan: The Ulster Society, 1987).
Harris, Rosemary. *Prejudice and Tolerance in Ulster – a Study of Neighbours and 'Strangers' in a Border Community* (Manchester: Manchester University Press, 1972).
Harrison, John. *The Scot in Ulster: Sketch of the History of the Scottish Population in Ulster* (Edinburgh: Blackwood, 1888).
Hast, D., and S. Scott. *Music in Ireland – Experiencing Music, Expressing Culture* (New York: Oxford, 2004).
Hastings, Gary. *With Fife and Drum* (Belfast: The Blackstaff Press, 2003).
Hebdidge, Dick. *Subculture – The Basis of Style* (New York: Methuen, 1979).
Henderson, Hamish. 'It Was in You That it A' Began', in Edward J. Cowan (ed.), *The People's Past* (Edinburgh: Polygon, 1980, 1991), pp. 4–29.

Henebry, Richard. *A Handbook of Irish Music* (Cork: Cork University Press, 1928).
Henry, Edward O. 'The Case for Ireland's Comhaltas Ceoltóirí Éireann', in *Ethnomusicology*, vol. 33, no. 1, 1989.
Heslinga, M.W. *The Irish Border as a Cultural Divide* (NV: Van Gorcum, 1964).
Hill, George. *An Historical Account of the Plantation in Ulster at the Commencement of the Seventeenth Century, 1608–1620* (Belfast: 1877).
Hyde, Douglas. *A Literary History of Ireland* (London: 1899).
Jarman, Neil. 'Troubled Images', in *Critique of Anthropology*, vol. 12, no. 2 (London: SAGE, 1992), pp. 133–65.
Johnson, David. *Music and Society in Lowland Scotland in the Eighteenth Century* (London: Oxford University Press, 1972).
Kearney, Hugh. *The British Isles – A History of Four Nations* (Cambridge: Cambridge University Press, 1984).
Kaemmer, John E. 'Between the Event and the Tradition: A New Look at Music in Sociocultural Systems', in *Ethnolmusicology*, vol. 24, no. 1 (Jan. 1980) (Illinois: University of Illinois Press, 1980), pp. 61–74.
Kedourie, Elie. *Nationalism* (London: Hutchinson, 1960).
Kennedy, Billy (ed.). *The Orange Institution* (Belfast: Grand Orange Lodge of Ireland, 1990).
—. *A Celebration – King William III, Prince of Orange, 1690–1990* (Orange Order of Ireland, Belfast: 1990).
Kluckhohn, R (ed.). *Culture and Behaviour: Collected Essays of Clyde Kluckhohn* (New York: The Free Press of Glencoe, Inc., 1962).
Larsen, Sidsel. 'The Glorious Twelfth – the Politics of Legitimation' and 'The two Sides of the House: Identity and Social Organisation', in *Kilbroney* (Manchester: Manchester University Press, 1982).
Leach, Edmund. *Culture and Communication – the Logic by which Symbols are Connected* (Cambridge: Cambridge University Press, 1976).
Lee, Joseph. *Ireland 1912–1985* (Cambridge: Cambridge University Press, 1991).
Levine, Lawrence. *Black Culture and Black Consciousness* (New York: Oxford University Press, 1977).
Leyton, Elliot R. *Conscious Models and Dispute Regulations in an Ulster Village* (Manchester: NS, 1966).
—. *Opposition and Integration in Ulster* (Manchester: NS, 1974).
Long, S.E. 'A Celebration: 1690–1990 – The Early Years', in *The Orange Institution* (Belfast: Grand Orange Lodge of Ireland, 1990).
Lovell, James. *Black Song – The Forge and The Flame* (New York: Paragon Books, 1986).
Lundh, Lise. *A Session is not a Performance: An Analysis of Traditional Music and Pub Sessions in Belfast* (Universitetet i Oslo, Lizenziatsarbeit, 1994).
Lythe, S.G.E. *The Economy of Scotland in its European Setting 1550–1625* (Edinburgh, Oliver and Boyd, 1960).
Mac Lua, B. *The Steadfast Rule – a History of the GAA Ban* (Dublin: 1967).
Mac Aoidh, C., Fiddle – Donegal, in F. Vallely (ed.), *The Companion to Irish Traditional Music* (Cork: Cork University Press, 1999), p. 126.
MacAoidh, Caomhín. *Between the Jigs and the Reels: The Donegal Fiddle Tradition* (Leitrim: Drumlin, 1994).

MacNeill, S. and F. Richardson. *Piobaireachd and Its Interpretation* (Edinburgh: John Donald, 1987).
Mandle, W.F. *The Gaelic Athletic Association and Irish Nationalist Politics 1884–1924* (Dublin: Gill & Macmillan, 1987).
Manson, W.L. *The Highland Bagpipe* (Edinburgh: 1901).
Manuel, Peter. *Popular Musics of the Non-Western World* (Oxford: Oxford University Press, 1988).
McCann, May. 'Music and Politics in Ireland: The Specificity of the Folk Revival in Belfast', in *British Journal of Ethnomusicology*, vol. 4 (1995), pp. 51–75.
McCarthy, M. *Passing it On: The Transmission of Music in Irish Culture* (Cork: Cork University Press, 1999).
McDowell, John H. 'The Mexican Corrido', in Bauman and Abrahams (eds), *And Other Neighbourly Names* (Austin: University of Texas, 1981).
McNamee, Peter (ed.). *Traditional Music – Whose Music?* (Belfast: Institute of Irish Studies, 1991).
McWhiney, Grady. *Cracker Culture* (Tuscaloosa: University of Alabama Press, 1988).
Merriam, Alan P. *Anthropology of Music* (Illinois: North-Western University Press, 1974).
Middleton, Richard. *Studying Popular Music* (Milton Keynes: Open University Press, 1990).
Milligan Fox, Charlotte. *Annals of the Irish Harpers* (London: 1911).
Mitchell, Pat (ed.), *The Dance Music of Seamus Ennis* (Dublin: NPU, 2007).
Moloney, C. 'Bunting, Edward', in F. Vallely (ed.), *CITM*, 1999, pp. 46–8.
—. (ed.). *The Irish Music Manuscripts of Edward Bunting (1773–1843): An Introduction and Catalogue* (Dublin: The Irish Traditional Music Archive, 2000).
Moore Pim, Herbert. *Unconquerable Ulster* (Belfast: Carswell, 1919).
Morgan, Hiram. 'Milesians, Ulstermen . . .', in *Linenhall Review*, vol. 18, no. 4 (1991), pp. 14–16.
Morris, Charles. *Signs, Language and Behaviour* (New York: George Braziller, 1955).
Morris, William. *Notes From Nowhere* (London: Longmans Green, 1918; New York: Routledge, 1972).
Morton, Robin. *Folksongs Sung in Ulster* (Cork: Mercier, 1970).
Moylan, T. 'Breathnach, Breandán (1912–85)', in F. Vallely (ed.), *CITM*, 1999, pp. 39–40.
Mulcahy, Michael, and Marie Fitzgibbon (eds). *The Voice of the People* (Dublin: O'Brien, 1982).
Mullen, Brian. BBC website – www.bbc.co.uk/ (2006).
—. *Swinging Shoulders – Dancing Feet* (forthcoming).
Munnelly, T., and H. Shields. 'Scots Ballad Influences in Ireland' in *Lore and Language, Proceedings of the tenth Symposium on European Ballad Research*, vol. 3, no. 4/5 (1981).
Nandy, Ashis. *The Intimate Enemy: Loss and Recovery of Self under Colonialism* (Delhi: Oxford University Press, 1983).
Neilson, Rev. William. *An Introduction to the Irish Language* (no date).

Nettl, Bruno. *Folk and Traditional Music of the Western Continents* (New Jersey: Prentice Hall, 1965).
Nettl, Bruno and Bohlman. *Comparative Musicology and Anthropology of Music* (Chicago: University of Chicago Press, 1991).
North, Peter. *Independent Review of Parades and Marches* (Belfast: HMSO, 1997).
Ó Bróithe, É., 'Song', entry in F. Vallely (ed.), *CITM*, 1999.
O'Boyle, Seán. *The Irish Song Tradition* (Dublin: Gilbert Dalton, 1974).
O'Brien, George. *The Four Green Fields* (Dublin: Talbot Press, 1936).
O'Brien, Richard. *The Irish Land Question* (London: Sampson Low, 1880).
Ó Canainn, Tomás. *Traditional Music in Ireland* (London: Routledge, 1978).
Ó Casaide, S. 'The Irish Language in Belfast, 1600–1850', in *Down and Connor Historical Society Journal II* (1929), pp. 4–63.
O'Doherty, Eamonn, and Allen Feldman. *The Northern Fiddler* (Belfast: The Blackstaff Press, 1979).
O'Donovan, Jeremiah. *The O'Growney Memorial Lecture*, Gaelic League Pamphlet No. 26 (Dublin: Gaelic League, 1902).
Ó Duibhín, C. *Irish in County Down since 1750* (Lecale: 1991).
O'Faoláin, Sean. *The Story of Ireland* (London, Collins, 1943).
Ó Murchú, Labhrás (ed.). *Treoir* (Dublin: CCÉ, 1968 to present).
—. *An Ród Seo Romhainn – A Future for Irish Traditional Music* (Cork: University College Traditional Music Society, 1987).
O'Neill, Francis. *Irish Folk Music: A Fascinating Hobby* (Chicago: Regan, 1910).
—. *Irish Minstrels and Musicians with Numerous Dissertations on Related Subjects* (Chicago: 1913; reprint with introduction by Breandán Breathnach, Cork: Mercier Press, 1987).
Opsahl, Torkel. *Report of the Opsahl Commission* (Dublin: Lilliput Press, 1993).
Ó Snodaigh, Pádraig. *Hidden Ulster* (Dublin: Clódhanna Teo., 1973).
Ó Tuama, Seán (ed.). *The Gaelic League Idea* (Cork: Mercier Press, 1972).
Ó Súilleabháin, M. Review of *The Melodic Tradition of Ireland* by James R. Cowdery (Kent, OH: Kent State University Press, 1990), in *Ethnomusicology*, vol. 37, no. 1 (Winter, 1993), pp. 109–12.
O'Sullivan, Dónal. *Carolan – The Life and Times of an Irish Harper* (London: RKP, 1958; Cork: Ossian, 2001).
O'Toole, Slugger. Web-search: 'pan nationalist conspiracy', site reference (2007 04) – http://66.102.9.104/search?q=cache:ghB-iI2MPkMJ:www.slugger-otoole.com/archives/2005/04/libel_update.php+pan-nationalist+conspiracy&hl=en&ct=clnk&cd=4&gl=ie.
Paisley, Ian. Quoted in *Chronology 1993* (Centre d'Études Irlandaises – Université Rennes 2, http://www.uhb.fr/langues/cei/chron93.htm 1993].
Pells, Richard. *Radical Visions and American Dreams – Culture and Social Thought in the Depression Years* (New York: Harper Torch Books, 1974).
Perceval-Maxwell, M. *The Scottish Migration to Ulster in the Reign of James 1* (London: Routledge & Kegan Paul, 1973).
Peterson, Richard A. *Creating Country Music – Fabricating Authenticity* (Chicago: University of Chicago Press, 1997).

Petrie, G. *The Petrie Collection of the Ancient Music of Ireland* (Dublin: The University Press, 1855. Also revised edition by David Cooper, Cork: Cork University Press, 2003).
Pollack, Andy. *A Citizen's Inquiry* (Dublin: Lilliput Press, 1993).
Porter, James. *The Traditional Music of Britain and Ireland – A Select Bibliography and Research Guide* (New York: H. Garland).
Pratt, Ray. *Rhythm and Resistance: Explorations in the Political Uses of Popular Music* (New York: Praeger, 1990).
Puirséal, P. *The GAA in its Time* (Dublin: 1982).
Purser, John. *Scotland's Music: A History of the Traditional and Classical Music of Scotland from the Earliest Times to the Present Day* (Edinburgh: Mainstream Publishing 1992).
Radford, Katy. *Loyal Sounds – Music as Marker of Identity in Protestant West Belfast* (Belfast: The Queen's University of Belfast, 2002).
Raven, Michael. *1,000 English Country Dance Tunes* (Stafford: Raven, 1984).
Reid, Briony. 'Patterns of Memory Fragmented: The Townland in Northern Ireland', paper given on the theme of 'Culture, Place and Identity' at The Irish Conference of Historians, University of Ulster, Magee campus, 22–25 May 2003.
Rising Sons of Down Flute Band, Donaghadee, County Down, www.risingsons.com, 2005.
Roberts, Brian. 'Subcultures, Cultures and Class', in *Culture, Ideology and Social Process – A Reader* (London: The Open University Press, 1981).
Robinson, Philip S. *The Plantation of Ulster* (Dublin: Gill & Macmillan, 1984).
Rose, Richard. *Governing Without Consensus: An Irish Perspective* (Boston, Beacon Press, 1971).
Rosenberg, Neil V (ed.). *Transforming Tradition* (Illinois: University of Illinois Press, 1993).
Scarlett, W.D. *The Economic and Social Effects of Partition on Clones* (County Monaghan) (Belfast: Queen's University, 1957) [Dissertation, Hons.].
Scholes, Percy. *The Oxford Companion to Music* (Oxford: Oxford University Press, 1987).
Schiller, Rina. *The Lambeg and the Bodhrán* (Belfast: Queen's University, Belfast, 2001).
Scullion, Fionnuala. 'History and Origins of the Lambeg Drum', in *Ulster Folklife*, no. 27, 1981.
Scott, Walter. *Minstrelsy of the Scottish Borders*, 18th century.
Sheehy, Jeanne. *The Rediscovery of Ireland's Past – The Celtic Revival: 1830–1930* (London: Thames & Hudson, 1980).
Shepard, Leslie. *The Broadside Ballad: A Study in Origins and Meaning* (London: Herbert Jenkins, 1962).
Shields, Hugh. *Narrative Singing in Ireland* (Dublin: Irish Academic Press, 1993).
Simon, A (ed.). *Das Berliner Phonogramm-Archiv 1900–2000 – Sammlungen der traditionellen Musik der Welt / The Berlin Phonogramm-Archiv 1900–2000 – Collections of Traditional Music of the World* (Berlin: VWB 2000).
Slobin, Mark. *Music in the Culture of Northern Afghanistan* (Arizona: University of Arizona Press, 1976).

Smyth, Clifford. *Rome our Enemy* (Bangor: Puritan Press, 1971).
Stokes, Martin. *Ethnicity, Identity and Music: The Musical Construction of Place* (Oxford: Berg, 1997).
Strauss, E. *Irish Nationalism and British Democracy* (London: Methuen, 1951).
Stumpf, Carl. 'Wissenschaftliche Wochenschrift für Wissenschaft, Kunst und Technik, 1908', in A. Simon, (ed.) *Das Berliner Phonogramm-Archiv 1900–2000* (Berlin: VWB, 2008).
Tansey, Séamus. 'Irish Traditional Music – the Melody of Ireland's Soul, its Evolution from the Environment, Land and People', in F. Vallely, E. Doherty, H. Hamilton and E. Vallely (eds), *Crosbhealach an Cheoil the Crossroads Conference – Tradition and Innovation in Traditional Irish Music* (Dublin: Whinstone, 1999).
Turino, Thomas. 'The Urban-Mestizo Charango Tradition in Southern Peru', in *Ethnomusicology* vol. 28, no. 2 (1984), pp. 253–70.
Uí Ógáin, R. Ennis, Séamus, the collector, in F. Vallely (ed.), *CITM*, 1999, pp. 118-119.
Uí Ógáin, Ríonach (ed.). *Mise an fear ceoil: Séamus Ennis – Dialann Taistil 1942-1946* (Indreabháin: Cló Iar-Chonnachta, 2007).
Vallely, Eithne. 'Education', in F. Vallely (ed.), *CITM*, 1999, pp. 113, 114.
—. 'Jackets on the Grass Verge', in *Causeway*, vol. 1, no. 1, 1993, p. 39.
Vallely, Fintan. *Fiddlesticks in the Closet: Ulster Protestant Suspicions of Traditional Music*, essay in J. Tonge and F. Neal (eds), *Irish Protestant Identities* (Manchester: Manchester University Press, 2008).
Vallely, Fintan. *Flute Routes to 21st-century Ireland* (PhD thesis, University College Dublin, 2004).
—. *From Fifth Column to Pillar of Society – Observations on the Political Implications of Popular Revival and Education in Irish Traditional Music in Modern Ireland* (Cork: Traditional Music Society, 2004).
—. 'Singing the Boundaries of Regional Distinctiveness: The Ulster-Scots Assembly of New Pedigree in Ulster Music' in MacCraith, M. and U. Kockel (eds), *Communicating Cultures* – Papers of ESRC Research Seminar in European Ethnology, 2002 (Berlin and London: LIT Verlag, 2003).
—. 'Knocking on the Castle Door – A Place for Traditional Music in Third Level Education? *JMI – The Journal of Music in Ireland*, 2002–7.
—. *Together in Time, the Life, Times and Music of John Kennedy of Cullybackey*. (Magherafelt: Lough Shore Traditions, 2001).
—. *Companion to Irish Traditional Music* [*CITM*] (Cork: Cork University Press, 1999).
— (ed.). *Sing Up!: Comic Songs and Satires of Modern Ireland* (Dublin: Dedalus Press, 2008).
Vallely, F., Charlie Piggott and Nutan. *The Blooming Meadows* (Dublin: Townhouse, 1998)
—. 'Politicians Are at the Crossroads, Not Musicians', in *Causeway* (Belfast: May 1994).
Waterman, Christopher. *Juju – A Social History and Ethnography* (Chicago: Chicago University Press, 1990).

Waters, John. *Jiving at the Crossroads* (Belfast: The Blackstaff Press, 1991).
Watson, W.J. *History of the Place-names of Scotland* (1926).
Wayfarer'.'Who Were the Celts?', in *Derry Journal* (Derry, 1992).
Wright, Louis B. *The Cultural Life of the American Colonies, 1607–1763* (New York: Harper, 1957).
Yankelovich, Daniel. *New Rules* (New York: Random House, 1981).
Yeats, G.,'Harp', in F. Vallely (ed.), *CITM*, 1999, pp. 169–172.
Zimmerman, Georges-Denis. *Songs of Irish Rebellion – Political Street Ballads and Rebel Songs 1780 –1900* (Dublin: Allen Figgis, 1967).

APPENDIX

Interviewees

Beattie, Michael, BBC TV, Northern Ireland
Bingham, Leslie, County Down, flute player
Musician 1, County Down
Musician 2, County Down
County Antrim, fiddler, piper
Crawford, Alec, County Antrim, accordionist
Crawford, Doris, County Antrim, pianist
Crockhart, Andy, Ulster Television producer
Dickson, Andy, Belfast, fiddler
Garvin, Wilbert, County Antrim, uilleann piper
Hastings, Gary, Belfast, flute player, writer
Healy, Michael, Alliance Party policy committee member
Kennedy, John, County Antrim, flute player, singer, teacher
McAdam, Geordie, Belfast, flute player, fiddler
McAuley, Tony, BBC Northern Ireland producer
Moulden, John, County Derry, song researcher
O'Doherty, Michael, Social, Democratic and Labour Party (SDLP) councillor
Patton, George, Belfast, Orange Order
Robinson, Philip, County Down, Ulster Folk Museum,
Sands, Colm, County Down, singer, songwriter
Singer – Belfast – Community worker
Spence, Gusty, Belfast, local politician

Personal Communications

Many personal insights from musicians, associates and friends of the author contributed to this text. These include Len Graham (singer); Joe Mulhearn (songwriter); Wilbert Garvin (piper); Robin Morton (singer & writer); PJ Flood (piper); Sam MacPhee (Director, St Anne's Gaelic College, Cape Breton, Nova Scotia, Canada); Paul Cranford (fiddler, publisher, Cape Breton); Dr Liz Doherty (researcher, fiddler); Mícheál Ó hAlúin (musician).

Index

References to illustrations are indicated by page numbers in italics.

A
accents 51
Adams, Gerry 41
Adler, Larry 66
aesthetics *see* artistic performance
American Civil Rights movement 65
American Civil War 58, 104
American folk music 64–6
American War of Independence 58
archaeology 44–5
Archer, William 105
artistic performance 77–8, 137–8
aural/oral transmission 7–8, 9–10, 120
authenticity 120–25
'Avondale' 106

B
Baez, Joan 66, 67
bagpipes 117
ballads 10, 28–9, 112
ballroom dancing 29
Ballymena Feis *27*, 27
band culture 45–6, 118, 140–41
barn dances 29
Barth, Frederick 143
BBC 48–9, 72
Behan, Dominic 106
Belfast (music scene) 26–7, 133
Belfast Folksong Club 133
Belfast Newsletter 48, 73
Belfast Telegraph 48
Bell, Carey 79
Bell, Des 143
Blacking, John 139, 145
Blatherwick, David 39

Bloody Sunday 149
bluegrass music 70
bomb threat, Jolly Judge bar 4–5, 53, 142
'Bould Orange Heroes of Comber' *100*, 102
bouzouki 25
Boyce, Jackie 34, 35
Boyle, Néillidh 129
Boys' Brigade 141
'Boys of Tandragee' *98*, 99
Breathnach, Breandán 138, 148
Breton music 70
'Bright Orange Heroes of Comber' *see* 'Bould Orange Heroes of Comber'
Britishness, concepts of *see* national identity
broadcasting *see* radio; television
Buckley, Anthony 58
Bunting, Edward 127, 148

C
cajun music 70
Campaign for Nuclear Disarmament (CND) 65, 134
Cape Breton Island 47, 70, 108, 113, 123
'Caper Fey' 97
Carson, Ciarán 66–7
Carter Family 66
cartoons 43–4
'Cath Chéim an Fhia' 102
Catholicism and identity 57–8
CCÉ *see* Comhaltas Ceoltóirí Éireann
céilí bands 29, *68*, 128, *152*

Celtic identity 81–2, 83–8, 93–6
Chopin, Frederic 79
cinema 124
Civil Rights movement 57–8, 134, 137
   see also American Civil Rights movement
Clancy Brothers, The 67
class representation (musicians) 13–14
class structure 54–5
CND see Campaign for Nuclear Disarmament
Coleman, Michael 123
'Come Out ye Black and Tans' 100
Comhaltas Ceoltóirí Éireann (CCÉ)
   and the *fleadh cheoil* 72, 87–8, 146
   and nationalism 85–8, 149
   and Northern/Protestant musicians 34, 80, 86–8, 149
   organised sessions 74
   and revivalism 16, 67, 130, 148
   Treoir 73, *86*, 86, *87*, 148
competitions 71–2
Cooper, David 102–4
Co-operation North 80
Counties Derry and Antrim Fiddlers Association 29
country music 70
Crooke, Elizabeth 44–5
Crosby, Bing 63
crossover music
   Ireland and Scotland 96–101, 108–14
   Orange and Green 102–7
cultural identity 39–49, 50–53, 122, 140–45
'Cultures of Ireland' conference 39

D
Dance Lexie Dance 89
dance music 2, 29, 128
dancing
   Orange Hall dances 28, 90, 128
   in Scotland 116
   set dancing 45, 89–90
   step dancing 27, 27–9, 89–90, 130
   as emblematic 140
Dancing at a Northern Crossroads (Lamb) 50
Dancing to History's Tune (Walker) 60
Deliverance 25
Dublin Institute of Technology 73

Dubliners, The 67
'Duke of Atholl's Rant' *101*
Dundalk Institute of Technology 73
Dylan, Bob 66, 67

E
Ediphone cylinders 120, *121*
education
   in music 72–3, 147–8
   segregation in 56
emblems 21, 43–5, 51, 140
English folk music 10, 67
English language songs 110, 112
Ennis, Séamus 138
entertainment formats 120–25
escapism 78–9
ethnicity 140–45
Examiner 73

F
Feis, Ballymena 27
Fenian, perception of traditional music as 32–8, 137, 139, 141–5, 146–7
Fitzgerald, Winston Scotty 123
fleadh cheoil 10, 72, 87–8, 130, 146
folk memory 83–8
folk music 2, 3–4, 7, 10, 63–7, 122–3, 134
   see also traditional music
Fraser, Simon 111–12

G
GAA see Gaelic Athletic Association
Gaelic Athletic Association 39, 42–3, 45–6, 85–6, 127–8
Gaelic identity see Celtic identity
Gaelic language 46–8, 94–5, 108–9, 127
Gaelic League 16, 47, 128, 147
Gaeltachtaí 47
Gallagher, Bridie 29
Garvin, Wilbert 29, *150*
gender representation (musicians) 13
'God Save Ireland' 104–5
gramophone 123–4
Guthrie, Woody 65, 66, 67

H
Harron, Maurice 5–6
Hastings, Rev. Gary 1, 102, 107
Heaney, Joe 66
Henebry, Richard 78

heritage 81–2, 83–8, 122
highland flings 29
Home Rule 18–19, 127
'Humours of Ballyconnell' *101*
hunger strikes 149
Hurt, Mississippi John 66
Hyde, Douglas *108*

I
identity
   Celtic 81–2, 83–8, 93–6
   cultural 39–49, 50–53, 122, 140–45
   and music 79–82, 122, 126–30
   national 39–49, 50–53, 79–81, 83–8, 126–30, 144–5
   political 17–24, 39–49, 85–8, 126–30, 132–5, 140–45
   religious 17–24, 54–61
Incredible String Band, The 67
industrialisation 118, 124
instruments *8*, 8–9, 36–7, 69, 96
internal rhyme 102
international scene 70–71, 132, 151
internet 73, 151
internment 88, 149
Irish dancing *see* step dancing
Irish language 46–8, 108–9, 127
Irish Minstrels and Musicians (O'Neill) 78
Irish Music magazine 73
Irish News, The 73
Irish Times, The 48, 49, 73
Irish Traditional Music Archive (ITMA) 7
Irish World Music Centre (IWMC) 73
Irishness *see* national identity
ITMA *see* Irish Traditional Music Archive
IWMC *see* Irish World Music Centre

J
Jackson, Aunt Molly 63
Jansch, Bert 67
Japanese musicians 70–71, *71*
jazz 128–9
jigs and reels 28
'Johnny the Jig' (sculpture) *33*
Jolly Judge bar, Newtownards (bomb threat) 4–5, 53, 142
Journal of Music in Ireland 73

K
Kaye, Danny 66
Kennedy, John 29
Kerr, Alex 29
Kingston Trio 66

L
Lallans culture 110, 112
Lamb, Charles 50
Lambeg drums *1*
'Lámh Dearg: Celtic Minstrels and Orange Songsters' (Cooper) 102–4
Leabhar Mór na Gaelige 94
Leadbelly 65
'Let the Dance Begin' (sculpture) *5*, 5–6
linen industry 118
Liverpool Céilí Band 68
Living Tradition, The 73
Lloyd, A.L. (Bert) 65–6, 67
Lomax, Alan 64, 65
Lomax, John 64, 65
London College of Music 72, 73
Loughnashade trumpets 1, 7
loyalism 18–19
'Lurgan Town' 106, 139
lyrics, political 14–16, 140

M
MacColl, Ewan 65–6, 67
Mac Gabhann, Dick 102
MacMahon, Tony 138
magazines 73, 151
Magill, Wilbert 5
manuscript music 120, 123
marching music 2, 29, 118, 140–41
Marxism 133–4
McGee, Brownie 65
McIlhatton, Mickey 29
McQuaid, John Charles 148
McSweeney, Rev. Patrick 44
media 48–9, 72, 73, 151
migration 93, 93–6, 108–14, 115–19
military two-steps 29
mixed marriages 55–6
'Mo Ghile Mhear' 105
Monroe, Bill 66
Mullen, Brian 102, 104–7
Munnelly, Tom 112

murals 51, 141, 143
Murphy, Jimmy 83
music hall 116, 120
music-pubs 138–9
musicians 12–14, 29–30
  see also performance; traditional music
'My Irish Molly O' 106

N
national identity 39–49, 50–53, 79–81, 83–8, 126–30, 144–5
nationalism 18, 126, 139, 149–50
Neilson, Samuel 19
New Christy Minstrels 66
newspapers 48–9, 73
Nigeria 79
'No Pope, Priest or Holy Water' 104–5
Northern Irish identity see national identity
nostalgia 83–4
Nova Scotia 47, 70, 108, 113, 123

O
O'Boyle, Cathal 102
O'Connell, Daniel 126
O'Donnell, Brian 32–3
'Ólaim Punch' 106
O'Neill, Francis 78, 148
oral/aural transmission 7–8, 9–10, 120
Orange Hall dances 28, 90, 128
'Orange Maid of Sligo' 105
Orange Order 18–19, 45–6, 118, 140–41
Orange parades 10, 45–6, 140–41
Ó Riada, Seán 137–8

P
Paine, Thomas 19
Paisley, Dr Ian 21, 42
pan-nationalism 41, 41–2
parades (Orange) 10, 45–6, 140–41
Partition 20, 20–21, 48–9
Patton, George 5, 140
performance
  artistic 77–8, 137–8
  professional 72, 138–9
Peter Paul and Mary 66
Petrie, George 102–3
Petrie Collection of Irish Music, The (Cooper) 102

Plantation of Ulster 17–18, 96, 109–11, 116
political identity 17–24, 39–49, 85–8, 126–30, 132–5, 140–45
political lyrics 14–16, 140
post-revival musicians 12–13
Praeger, Rosamund 33
pre-revival musicians 12
press see newspapers
professional performance 72, 138–9
Protestantism and identity 58–60
Provisional IRA 94
Punch magazine 43–4

Q
Queen's University, Belfast 73

R
racial identity see national identity
radio 115, 120, 121, 124, 128, 130, 151
'Rakish Paddy' 97
Rea, John 89
recording see sound recording
records 120, 123–4, 128, 130
Red Hand Commando 4–5
reels see jigs and reels
regional bias 25–6
religious identity 17–24, 54–61
Repeal movement 126
republicanism 19–20, 133
revivalism 3, 16, 66–7, 68–9, 126–35, 148–9
revivalist musicians 12–13
Rights of Man, The (Paine) 19
Riverdance 89
Rodgers, Jimmie 64, 66
Root, George 104
Royal Irish Academy of Music 44–5, 72
RTÉ 34, 48
rural performance 75, 124–5
rural/urban representation (musicians) 13–14
Russell, Thomas 19

S
'Sash My Father Wore' 102, 106
Scotland and Ireland
  crossover music 96–101, 108–14
  cultural links 93–6, 108–14, 116–17
Scottish assembly 94

Scottish Gaelic 46–7, 94–5, 108–9
Scottish lowland culture 110, 112
Scottish music 2–4, 10, 22, 29, 70, 81, 95–6, 117
  see also crossover music
Sea Scouts 141
sean-nós 1, 66
Seeger, Peggy 65–6
Seeger, Pete 65
sessions 69–71, *70*, 72, 74–5, 138–9
set dancing 45, 89–90
Shand, Jimmy 128
'Shanghai March' *98*, 99
Shankill Road 27, 28
sheet music 120, 123
Shields, Hugh 112
socialism 133–4, 146
Songs of County Down (O'Boyle) 102
'Sons of Levi' 105
sound recording 115, 120, 123–4
South Africa 145
'Spanish Lady' 105
sponsorship 138–9
sport 42–3
step dancing *27*, 27–8, 89–90, 130
Stewart, Neil 108
Stumpf, Carl 44
style of play 120–25
Sullivan, T.D. 104
Sunday School 141
Sunday Tribune 73
'Swallow's Tail' *99*
symbols *see* emblems

T
Taylor, John 21, 50, 51–3
teaching *see* education
television 32–4, 48–9, 72, 121, 124, 151
Temperance movement 118, 126
Terry, Sonny 65
third-level education 73
Tone, Wolfe 19
'Town of Garvagh' *100*
trade unionism 134, 146
traditional music
  artistic performance 77–8, 137–8
  authenticity 120–25
  competitions 71–2
  dance music 2, 29
  defined 7–8
  distinguished from folk 7
  education 72–3
  as escapism 78–9
  and heritage 81–2, 83–8
  and identity 79–82, 122, 126–30
  instruments 8, 8–9, 36–7, 69, 96, 116–17
  international scene 70–71, 132, 151
  modern context 68–75, 136–9, 150–51, 152–4
  newspaper coverage 73
  perceived as Fenian 32–8, 137, 139, 141–5, 146–7
  professional performance 72, 138–9
  regional bias 25–6
  as representing Irishness 26, 137
  revivalism 3, 16, 66–7, 68–9, 126–35, 148–9
  rural performance 75
  sessions 69–71, *70*, 72, 74–5, 138–9
  sponsorship 138–9
  style of play 120–25
  television coverage 32–4, 72, 151
  transmission 7–8, 9–10, 108–14, 120, 147–8
  urban performance 74–5
  see also folk music
'Tramp, Tramp, Tramp the Boys are Marching' 104
transmission 7–8, 9–10, 108–14, 120, 147–8
Treoir 73, *86*, 86, *87*, 148
Troubles, the 57–8, 134, 137, 149

U
Ulster (usage of term) 20–21
Ulster identity *see* Northern Irish identity
Ulster-Scots Fowk Orchestra 112
Ulster-Scots movement 2, 3–4, 22–4, 61–2, 154
Ulster Television (UTV) 32–3, 49, 72
unionism 18
United Irishmen 19, 126
University College Cork 73
University College Dublin 73
University of Limerick 73
University of Ulster 73
urban performance 74–5

urban/rural representation (musicians) 13–14
UTV *see* Ulster Television

W
Walker, Brian 60
War of Independence 128
  see also American War of Independence
Waterford Institute of Technology 73
Waters, Muddy 66
Watersons, The 67
Watson, Doc 66
Weavers, The 63, 65, 66
Weir, Judith 153
West of Ireland 25–6
'Whose Music?' conference 68, 80, 102, 137
Williams, Hank 66
With Fife and Drum (Hastings) 1, 107

Y
YMCA 141

Z
Zorba the Greek 25